Dear Reader:

The book you are a[...] the St. Martin's Tr[...] *York Times* calls "th[...] offer you a fascinating account of the latest, most sensational crime that has captured the national attention. St. Martin's is the publisher of bestselling true crime author and crime journalist Kieran Crowley, who explores the dark, deadly links between a prominent Manhattan surgeon and the disappearance of his wife fifteen years earlier in THE SURGEON'S WIFE. Suzy Spencer's BREAKING POINT guides readers through the tortuous twists and turns in the case of Andrea Yates, the Houston mother who drowned her five young children in the family's bathtub. In Edgar Award-nominated DARK DREAMS, legendary FBI profiler Roy Hazelwood and bestselling crime author Stephen G. Michaud shine light on the inner workings of America's most violent and depraved murderers. In the book you now hold, INTO THE WATER, Diane Fanning explores the twisted world of a serial killer—and laments the lives and love that was lost.

St. Martin's True Crime Library gives you the stories behind the headlines. Our authors take you right to the scene of the crime and into the minds of the most notorious murderers to show you what really makes them tick. St. Martin's True Crime Library paperbacks are better than the most terrifying thriller, because it's all true! The next time you want a crackling good read, make sure it's got the St. Martin's True Crime Library logo on the spine—you'll be up all night!

Charles E. Spicer, Jr.
Executive Editor, St. Martin's True Crime Library

...are about to read is the latest bestseller from
...The Crime Library, the imprint the New
...calls ...the leader in true crime". Each month, we

FIGHT OR FLIGHT

One mile, two miles, then Evonitz spotted the flashing lights racing toward him—he knew they had him in their sights again. Joy transformed into panic and despair. He was clocked at speeds of up to 120 miles per hour.

At Route 41 and Tenth Street, he slowed at a red light as he approached three lanes of stopped traffic. Then, he blasted through the intersection—sliding between two cars stopped at the light. He missed them both by a whisper.

Up ahead, three officers each picked a spot and pulled stop strips of tire-ripping Teflon nails out of their trunks. The strips lay in wait in the inside lanes of the street. Evonitz flew across them, blowing out tires with a roar. Three of his tires were flat. He lost control of his car, striking the curb. He bounced back on the roadway. He kept going forward on his rims, ricocheting from one curb to the other. Rubber from his front left tire flew off in all directions hitting guardrails and patrol cars with a denting thud. The police no longer were hampered in their chase by his extinguished headlights—the metal rims of his Escort sprayed sparks, lighting his trail.

The chase was so frenzied and determined that the police did not have time to pull the stop strips from the road before five or six of their own vehicles flew across them and had their tires blown, too.

Now Evonitz's disabled car had slowed to the point that some officers were pursuing him on foot. He tried desperately to cross the median. His car conquered the curb, but knocked off all of the rubber on a front tire in the process. The rim dug into the grass and dirt, and stopped him in his tracks.

Adrenaline pumped to the max, Evonitz was ready for fight or flight. He stuck one hand out the driver's-side window. In the other hand, he held a gun. . . .

TITLES BY DIANE FANNING

Through the Window
Into the Water

FROM THE TRUE CRIME LIBRARY OF ST. MARTIN'S PAPERBACKS

INTO
THE
WATER

**THE STORY OF SERIAL KILLER
RICHARD MARC EVONITZ**

Diane Fanning

St. Martin's Paperbacks

INTO THE WATER

Copyright © 2004 by Diane Fanning.

Cover photograph of water © SIME/eStock Photo.

All rights reserved. No part of this book may be used or reproduced in any manner whatsoever without written permission except in the case of brief quotations embodied in critical articles or reviews. For information address St. Martin's Press, 175 Fifth Avenue, New York, N.Y. 10010.

ISBN: 0-312-98526-6

Printed in the United States of America

St. Martin's Paperbacks edition / June 2004

10 9 8 7 6 5 4 3 2 1

THIS BOOK IS DEDICATED WITH ADMIRATION TO
Kara
AND WITH DEEP REGRET TO
THE WOMEN WE WILL NEVER KNOW:
Kristin Lisk
Kati Lisk
Sofia Silva

Acknowledgments

I have an overwhelming appreciation for everyone who took the time to talk to me about pivotal events in their lives or careers as I conducted the research into this story.

My thanks to Carol and Melissa Britt, Danny Minter, Pat Stanley, Adrienne Hayden, Angie Frantz, Kieth Raba and all the many other folks in Spotsylvania County who shared their experiences with me but who chose to remain nameless.

In Columbia, South Carolina, there are a number of people in this book who are identified only by their first names to protect the privacy of a brave young girl named Kara. Thanks to Debra and Cindy for giving me the personal perspective of the harrowing event that occurred there. And thanks to Alan Hitchcox, editor of *Hydraulics & Pneumatics* magazine.

I extend my appreciation to the relatives of Richard Marc Evonitz: Tess Ragin, Joe Evonitz, Kristen Weyand, Jennifer Evonitz and Jeffrey Weyand, who shared the shock and pain they experienced in learning the truth about an important person in their lives.

William Neeley, Commonwealth's Attorney for Spotsylvania County, Sanda Wasser of the records room in the office of the clerk of circuit court in Spotsylvania, April Warford in the clerk of court office at the Charleston County Criminal Court, the clerk of court's office in the criminal division of the Clay County Circuit Court, Patricia Eckard of the Placer County Superior Court in California, Norfolk Commonwealth Attorney's Office, and Pam Liles of the Charleston *Post and Courier* provided invaluable assistance in preparation for this book.

The excellent journalistic coverage provided by a host of reporters at the Fredericksburg *Free Lance–Star* constructed a road map I could follow in the earliest stages of my research. Thanks to you all—with a special nod to American University Journalism Professor Rose Ann Robertson, who worked on the newspaper's Web site during the summer of Evonitz's capture.

There is one group of people whose information and insight was of paramount importance—the members of law enforcement. In Virginia, thanks to Major Howard Smith and Detective Twyla Demoranville of the Spotsylvania County Sheriff's Department, Captain Steve Dempsey of the King George Sheriff's Department, Captain David Hines and Lieutenant Doug Goodman of the Hanover County Sheriff's Department, Lucy Caldwell of the Virginia State Police, and Detective Sam Newsome and Sergeant Kim Chinn of the Prince William Police Department.

In South Carolina, hats off to Major Howell "Holly" Siniard and Sheriff Leon Lott of the Richland County Sheriff's Department; Captain John Allard of the Lexington County Sheriff's Department; Chief Roddy Perry, Mount Pleasant Police Department; Eugene Frazier, retired detective, Charleston County Police Department; Lt. Chris Morgan, Raleigh Police Department; Captain Rene Williams of the Orangeburg County Sheriff's Department and Captain Dwayne Courtney, Aiken police.

In Florida, thanks to Jay Frank of the Sarasota Police Department, Dave Bristo of the Manatee County Sheriff's Department, Mary Justino of the Clay County Sheriff's Department and Lt. Joe Paez of the Hernando County Sheriff's Office.

In Maine, thanks to Stephen McCausland of the state police. In West Virginia, I extend my gratitude to First Sergeant Don Benson of the state police.

A special note of gratitude to former FBI profilers Robert K. Ressler and Greg McCrary—thank you for your willingness to share the wealth of your knowledge.

To my agent Jane Dystal, my editor Joe Cleemann and executive editor at St. Martin's Paperbacks, Charles Spicer—thank you for making this book possible.

And finally, to my husband, Wayne—you are my rock.

> *"If you want to understand the artist, you have to look at the painting."*
>
> John Douglas, former FBI profiler,
> from his book *Mind Hunter*

Chapter 1

Richard Marc Evonitz's eyes popped open in alarm. Something was wrong. Loud noises at the front door had jerked him from his dreams, but the details did not register in his sleep-fogged brain. He was alone in his bed. Where was she?

He tossed the sheets and blankets, hoping to make a lie of the emptiness beside him. He dropped to the floor on his knees and peered under the bed. Jumping to his feet, he pulled open the closet, shoved aside his clothes. No one there. In the bathroom, he whisked back the shower curtain. No one. He covered the rest of his apartment in seconds.

There was no sign of the girl.

He raced from window to window but did not catch a glimpse of her fleeing form outside. The clock was ticking. He had to move fast. Before the red and blue lights descended in an urgent rush.

He opened a bag. Tossed in his clothes and toiletries with little thought. He focused on his escape—on possible obstacles, and how to overcome them. First, he needed to get out. He grabbed his cell phone, his handgun. It was time.

He edged open the door, scanning everywhere. Then, he froze, closed his eyes and listened for the distant approach of sirens. All clear. He sprinted to his '96 silver Ford Escort.

He threw his personal belongings in the back seat—except

for the cell phone and the gun. He placed those on the passenger seat up front. He eased out of the parking lot, trying not to draw any attention. He stopped at a nearby Wal-Mart and, using his company credit card, picked up some supplies for the road. Then, he jack-rabbited to Interstate 26 and merged into the traffic headed toward Charleston.

When his mind strayed and panic rode shotgun, his foot got heavy on the accelerator. Then his awareness snapped back and he'd ease up—he could not risk being stopped for speeding. His eyes were wed to the rearview mirror—searching for pursuers. His ears tuned in to hear whispered wails of approaching doom.

When he hit Orangeburg, he called the Irmo home of the older of his sisters, Kristen Weyand, and begged for her help. She had made a lifetime habit of standing up for her siblings. She raced to his side now. She met him at a McDonald's and then booked a room for four nights in her name at Days Inn—paying cash and requesting lodging in the back, away from the highway.

She knew he was in trouble. The extent of it was far beyond her ability to imagine. She helped her brother unload his car and then returned to her own home. It was Tuesday evening, June 25, 2002.

All day Wednesday, Evonitz hibernated in his room—jumping at every passing footstep, cringing at every approaching car. He tried to reach his wife—he wanted her to join him so that they could leave the country together. He placed a call to his younger sister Jennifer in Bradenton, Florida. Maybe he should head that way. Get the state of Georgia in between him and the lawmen of South Carolina.

Jennifer would help him melt into the landscape. Now, he had a plan. He'd finalize it in the morning.

Shortly before 10 A.M. on Thursday, June 27, Evonitz startled awake. Was it just a jumpy attack of paranoia? Or did he hear the shrill shriek of a siren, and fear it was calling his name as its sound came closer and closer? Or did he answer the phone and get the word that the cops were on the way? Whatever drove him, he sensed he did not have a second to lose. He fled the room, abandoning his belongings. Police would not enter his hideout for three more hours.

He continued down Interstate 26 until it intersected with Interstate 95. He sped down that highway to the state line. Before leaving South Carolina, he stopped in Hardeeville to gas up. He withdrew $300 from his account at South Carolina Bank and Trust from an ATM on Highway 17 in Jasper County. Police were tracking his whereabouts through his banking transaction and his cell phone calls. They could not get a fix on his cell phone, though, because whenever he was not using it, he turned it off.

While traversing coastal Georgia, he called Kristen to explain his departure and confess his sins. He told her that he was ashamed of what had happened in Columbia. Much of his conversation was disjointed and naked of details.

He crossed the Georgia state line and entered Florida. Soon after, he cut over to I-75 via I-10. Then he called Jennifer again from near Jacksonville. She agreed to meet him at an IHOP not far from Bradenton. He knew he could count on her.

But he did not count on the power of her conscience. He thought his downfall would come through a telephone tap. Believing that the lines of his family members in Columbia were monitored by law enforcement, he took precautions. He assumed that Jennifer's phone—two states away from the scene of his crime—would be safe. Nonetheless, he did not take any chances. He weighed and coded every word. But a phone tap was not his problem—Jennifer's strong sense of right and wrong was.

As he and his sister made plans for a rendezvous at IHOP, the men who hunted him pinpointed his arrival in Florida. They drew the conclusion that he was headed to Bradenton. Their suspicions were confirmed when Jennifer reported the impending meeting to the Sarasota office of the FBI.

The information was passed along to the Manatee County Sheriff's Department, the law enforcement agency with jurisdiction in the area. Deputies Timothy Hartman and Bret Owen rolled their cars into the IHOP parking lot, but could find no sign of the wanted man.

Richard Marc Evonitz spotted them when he arrived. He did not know if they were there for him or if their presence was mere coincidence, but he was taking no chances. He pulled into the strip of stores across the street and parked behind the Outerlimits nightclub. He called Jennifer, now convinced his calls to her were being overheard, too. He left a veiled message on her answering machine: "I'm at the opposite location." He hoped she would understand and meet him across the street.

He tarried overlong awaiting his sister's arrival. The police fanned out and searched the area. While driving south behind a pawn shop, Deputy Owen spotted Evonitz's car. He turned into the parking lot of Ma Fudpuckers Bar and Grill and saw the Ford Escort parked on the side of the building. He came to a stop, trained his spotlight on the vehicle and took cover behind his car.

Evonitz jerked out of the parking lot and down Route 41. He floored his Escort toward Sarasota. Deputy Hartman was still behind the wheel. He flew off, taking first position for the chase. When Owen got back into his patrol car, he followed, assuming second position. The number of pursuing vehicles increased with every mile.

It was after 10 at night and Evonitz killed his headlights in an attempt to disappear. His darkened vehicle wove in and out of lanes at speeds exceeding ninety miles per hour. He shot across the median strip and headed straight into the oncoming rush. Horns blared as cars peeled off to each side like synchronized swimmers at high speed.

Hartman kept close contact with Sergeant Paul Fieber at headquarters, reporting driving conditions, speeds and the suspect's erratic driving patterns. When he reached Whitfield Avenue, Fieber called off the pursuit because of its danger to the public.

Evonitz thought that his ploy succeeded—his mission was accomplished. He believed that with his daring driving, he had lost his pursuers. He had a moment of thrilling jubilation.

The Manatee County Sheriff's Department issued a

BOLO—a "Be on the lookout" request—warning other law enforcement entities in the area. Before the Sarasota Police Department could send the information out to the men on patrol, Officers Thomas Shanafelt and Thomas Quinlan in the 2900 block of North Tamiami Trail saw a vehicle speeding at 100 miles per hour heading south on the northbound side of the four-lane divided highway. Unaware of who they were chasing, the patrolmen hit their lights and picked up the pursuit.

One mile, two miles, then Evonitz spotted the flashing lights racing toward him—he knew they had him in their sights again. Joy transformed into panic and despair. He was clocked at speeds of up to 120 miles per hour.

At Route 41 and Tenth Street, he slowed at a red light as he approached three lanes of stopped traffic. Then, he blasted through the intersection—sliding between two cars stopped at the light. He missed them both by a whisper.

By now, Officers William Schwenk, Timothy Bain and Lieutenant Paul Sutton had joined Shanafelt and Quinlan in the chase.

Up ahead, Officers Derrick Gilbert, Todd Thurow and Rick Rivera each picked a spot and pulled stop strips of tire-ripping Teflon nails out of their trunks. The strips lay in wait in the inside lanes at the 600, 400 and 100 blocks of North Tamiami Trail. Evonitz flew across them, blowing out tires with a roar. Three of his tires were flat. He lost control of his car, striking the outside lane curb. He bounced back on the roadway. He kept going forward on his rims, ricocheting from one curb to the other. Rubber from his front left tire flew off in all directions hitting guardrails and patrol cars with a denting thud. The police no longer were hampered in their chase by his extinguished headlights—the metal rims of his Escort sprayed sparks, lighting his trail.

The chase was so frenzied and determined that the police did not have time to pull the stop strips from the road before five or six of their own vehicles flew across them and had their tires blown, too. Back at headquarters, Sergeant Curt Holmes monitored the pursuit and called in resources.

Evonitz turned off of North Tamiami Trail and onto Bayfront Drive. Now his disabled car had slowed to the point that some officers were pursuing him on foot. In the exclusive Sarasota Bayfront area, near the entrance to Marina Jack's restaurant and just yards from one-million-dollar condos, he tried to cross the median. His car conquered the curb, but knocked off all of the rubber remains on the passenger-side front tire in the process. The rim dug into the grass and dirt, and stopped him in his tracks.

Adrenaline pumped to the max, Evonitz was ready for fight or flight. Immediately, a swollen police force now including fourteen additional officers, Jim Kerul, Maria Llovio, Greg Kitsos, Pat Robinson, Charles Riffe, Danny Robbins, Doug Vollmer, Rex Troche, Michael Jackson, Kevin Schafer, Mike Jolly, Donzia Franklin, Ryan Stimpert and John Todd, surrounded Evonitz with a fifteen-foot perimeter.

He stuck one hand out the driver's-side window. In the other hand, he held a gun.

"More often than not, the typical psychopath will seem particularly agreeable and make a distinctly positive impression when he is first encountered. Alert and friendly in his attitude, he is easy to talk with and seems to have a good many genuine interests. There is nothing at all odd or queer about him, and in every respect he tends to embody the concept of a well-adjusted, happy person."

Hervey Cleckley, M.D., from *The Mask of Sanity*

Chapter 2

Luxurious waterfront hotels and condos towered around Richard Marc Evonitz as he sat inside his car. Bright city lights illuminated his Ford Escort like a luxury model on the showroom floor. The fronds of towering palm trees formed a majestic canopy over his head. And yet, there he was, cornered like a common purse-snatcher pursued to the end of a dark, dirty, dead-end alley.

Who was this man? A social outcast shunned by family and scorned by acquaintances? A withdrawn individual living alone and lonely?

No. He was, to all outward appearances, a normal man. A man who was loved by his mother, cherished by his sisters and well-liked by his friends. Certainly he had his personal quirks—who didn't?—but these eccentricities only served to make him more interesting. He concealed his dark side from everyone except his wives and his victims.

To most he encountered, Richard Marc Evonitz was perfectly normal—simply human. He was never the object of suspicion or concern. He was a reasonably attractive man—always well-groomed and neatly dressed.

He was a bright child who conquered reading before many his age could form a complete sentence. He soaked up knowledge from every available source like a dry sponge in warm water.

Family members recalled his perennial acts of kindness, his warmth, his compassion. Friends remembered his willingness to help find solutions for home improvement projects. Neighborhood kids found him helpful when a bicycle chain slipped or a wheel fell off a skateboard.

He served eight years in the U.S. Navy, and left the service with an honorable discharge and multiple commendations. From there, he moved into an industrial career where he found success both in sales and with his innovative ideas. In his heart, he was an inventor—drawing out detailed plans and building prototypes.

Evonitz was an articulate communicator who was involved in his community and committed to his work. As president of the South Oaks Neighborhood Association, he led the fight to stop rezoning near his subdivision. His letter to the editor published in the local newspaper made a strong case in support of gays in the military. He went beyond the call of duty at work, too—co-authoring a technical piece that ran in a trade publication.

He was a gregarious man who presented a normal, human face to the world. He was the kind of guy who would share a beer and talk at length to his neighbors in their front yards until mosquitoes drove them all indoors. He invited them to cookouts in his backyard and attended parties at their homes. He was just another guy-next-door.

How then did he become the object of a multi-state manhunt? How did someone who seemed so ordinary end up surrounded by men with drawn guns in an exclusive neighborhood in the heart of the night?

> *"It appears that this type of violence is caused by a not well understood combination of nature and nurture. Some people seem to be genetically predisposed to violence and when those people are subjected to an abusive rearing environment, we are virtually guaranteed of creating a monster. On the other hand, there are serial killers who appear to have come from a normal family with no trauma in their background, so the development of these offenders is one of the not well understood phenomena that mental health professionals are looking at because of its obvious significance."*

Greg McCrary, former FBI profiler, on *FredTalk*

Chapter 3

Hester "Tess" Ragin and Joe Evonitz met while working in the same office at Fort Jackson in Columbia, South Carolina. Fort Jackson was born to fill the training needs of the World War I fighting force in June of 1917. It was constructed on 1,200 acres of land donated by the citizens of Columbia to the federal government. In two months' time, the Sixth National Cantonment—one of sixteen developed to support the war effort—had grown from a scrub pine and oak forest to Camp Jackson, a training facility for 10,000 troops complete with a trolley line and hundreds of buildings. In eight months, construction was complete, but after the Armistice was signed in 1918, the camp went idle. It was little used until the drums of war began their relentless beat in 1939.

When Tess and Joe worked there more than a decade after the war, Fort Jackson was a hodgepodge of mostly temporary buildings and old wooden barracks to house the troops. Tess was a local girl with a civil service job. Joe was in the Army, stationed at Fort Campbell in Kentucky, on temporary assignment in South Carolina. His home was Perth Amboy, New Jersey. The attraction between Joe and Tess was instant and mutual. Romance bloomed in the ramshackle environs of a utilitarian Quonset hut office.

On December 6, 1961, they married in a Methodist church in Lexington, South Carolina. Joe returned to Fort Campbell for a few months soon after the ceremony. His stint in the Army ended in June of 1962. After his discharge, the newlywed couple moved into Joe's mother's apartment overlooking the New Jersey Turnpike just outside of Perth Amboy.

In the summer of 1963, Tess had a new civil service job in the finance and accounting department at Raritan Arsenal in Metuchen, New Jersey. She was pregnant with her first child and about to go on maternity leave. Joe, who was working for a bus company, lost his job, plunging the expectant couple into dire financial straits. Joe insisted that Tess call her parents and ask them to send money for their living expenses—he felt entitled to their support. Tess, humiliated and reluctant, placed the call begging her family for help.

Instead of sending money, her parents drove up to New Jersey, picked up their daughter and took her home. Joe made his way south and to his wife's side a few days before she went into labor. Their first child, Richard Marc Edward Evonitz was born on July 29, 1963, at Providence Hospital in Columbia, South Carolina. Since Joe's brother was also named Richard, the family called the new baby Marc from the start.

By this time, Joe knew that he made a miserable mistake when he married Tess, he said later. However, since he was from a broken home, he knew how difficult divorce was on the children. He was determined to keep his family together. His internal conflict made it easy for him to use alcohol for a crutch. His drinking problem escalated and caused him to lose one job after another.

Despite his unhappiness with his marriage, Joe loved little Marc. His child's intelligence filled him with pride and amazement. "He had linear thinking even when he was a baby. When he made up his mind he wanted to do something, he worked at it until he did it," Joe said.

Once, when Marc was still young enough to be crawling around on the floor, a kitchen chair captured his undivided attention. No one suspected what he had in mind as he examined and fiddled with the chair. A little later that day, Joe sat down on the object of Marc's attention and was dumped on the floor as it broke into pieces. He then realized that Marc—somehow—had managed to remove every screw on the chair that was within his reach.

Marc developed a strong attachment to a Mickey Mouse hand puppet when he was a toddler. Joe entertained him for hours talking through the puppet. It seemed as if Marc believed the puppet was a living, breathing, talking creature. To test this idea, Joe threw Mickey across the room, where he flopped in a lifeless heap beside the floorboard. The little tyke erupted into an anguished torrent of tears. Joe's first instinct was to comfort his son, but Marc was inconsolable. Joe rushed across the room, retrieved the puppet, snuggled it onto his hand and made it punch him in the nose and verbally rebuke him for his behavior. Soon, Marc's sobs segued into smiles when he was convinced his puppet had come to no harm.

When Marc was 2 years old and Joe was unemployed again, the Evonitz family moved back to Joe's mother's place in Perth Amboy. The little boy did not have many children to play with in the apartment complex, and seeing others was a big treat. As often as she could, Tess took him down to the park, where Marc would exclaim, "Oooooh, kids!" and run off to play.

On his first Halloween trick-or-treating excursion, Marc was very confused. His parents sent him up to front doors and he would walk away baffled. After the fourth house, he finally looked down in his bag and saw the candy. At last, he got it. "I like this."

Marc was an exuberant young boy who was comfortable with strangers. On his fourth birthday, he went to the grocery store with his mother and stopped every shopper to say, "Hi! I'm four years old." His two big loves were Batman and Speed Racer.

Marc was the only child until July 1968, when his sister Kristen was born at Perth Amboy Hospital. Marc turned 5 that same month. He was enthralled with her, spending hours by her side. He erupted in laughter at every little thing she did.

Joe noticed his son's early interest in automobiles and bought him Matchbox cars by the dozen. By the time he was 5, Marc could name the make and model of every one of the miniatures in his collection. Joe and his brother, Richard, sat on the sofa by the window in their mother's living room one afternoon. As they talked and listened to the whizzing traffic in the background, the young boy climbed up between the two men and looked through the glass to the highway below. To the entertainment and astonishment of his Uncle Richard, Marc demonstrated his ability to match the small models to the real thing—identifying each and every car that drove down the road.

The following May, Joe lost another job and the family moved back to South Carolina. Tess's mother said, "Joe always celebrated having a new child by losing his job." There, the household grew by one more in March of 1971 when Jennifer was born in Providence Hospital.

By now, Marc was 8 years old and girls—even his sisters—were more often considered an annoyance. Three-year-old Kristen, in typical little-sister fashion, was in awe of her older brother and wanted to follow him everywhere.

She would turn her little pleading face on Marc and his friend and beg, "Please. I want to go. I want to go. Please."

"No," Marc said.

"Aw, let her go," his friend said.

"No. That might work on you but not on me."

Marc always took exceptional care of his toys and books. Like younger siblings everywhere, Kristen and Jennifer scribbled in his books and tore up his toys. Marc was so outraged by this behavior, he made it the subject of a school essay.

Nonetheless, Jennifer remembered him as a good brother. She recalled many days when Marc would entertain her by speaking through her stuffed animals with a broad variety of funny voices.

Religion was not a strong influence in their home—Tess was a nominal Methodist and, until he converted to Buddhism in the mid-80s, Joe did not have much in the way of religious convictions. The children's maternal grandparents, however, often took the kids to Sunday school and morning services at the Methodist church. Afterwards, they would take their grandchildren out for a meal.

Joe placed a high premium on education in his home. "He was an intelligent man," Jennifer said. "He gave me a good education in life—both in street smarts and in book smarts."

Joe tried to teach all three children to read long before they went to school. Marc was a quick learner. At first, he pretended to have the ability by memorizing stories that were read to him and reciting them back as he turned the pages. Soon after, the actual recognition of words followed. In time, he read family's set of encyclopedias cover to cover, from A to Z.

Jennifer was as adept at reading as Marc. Unknown to anyone in her early years, however, little Kristen was dyslexic. Her inability to read made her father furious and turned her into a target. He berated her, calling her "stupid" again and again. He often used that insult with other family members, but threw it in Kristen's face most of all. Years later, one teacher recognized Kristen's problem and enrolled her in a special summer program that taught her the coping mechanisms she needed to read with competence.

Marc appeared to be a typical, normal boy—a member of the Boy Scouts, an active participant in Little League baseball and a good student. He was often seen flashing from one side of his neighborhood to another on the back of his skateboard. The family continued its pattern of frequent moves. Joe would get fired or quit his job. The money would run out, resulting in eviction from their home, and the family would settle in another spot. Marc attended three different elementary schools: Satchel Ford, Lyons and Forest Lake.

Beneath the façade of normalcy, the family hid a dark secret—the chaos in this home was out of control. According to Tess, Joe's behavior had a predictable pattern: get drunk, get nasty, pass out, wake up and be even worse. The slightest thing would set him off.

He yelled a lot. His favorite insult was "moron." He used the word on everyone in the family. He had a habit of calling people all over the country when he was drinking—racking up long distance bills that the strapped family could ill afford. Tess often removed the phones from the home and placed them in her car when she went to work. When she did, she knew her return home would earn her more abuse.

According to Tess, the physical violence escalated dramatically when Tess was pregnant with Jennifer. It turned what should have been a joyful time into nine nightmare months. The physical battering was not reserved solely for his wife.

On one occasion, Marc spilled dog food from the bag onto the floor. Joe flew into a rage—chasing the young boy out of the house. Marc outran him that time.

Another time, Kristen was sitting in a wicker chair and did not respond quickly enough to Joe's orders. He grabbed the chair and shook it as he yelled at her, then he knocked her and the chair flat. As she fell, the back of her head collided with the sharp corner of the television set, and blood flowed. She was rushed to the emergency room. Joe lied and said it was an accident. Tess backed up his lie. Kristen, Jennifer and Marc remained silent.

One hellish Christmas Eve, Tess said, Joe had his hands around her throat and was squeezing hard. She was certain he was going to kill her that night.

Tess, however, was unaware of the many acts of abuse that occurred while she was at work. The children kept those incidents to themselves. Only when they were adults did they share the stories they had hidden from her all those years. Tess was horrified when she heard of the time that Joe hoisted Kristen in the air and slammed her against the wall.

As late as June 2002, Tess was still learning more about

the horror in her home. She comforted her crying 38-year-old son as he related even more incidents of abuse by his father.

"I don't know if there was one particular moment that it clicked for me," Jennifer said. "But when I was in the fifth grade, I began to realize that other people did not live like that."

She said that between their nomadic existence and her total lack of self-esteem, making friends was very difficult. Even when they did, the three kids avoided bringing their friends to their house as a general rule. "Occasionally, I would bring a friend home and Dad would not behave as usual," Jennifer said. "They thought he was so charming and so funny. And that hurt me."

MARC ATTENDED Fairwold Middle School, now Sanders Middle, in Columbia. He was a quiet student, not popular among his peers or memorable to his teachers. Like many children of alcoholics, he built a wall between himself and the outside world to keep his family's secrets intact.

He demonstrated his ability to design and construct early on. When he was just 12 years old, he built "tater" and "onion" boxes from wood. With his father, he set up a stand and sold them quicker than he could put them together.

Marc attended Keenan High School where, at the end of his freshman year, he made the list of outstanding students chosen by staff and faculty at the school. He transferred to Irmo High in the summer of 1979. The next year, he took extra classes in the summer session and graduated from high school when he was 16. There was no history of disciplinary problems—no indication of the aberrant behavior that was to come.

KRISTEN CLAIMED the family dynamic was inconsistent and unstable. It was highlighted by frequent moves and the emotional disruptions that ensued. It was so chaotic that she did not know where her brother and sister were born. "I know it was somewhere in the state [South Carolina], but I could not tell you where."

She also said that Joe created a violent and abusive environment in the home and that Marc received the brunt of this brutish behavior because of his attempts to protect his mother and his sisters.

"We lived in a prison," Jennifer said. "He was a very controlling person. He wanted us to make straight A's. If we didn't, we were stupid. It was all about power and control. 'You'll get an A or you'll get a beating.' I see him as a sadistic man who got pleasure—I know I saw the pleasure in his face—out of making us miserable."

About her mother, Jennifer said, "She tried her best, but she had checked out a long time ago—both mentally and emotionally. We all had to check out to some degree."

Joe admits he was verbally abusive—he yelled at his wife and kids often, and his negative remarks were a constant cloud hanging over the home. But, he insisted, he was not physically abusive. There was only one occasion when he hit anyone in the family. That incident, he claimed, occurred when Tess admitted she was cheating on him.

*"The disorganized offender is socially inadequate. Often he
has never married, lives alone or with a parental figure, and
lives in close proximity to the crime scene. The offender is
fearful of people, and may have developed a well-defined
delusional system. He acts impulsively under stress, finding
a victim usually within his own geographical area."*

Robert K. Ressler, Ann W. Burgess and John E. Douglas
Sexual Homicide: Patterns and Motives

Chapter 4

In 1975, Perry Deveaux was 17 years old. An African-
American male of limited intelligence, he lived in the Mount
Pleasant area near Charleston, South Carolina, at his grandmother's home on Venning Road. The path of his life did not
seem destined to intersect the road traveled by the Evonitz
family, but the twists and turns of fate created a crooked
crossroads of connection.

Deveaux worked on a garbage truck hauling trash from
the Isle of Palms and Sullivans Island. Next to the house was
a horse stable on Rifle Range Road where, for years, he had
cleaned stalls to make extra money.

Over time, he and many of the riders who came to the sta-
bles got to know one another well enough to exchange greetings and engage in brief conversations in passing. One of the
riders was 23-year-old Kathleen Sanderlin of Sullivans Island,
a fifth grade schoolteacher at Harbor View Elementary School
on James Island.

Kathleen mounted her horse on the afternoon of November 28 and cantered out of the stable for a relaxing ride
through the countryside. Deveaux started drinking early that

day and kept it up unabated. Mid-afternoon, he walked up to Gold's grocery store to refuel. There he bought a quart container of Budweiser beer. He guzzled it straight out of the bottle on his way back from the store.

Then he saw her. He narrowed his eyes—zeroing in on Kathleen out riding alone in the isolated rural area. When he greeted her, he saw the fear flash in her eyes. Beyond the safe, populated confines of the stable, her comfort level with this simple young man dissipated like a drop of water on a griddle-hot pavement.

Deveaux jumped forward, startling both the horse and the rider, his movements too sudden for them to react or flee. He grabbed Kathleen's arm and jerked her out of her saddle. He tossed her like a sack of garbage to the ground.

She crumpled in a heap—for a moment too stunned and disbelieving to respond. Then Deveaux flashed a knife and she screamed for help. When she did, Deveaux got on top of her. He stabbed her, yelling, "Shut up! Shut up! Shut up!" with each swing of the knife blade. He stabbed her in the abdomen, in her side, across her hands and arms. Then, he stabbed her in the throat—severing her vocal cords—and the screaming stopped.

He cut off her dress and her panties with the same knife and ripped them out of his way. He unzipped his pants. He raped her with a savage intensity. When he was through, her body was riddled with twenty-seven wounds, including the defensive cuts on her hands and arms. He threw the knife as far as he could and fled the scene. He did not know when he left her if she was alive or dead. And he did not care.

Another person on horseback spotted Kathleen's horse early that evening wandering back to the stable with empty stirrups jingling at its sides. The rider headed out expecting to find a thrown Kathleen limping back on foot. Instead, he discovered Kathleen's ravaged, lifeless body abandoned in dense undergrowth along Four Mile Road, a dirt road in the Cooper area near Mount Pleasant. She was rushed to Medical University Hospital where she was pronounced dead on arrival.

• • •

EUGENE FRAZIER joined the Charleston County Police Department in the early sixties. He was an ex-Marine and one of the first African Americans on the force.

Racism was not a stranger to police departments across the country at that time. Frazier combated this prejudice and earned his success by working harder and longer and caring more than his white counterparts.

The first twelve years of his career, he was a patrolman. In his last assignment in that capacity, his beat included the area where Perry Deveaux lived with his grandmother. In 1975, when Kathleen Sanderlin was murdered, Frazier was a detective. He was called to the scene.

Perry Deveaux came to his mind right away when he saw Kathleen's ravaged body. Frazier had gotten to know a lot of the people in this rural area when he was on patrol. He remembered Deveaux as a naïve, slow-witted but deadly young man. Frazier knew that Deveaux lived just a quarter of a mile from the spot where the homicide was committed. Frazier also remembered Deveaux's fascination with white females—his constant litany of "I'm gonna get me a white woman."

After the gruesome discovery of the body, Corporal Eugene Frazier and Corporal Curt Parsley went out to Deveaux's grandmother's house. They knew that an empty quart bottle of Budweiser was found at the scene of the murder. At Gold's, they learned that Deveaux had purchased a similar bottle that afternoon. They had also located two witnesses who had seen Deveaux emerge from the woods that day at the approximate time of the murder and near the location of Kathleen's body. When he arrived at the young man's home, Corporal Frazier also noticed fresh scratch marks on both of Deveaux's hands and arms—scratch marks consistent with the vines and bushes where the victim had been found.

Unfortunately, the captain of the detectives, an unabashed racist who did not feel that blacks were capable of doing the job, accompanied Frazier and Parsley to Perry

Deveaux's grandmother's house. In Frazier's opinion, the captain felt he could easily outwit an old black woman.

He played a cat-and-mouse game with her in her front yard—teasing and pulling back. Frazier pleaded with him to stop and just take Deveaux in to the station for questioning. But the captain would not relent. Eventually, his game alarmed the grandmother, who called a prominent defense attorney and former prosecutor.

The officers did take Deveaux in to the station, but now his lawyer was present, preventing him from answering the most important questions. Frazier was certain that, without an attorney, Deveaux would have confessed that night.

Instead, the suspect denied any involvement in the homicide and there was not enough evidence to charge him with the crime. Frazier released him with great reluctance.

But the investigator was convinced of Deveaux's guilt. He pursued him with the single-minded intensity of a cat stalking a mouse.

First, he contacted Ronald Heyward, an informant he had worked with on other cases. Heyward got a job working in the sanitation department with Deveaux. The plan was to befriend the suspect and get him to confess to the murder. Heyward reached out to Deveaux and was making progress in building a relationship. Deveaux made comments to Heyward that bolstered Frazier's suspicions.

Then, the captain of the detectives pulled the plug. He did not like Frazier's plan. In fact, he did not like any of his ideas. The captain's approach was to pick up every young black male in the area. And he did just that with the help of two white detectives. Each suspect was interrogated and strapped to a lie detector machine. Frazier was eased off of the case.

THE RESIDENTS of the community at first offered a $5000 reward, which over time grew to $15,000, for information that would lead to the discovery of Kathleen Sanderlin's murderer. A year and a half after her death, Charleston house delegation chairman Robert R. Woods, of the South Carolina

State Legislature, formed a committee to review the criminal investigation in the homicide of Kathleen and one other unsolved killing.

Despite the combined efforts of the community, the politicians and the investigators, Deveaux eluded justice for nearly six years. Twenty years later, a rumor about actions taken by Wesley Buckheister, the victim's brother, still circulated through Charleston. Residents said that Wesley was frustrated—and his frustration grew exponentially with each passing year. One day, they conjectured, when the thirst for justice had dried up his self-control, he ran down Deveaux with his car and broke the man's leg.

The rumor was repeated with a secret admiration for Wesley's loss of control, but it had no basis in fact. No altercations ever occurred between any members of the Deveaux and Buckheister families.

ALTHOUGH HE was no longer on the case, the dogged Detective Frazier was haunted by it. It was a brutal murder and he wanted to hold the perpetrator responsible for his actions. "It didn't bother Deveaux at all," he said. "It was no different to him than slaughtering a hog."

In this frame of mind, Frazier was ready when Charlie Condon was elected to the Ninth Circuit Solicitor's Office in 1981. Condon pulled the files on unsolved homicides in his jurisdiction. He looked at the Kathleen Sanderlin reports and saw Eugene Frazier's name on them as the original investigator.

Condon called Frazier into his office, looked him in the eye and asked, "After all these years, do you think this case can be solved?"

"Yes," Frazier said. "If I work on special assignment out of your office and have no interference from the Charleston County Police."

The prosecutor made the inter-office arrangements through the police chief. Eugene Frazier was on the case again.

As before, his first move was contacting his informant,

Ronald Heyward. Heyward renewed his relationship with Deveaux. It was a simple thing to get close to the young man again—he was hungry for a role model, eager to be seen as a tough guy. The two men went to the movies together and became drinking buddies. Soon, Deveaux was sharing intimate details about his family with his new friend.

Following Frazier's master plan, Heyward wove a tale designed to ensnare Deveaux. Heyward told him that he'd been involved in a killing up in Chicago and had some trouble with it. Now, a drug dealer and pimp wanted him to bump off a prostitute and he needed someone to help him.

Deveaux was ready and eager to be his partner. Heyward said that he'd have to check it out with the pimp. Then, he raced to meet with Frazier. Frazier, meanwhile, had the perfect pimp candidate waiting on the sidelines. His name was Rollo Brown.

Brown, a Charleston County police detective, was typecast for the role. He had a full head of Jeri-curls. He pulled on a treasure chest of gold chains and sported a flashy gold watch. The only other thing Brown needed was the right swagger and he had that nailed, too.

On June 9, 1981, the set-up was complete. Heyward lured Deveaux into a motel room equipped with video cameras and audio pick-up. There he introduced him to the so-called pimp and drug dealer, Rollo Brown. To complete a credible picture of his role, the room was decorated with white and black women posing as prostitutes. When Deveaux saw them, he was tongue-tied and the scene was set.

Brown dismissed the ladies and turned to Deveaux. "My man here told me you wanted to do this thing. How do I know you're trustworthy?" He insisted that before they could give Deveaux the job, they had to have proof that he was capable of murdering a woman—they had to know that he had killed before.

Deveaux fell for the ploy, revealing information about the 1975 killing of Kathleen Sanderlin that the police had never released to the public, including the unknown fact that

Kathleen's pubic hair was a different shade from the dark brown hair on her head.

Deveaux said, "You know she was scared. The horse was about from here to that chair over there and I snatched her like this here."

"You just snatched her off her horse?" Detective Brown asked.

"Yes, I did. When I snatched her off, she started screaming. [. . .] And then she rolled back over and she was trying to scratch me because I was holding her. [. . .] And I said, 'Now, you shut up.' I jerked her on the side and I do like this."

"You stick her? Where at?"

"I stick her here first."

"In the throat?"

"Uh-huh, where she couldn't scream no more. Then right back around, I stick her in the navel part, then after I do it, I turned her around like this here and stick the back part."

It was the stab wound to the abdomen that the autopsy concluded had caused her death when it severed an artery. Deveaux also described the type of knife he used when he stabbed her and cut off her dress and panties. He also identified the side where the slices to the clothing were made.

When Brown agreed to allow Deveaux to participate in the upcoming phony murder, Deveaux said, "Before I kill her, I want to have sex with her."

The deal was struck. A couple of days later, Deveaux was heading down the road believing that he was going to get his advance money for the killing. Detectives Eugene Frazier and William Grier pulled him over on Savannah Highway. He was arrested and charged with murder.

Roddy Perry, the last partner Frazier worked with before his retirement, said, "Frazier taught me a lot. He was an excellent investigator. He would not stop until he solved a case. Some cops would get eight to ten leads that would go nowhere, and give up. Gene was not one of those guys. He'd work even harder after he had the suspect behind bars to make sure everything was just right for the trial. His rate of conviction was amazing." Perry went on to become the chief of police in Mount Pleasant, South Carolina.

DEVEAUX WAS released on bond in July. On January 22, at the request of Public Defender Michael P. O'Connelly, the court ordered the Department of Mental Retardation to examine Deveaux to determine if he was capable of understanding the proceedings and able to assist in his defense. After they did so, the department was prepared to testify to Deveaux's competence to stand trial.

His attorneys were convinced that if he faced a trial, he would be convicted and had a strong probability of receiving the death penalty. Prosecutors were concerned that Deveaux might elude justice, since the murder weapon had never been found. With both sides facing the possibility of undesirable scenarios, the defense was able to work a deal with the prosecution. Perry Deveaux agreed to plead guilty and, in exchange, the prosecution offered a life sentence.

On the morning of February 24, he was due in the courtroom to enter his plea. He had started drinking early that day—by his own admission, he had already had three beers by the time he arrived in the courtroom. The judge postponed the hearing until that afternoon to make sure Deveaux was sober.

When the bench announced the imposition of a life sentence, an unidentified woman at the proceedings, presumed to be Deveaux's companion, passed out cold. She was carried from the courtroom. Deveaux took up residence at the Lieber Correctional Institute on March 1, 1982.

By current law, instituted in 1977, an inmate receiving a life sentence had to serve a minimum of twenty years before being eligible for parole. However, since Deveaux's crime was committed in 1975, his eligibility would be set by the old law—he would be up for parole in ten short years.

BY 1982, Tess Evonitz had been trying to get Joe out of her life for years. One time, she took him up to his brother

Richard's home in Fredericksburg, Virginia, and left him there. When he came back to Columbia for a visit, Tess allowed him to sweet-talk her into letting him stay.

She was working as a telephone operator at that time. She, along with many of her co-workers, talked to Perry Deveaux and other prisoners on the phone during slow times at the office.

Deveaux told Tess that, despite his confession, he was an innocent man. He said that police had kept him in the interrogation room for hours. He was tired and defeated. When the officers told him that if he signed a confession, he could go home, he fell for it. He signed it and was put under arrest.

Tess knew Deveaux's low IQ made him susceptible to such a ploy. She also knew that fairness was often not part of the game in the prosecution of black-on-white crimes. She found his story credible and was convinced of his innocence.

> *"Although the families initially appear to be functional with both parents present, a number of problems appear with the parents' background to indicate they had their own stresses and problems to deal with in addition to raising children. The family histories of thirty-six murderers revealed that multiple problems existed in family structure. [. . .] Nearly 70 percent of the families had histories of alcohol abuse [. . .]"*
>
> Robert K. Ressler, Ann W. Burgess and John E. Douglas
> *Sexual Homicide: Patterns and Motives*

Chapter 5

Marc Evonitz did not enroll in any higher education classes, but instead worked a series of unsatisfying jobs in the area for a couple of years. When he was the manager of a Jiffy Lube, his father said, he started hanging around with a bad group of "jail birds." The one that bothered Joe the most was a guy named Billy, who served seven years in prison for robbery and whose life ended in suicide a few years later. "There was something evil about Billy that I didn't like," he said. "Billy and Marc went to Florida. When they came back, there was something different about Marc." Since that day, Joe has often wondered just what happened on that trip.

Jennifer, on the other hand, insists there was nothing unusual about Billy—Marc had been in trouble long before meeting him. "Dad rants and raves about Billy because he does not want to take personal responsibility for the fact that Marc was into drugs, into alcohol and breaking into houses."

In one incident, police questioned Marc about a break-in at the Evonitzes' next-door neighbor's house. Some collectible coins and valuables were stolen. Marc denied any involvement and his mother believed him. Police never found sufficient evidence to prosecute. Years later during a massive spring cleaning, Tess and Jennifer found some of the stolen coins. To Jennifer, the discovery was no surprise, but Tess was shocked to learn that Marc was responsible.

Marc had also developed a habit of kiting checks. He had a series of run-ins with people he'd cheated. It reached a crisis point when he wrote a rubber check for $350 to Kmart. The manager there, Joe said, wanted to put his son in jail. Joe told Marc he had to get out of his house because he was a criminal. Joe gave Marc a choice: Join the service or pack up your bags and live on the street. "I was happy for Marc because he was getting away from our dad," Jennifer said. "But I was sad to see him go because he protected us."

In February 1984, he joined the U.S. Navy beginning his tour of duty with basic training at Naval Station San Diego. He was glad to be out of the house, but felt guilty for leaving his mother and sisters behind. Joe was confident that a stint in the service would straighten his son out.

TESS ADMITTED that developing an emotional attachment on the telephone with Perry Deveaux was pretty stupid. But many desperate women make foolish choices. She saw this relationship as a vehicle for getting out of her marriage to Joe.

Although he had limited mental abilities, Deveaux was an amusing companion. He made this battered woman feel better about herself. Tess felt attractive for the first time in a long time. She spent a lot of her time writing papers and letters on Deveaux's behalf, and became an active member of CURE—Citizens United for the Rehabilitation of Errants— a national grassroots organization dedicated to the reduction of crime through the reform of the criminal justice system. Prisoners, former prisoners and families of prisoners are the bulk of the membership of CURE. The goals of the organization are to use prisons only for those who have to be in them and to provide those inmates with all the rehabilitative opportunities they need to turn their lives around.

Soon, Joe felt certain that his wife was having an affair. One day, the phone rang. The caller asked to speak to Tess. Joe's anger ratcheted up to violence when Tess confirmed that she had a strong attachment to Deveaux. Joe backhanded her when she insisted on taking the call. She staggered back from the blow, a tiny bead of blood forming in the corner of her lips. With a glare that could melt stone, she turned away from Joe and picked up the telephone.

Joe left the home, borrowing Marc's car. That vehicle became his only shelter. Amid piles of clothing, fast food wrappers and empty bottles of booze, Joe camped out in cramped quarters, slipping further down the road to his own destruction. He stole Tess' income tax refund check from her mailbox, signed her name and cashed it. Then he headed to northern Virginia. She never pressed charges for the theft—she was too glad to see him go. When the money he stole from Tess ran out, Joe hit rock bottom in his dissolute life of drunkenness and despair. He turned to the Salvation Army shelter for assistance. They dried him out and soon got him a job working at a fast food restaurant.

In that eatery, he met Ezghaharia, who came to the United States from northern Ethiopia to visit family members here. Her English was rudimentary—so much so, she had trouble forming a sentence. But despite the communications barrier, Joe and Ezghaharia developed a strong rapport. All the while, a hole in Joe's stomach, born of alcohol abuse, was wreaking havoc on his body. He said he was close to death the day Ezghaharia rushed him to the hospital.

Joe and Tess filed for divorce. When it was final, Tess married Perry Deveaux at Lieber Correctional Institute where he was serving his life sentence for the 1975 murder. The odd couple spent many enjoyable hours together in the visitors' area. An interactive social life blossomed among the frequent attendees there. In the group of visitors, Tess had fond memories of the nice people she had met.

Tess invested massive amounts of time and energy in an

attempt to set Perry free. Marriage altered her last name, but that was not enough for Tess. She went to court and had her name legally changed to Lorraine Deveaux.

JOE AND Ezghaharia were married by a justice of the peace, and jump-started their life together in northern Virginia. Finding housing was not easy for an integrated couple in that state in the 80s, but they managed. She got a job at the telephone company and he drove a cab.

When Jennifer met Ezghaharia, she was shocked to discover that her new stepmother was a black woman. The racial difference did not bother her, but, Jennifer said, "We grew up for years with him ranting and raving the 'N' word. And originally when he told the family about her, he said that she was from Ethiopia but was a Caucasian."

Marc had more contact with her over the years than Jennifer did, and he liked her a lot. She always annoyed Jennifer, though, with her constant litany of "Why don't you call your father?" Jennifer never answered that question because she was certain that if she did, she would not be believed. She did, however, have some admiration for Ezghaharia. "She was a workhorse who had three jobs and had figured out how to put my father in his place. He needed her."

MARC LEFT the base in San Diego in August of 1985 when he transferred to the U.S.S. Koelsch, a frigate based at Naval Station Mayport near Jacksonville, Florida.

The Challenger shuttle's tenth flight launched into space from its pad in Florida on January 28, 1986, at 11:38 A.M. On board was the first private citizen ever to go into space, high school teacher Christa McAuliffe. Their mission was scheduled to last six days and thirty-four minutes.

Seventy-three seconds into the flight, at an altitude of 48,000 feet, communication to the command center ceased. The orbiter broke in two in an explosive burn of hydrogen and oxygen propellants. For twenty-five more seconds, the shuttle continued its upward trajectory, reaching 65,000 feet. Then, it plummeted down at 207 miles per hour, hitting the ocean surface less than three minutes after the break-up.

The U.S.S. Koelsch was called into duty. Their sonar technician was Petty Officer Richard Marc Evonitz. Their charge—to search for the wreckage of the Challenger crew cabin—left a footprint in history. Involved in such a dramatic event, Evonitz found success and enjoyment with the Navy.

His job satisfaction was not enough to prop him up through personal tragedy, though. He staggered under a great loss in September 1986. Hester Ragin, his maternal grandmother, passed away. He had been very close to her all throughout his childhood. This relationship continued after he became an adult. His grandmother wrote to him every week while he was in the service. Her death left a hole in his heart that nothing could fill.

Now, inside his head, the synapses were misfiring— leading Evonitz to actions that would doom the rest of his naval career to stagnant mediocrity.

"Most serial offenders evolve to that level of violence. They transition through lesser sexual crimes such as flashing or exhibitionism, peeping and prowling type activities, obscene phone calls or those type of nuisance offenses. Some sexual offenders plateau off at those lesser crimes."

Greg McCrary, former FBI profiler, on *FredTalk*

Chapter 6

On the southern outskirts of Jacksonville, Florida, lies the community of Orange Park in Clay County. The county is bordered on the east by the St. Johns River and covers over 600 square miles. In the 80s, it was home to 106,000 people—92% of them white. Orange Park nestles against this river and is one of only four incorporated municipalities in the county.

Fifteen-year-old resident Kelli Ballard was walking on her street with her 3-year-old sister on January 3, 1987, at about 4:30 P.M. As they approached and prepared to cross Bellair Boulevard, a '74 beige four-door Dodge with South Carolina plates stopped in their path. Inside the car was off-duty Navy man Richard Marc Evonitz.

He peered straight at Kelli's face. When his unblinking stare got her attention, he looked down in his lap. Kelli's eyes followed his. She was shocked to see that his erect penis was out of his pants and in his hand. He stroked it as he pinned her to the spot with his eyes and within seconds he ejaculated. Kelli burst into tears. Fortunately, her little sister was too short to see inside the car.

A few yards away, 13-year-old William Rosemark, 14-year-old Keith Korwaski and 10-year-old Christopher Ship were riding their bicycles. They were not close enough to see what Kelli saw, but they did notice the driver. When Evonitz jerked away from the intersection, he terrified the boys—coming straight at them before he swerved away at the last possible moment. Kelli raced home and sobbed out the story to her mother, Nancy.

The next day, Kelli was out with her mom when she saw Evonitz again. She recognized him and remembered the license plate number. As they watched, he pulled into the Morgan Plaza shopping strip and entered Movie Land, a video rental business. Nancy called the police.

A Sergeant Scherer responded to the location and noticed that the beige Dodge with South Carolina plates was still in the parking lot, but no one was near it. He entered the business and asked for the manager. As he talked to him, Scherer saw a man about 5'8" tall, approximately 25 years of age with dark hair and a moustache, leave the store. The yet-unidentified man got into the Dodge and drove away.

The clerk at Movie Land provided the officer with a duplicate of their file copy of Evonitz's driver's license and the information that he was stationed aboard the U.S.S. Koelsch. Scherer and Investigator Lawrence then went to the victim's home on Kevin Drive to follow up on the report.

The Clay County Sheriff's Department contacted Naval Investigative Services Agent Jim Black on January 8. Black informed them that the ship was now out to sea and he did not know when it was scheduled to return. He promised to call when he knew the date.

The drivers' license bureau in Tallahassee, Florida, provided investigators with a copy of Evonitz's identification photo. Lawrence put together a photo spread of six white males with dark hair and moustaches. Kelli pointed to the bottom middle picture in the six-pack. She positively identified Richard Marc Evonitz.

On January 16, Black called Clay County. The U.S.S. Koelsch was due back in port on February 9 and was scheduled to remain there until March 16. Tim Collins of the state attorney's office drew up an affidavit charging Evonitz with a lewd/lascivious act in the presence of a minor child. An arrest warrant was issued on February 9.

The U.S.S. Koelsch docked a day early. By the time the arrest warrant was available, Evonitz was in the base hospital—admitted for a case of hepatitis. Five days later, he was released and delivered to the sheriff's department. After being advised of his rights, he gave a statement confessing his guilt.

Evonitz told Lawrence that he "[. . .] ha[d] a problem with masturbating in front of girls." When he felt the urge, he drove around looking for a young victim.

He also explained that when the ship was in port he liked to get way from his crowded, noisy quarters when he could. On January 3, he got a motel room on Interstate 295. In his statement, he said, "I went out to get something to eat after having rented a VCR and movies. I watched one of the movies before leaving and went out to go for a burger. However, after leaving the room, I felt compelled to drive and look for a brunette of around 18 or 19. I found her walking on the road and pulled up next to her. I had my pants unzipped and was masturbating. She turned away and I left."

Evonitz was arrested and booked in the Clay County Jail. The judge released him on his own recognizance.

On June 30, Evonitz pleaded no contest to the charge that he did "[. . .] knowingly commit a lewd or lascivious act, to wit: masturbation in the presence of Kelli Ballard, a child under 16 years of age, contrary to the provisions of Section 800.04, Florida Statutes."

The court did not issue a final verdict. The judge did, however, place him on probation for three years and ordered him to pay $200 in state costs and $52.50 in court costs. As a condition of his probation, he was required to receive a mental health evaluation and treatment, including psycho-sexual counseling, as directed by his probation officer. In addition, Evonitz needed to pay the state of Florida $30 per month toward the cost of his supervision.

The incident marred his rise in the Navy. Evonitz had emerged from boot camp and training as a Sonar Technician Seaman. He was promoted to Petty Officer 3rd class, then to

2nd class and then 1st class. As a result of this crime, he was bumped down to Petty Officer 2nd class, where he remained until the end of his naval career.

Tess was aware that Marc had gotten into some trouble in Florida and knew that he was on probation. Marc covered up the sexual nature of his crime with a story that he had gotten into a fight outside of a bar and had beaten a guy up.

Jennifer thought Marc's demotion in the service had something to do with marijuana or a fight. "I had no idea that he had exposed himself to a child," she said.

His father did not even know there was a problem until years after his son left the Navy. Marc was visiting Joe and his wife in northern Virginia when he let slip a vague remark about some trouble he had in the service. Joe asked, "What trouble?" Marc wove a complicated tale about an 18-year-old kid who chased him and almost ran into his car. "He then told me," Joe said, " 'I got out of my car, grabbed a tire iron, chased him down and beat him up.' "

In March and April of 1988, the Navy placed Evonitz in their alcohol rehabilitation center for treatment. He then returned to the U.S.S. Koelsch at Mayport until the Navy decided to remove the ship from service and sell it to Pakistan. In May, Evonitz and the rest of the crew took the ship to Bath Iron Works dry dock in Portland, Maine. There, they removed any equipment from the ship that they did not want the Pakistanis to have.

BONNIE LOU GOWER, a smart, pretty girl with dark brown hair, lived with her mother two doors down from the Evonitz family home. She and Jennifer were about the same age, and Bonnie was a constant sight going in and out of Jennifer's room. Her mother, Betty Gower, was a psychologist in the South Carolina prison system. Bonnie barely knew her father. While she was growing up, he was serving time in jail in Ohio for the statutory rape of a 16-year-old.

As a young adolescent, Bonnie was drawn to the older

boy next door. She and Marc started corresponding when she was just 14 years old. Their letters led them into a romantic relationship, and they dated whenever Marc came home on leave. Jennifer was bothered that Marc was attracted to someone so young, but it did not set off any alarms in her head at that time.

On August 11, 1988, while Marc was on leave from the base in Maine and Bonnie was only 16 years old, the two were married on the campus of the University of South Carolina in the Rutledge Chapel. Joe Evonitz was not invited to the wedding. The couple then flew up to Portland.

Bonnie was an innocent and naïve young bride. Marc had no difficulty convincing her that their sex life was normal. Bonnie later told investigators that she believed there was nothing out of the ordinary about her husband coming home, blindfolding her, tying her to the bed and raping her for three hours.

When the work was completed on the U.S.S. Koelsch, the ship and crew traveled to Charleston, South Carolina, to await the ship's sale. Within a couple of months, it was gone and Marc was transferred back to San Diego. In November of 1989, Evonitz re-enlisted with the Navy for another three years.

THE RELATIONSHIP between Bonnie and her mother-in-law was strained. Tess saw her as a pretty but egotistical girl who whined all the time. She thought her son devoted an inordinate amount of energy in trying to please her. She said that Bonnie used the excuse of long fake nails to get out of housework, and that Marc obliged her by doing all of the work around their home.

Tess and Jennifer visited the couple in San Diego in 1991. It was not a pleasant stay for Tess. She felt that Bonnie seemed to resent her presence. When an excursion was planned to Los Angeles, Bonnie did not want to go, and asked her husband, "Why do we have to go there?"

"Mom wants to go. She wants to see Hollywood."

"Why do we always have to go where she wants to go?" she retorted.

In the end, Marc, Jennifer and Tess made the trip. But Bonnie stayed at home.

When Tess went back to South Carolina, Jennifer remained in California. She and Bonnie's older brother each claimed a bedroom in the couple's condo and helped with the rent and other household expenses.

Jennifer agreed with her mother that Bonnie was prissy and whiney. "But," she said, "she was a pretty good home-maker for Marc. She cooked and cleaned, and he loved her deeply."

On November 16, 1992, Marc left the Navy with an honorable discharge, a Navy Achievement Medal for leadership, a Navy Good Conduct Medal, two Coast Guard Meritorious Unit Ribbons, a Sea Service Deployment Ribbon and a National Defense Service Medal. The couple came back to Columbia, South Carolina. But they did not stay long.

Bonnie had attended beautician school in California and had certification there. In South Carolina, though, the board requirements for that profession were more rigid, and she would be required to take more classes before she could work. The commonwealth of Virginia, however, would accept the California certification. Since Marc had a good relationship with his Uncle Richard, the couple decided to move near him in the Spotsylvania area.

"Spotsylvania is a vibrant county! We honor the past and look forward to the future."

Martha C. Carter, curator, Spotsylvania County Museum

Chapter 7

Bonnie and Marc moved to Sunburst Lane in Spotsylvania, Virginia, in January 1993. The Rappahannock and Rapidan Rivers to the north and the North Anna River to the south wrapped around the boundaries of Spotsylvania County. Virginia Power built a dam across the southern river in 1972, creating the 9600-acre Lake Anna. Located on the Interstate 95 corridor midway between Washington, D.C., and Richmond, Virginia, the county was a commuter refuge and a retirement haven. The preponderance of former FBI personnel was often highlighted in the press.

Spotsylvania County's 407 square miles echoed with the ghosts of Civil War history—four major battles and the death of Stonewall Jackson happened there. Throughout most of the country, Jackson had long been forgotten in the dusty attic of the past. But in Virginia, he was still very much alive. Jackson-Lee-King Day was a state holiday every January until 2001. It was established originally to remember two Confederate heroes, Stonewall Jackson and Robert E. Lee. When the push for a day to commemorate the life and work of civil rights leader Martin Luther King, Jr., thrust forward on the political scene, Virginia created a puzzling combination—tacking King on to this existing holiday for generals of the Confederacy on the state calendar.

Frenzied interstates and miles and miles of bucolic byways surrounded the county's largest city, Fredericksburg, home to fewer than 20,000. A drive south to the town of Spotsylvania began on these interstates, but soon turned off to smaller state routes across rolling hills and lush greenery.

From sterile beltways streaming with cars to busy highways with strip malls, gas stations and a maze of electrical poles and wiring, it is always a short distance to nowhere. Side roads lead to wilderness in record time. Whizzing tires and honking horns quickly give way to undulating roads flanked by fields, forests and the occasional farmhouse.

In spring, Mother Nature smiles on Virginia, revealing hillsides of wild pink lady slippers and abundant patches of violets that wend like a river through the woods. Dogwood trees splash a blinding white in every direction. Lanky Judas trees accent this brightness with their pearly pink blossoms. Crabapple trees fill the air with an intoxicating sweetness from their fragile blooms.

In the humid summer months, undeveloped land in these rural areas in this part of Virginia transforms into temperate jungles of oaks, poplars and loblolly pine entombed in a thick shroud of kudzu vines, Virginia creeper and poison ivy. A thick undergrowth of indeterminate weeds, worthless shrubs, blackberry brambles and paradise trees pulses with wildness and crowds the roads as if threatening to reclaim them.

The leaves turn, on trees, vines and shrubs alike with the coming of fall. Their glorious brilliance screams a short-lived symphony of red, gold, orange and yellow accented by the plump purples of the ever-present pokeberries.

One by one, the leaves fall. A cold and gusty front pushes through and all the leaves are gone. What remains is a stark, gray, unforgiving landscape. Trees stripped bare but for the thick sinuous vines that drape across them, around them, through them. The vines, in their nakedness, look like huge gnarled cables determined to pull the trees to the ground with their collective weight.

Without warning, the wilderness once again gave way to civilization. At the heart of Spotsylvania County is the

Spotsylvania Court House area. The Virginia Historic Landmark Commission designated it as an Historic District in
1983. The Civil War battle waged at the spot heralded the beginning of the fall of the Confederacy.

The historic enclave is home to the old courthouse built
in 1839; the Old Berea Christian Church, now a museum;
and the Spotswood Inn, a popular stop for travelers as early
as 1820. The Courthouse also fulfilled a mission as headquarters for General Jubal Early and an observation post for
General Robert E. Lee during the Civil War and later served
as a school, a post office and a tavern. The current owners,
the law firm of Jarrell, Hicks & Sasser, restored it to its original dignity.

On the grounds of the district are the remaining vestiges of
the old original county jail. Built in 1781, it was transferred
brick-by-brick to the courthouse district and reconstructed.
After a fire, a few years later, its bricks became a wall on the
courthouse lawn. The next jail, built in 1856, was condemned
in 1948 and now, in its renovated state, houses office space
and storage for the local government. The County Courthouse
complex with the sheriff's department and Commonwealth's
Attorney's Office wrap around and are housed inside the old
buildings. There is a sense of rural serenity on these grounds
with an undercurrent of practical purposefulness.

In this backdrop of bloody history and cozy country,
Richard Marc Evonitz found his new home.

BY APRIL, Bonnie was working as a hairdresser and
Evonitz had a job at Kaeser Compressors on Sigma Drive in
Fredericksburg. This privately owned German company
manufactured a unique line of air compressors, air tools and
vacuum products including rotary screw compressors, oil-
less reciprocating compressors and rotary lobe blowers.

Their products are used in every area of manufacturing
and processing, including the metal, automotive, chemical,
plastic, pharmaceutical, aerospace, computer, printing and

textile industries. The equipment designed for commercial applications is used in body shops, car dealerships, repair and machine shops.

Non-industrial facilities like hospitals, laboratories and dental offices rely on these products to supply their air system needs. Their tool line is used to drill and chip rock and dig trenches.

"It was 'staged' to be a family-type situation. However, it was a very tense work environment with mostly German managers and American workers. We had to hang together, and most everyone [. . .] got along well," said a former employee who worked at the company at the same time as Evonitz. "I understand that over the last few years they've relaxed their standards to accommodate their people, but this is the same place that fired entire departments for standing up for one another. Oh, and personal chitchat is unacceptable unless it's before you come in or after you leave. Very different from American culture—no standing around the water cooler there!"

Evonitz worked in the applications department with close ties to the technical aspects of the business—working with a draftsman named Mark to ensure the correctness of the technical documentation. Mark "wore crosses and was very devout in his religion," a former worker said. "[. . .] While Evonitz made fun of Mark and was constantly cursing and using the f-word, they somehow forged a daily working relationship.

"I don't think Mark liked the situation, and often felt that he was trying to overcompensate for Evonitz's rudeness and abusiveness with his religious zealousness. I was never sure how they actually did get along.

"My first encounter with Evonitz was when I had to pass one of my customers to him to explain a problem with the documentation. The customer tech was trying to fix their compressor based on Evonitz's documentation, but it was incorrect. The first inclination that I received that things weren't right was when the customer called back to complain of Evonitz's rudeness and said that he went off on him for finding the mistake. I smoothed things over, but never fully trusted Evonitz's judgment after that, and was careful to send my customers to one of the other applications people, although there were few.

"Kaeser was a very small company with less than eighty employees, so everyone knew everyone. But, the company was split physically into two locations in their old building, so I didn't have day-to-day dealings with Evonitz. However, I smoked and he smoked and he would stand outside muttering to himself a lot," he said. "When he was outside smoking with the regular smoking group, he had little to say, stood off to the side and smoked several cigs in a short time."

Evonitz reportedly had difficulties with anger management when he faced frustrating situations. "I remember when he called our computer tech to try to get back a document he deleted," a former co-worker recalled. "At the time, we had this basic computer system with no backups. Not her fault; she was new and did do many things to bring us into the twentieth century. But Evonitz went off on her, calling her names and throwing books around the office. He had deleted the file and wanted her to create miracles. I think he was reprimanded for that, because many people saw and heard it, and from that point on I just avoided him when possible.

"Most of the women," he continued, "stayed away from him due to his temper and rudeness. He made tasteless jokes and insinuations. [. . .] He had long fingernails, filed long and pointy like a woman's—not squared off and fairly short like a man's. He wore flashy gold necklaces and rings and just looked like an off-the-screen gigolo type. [. . .] He looked a little weasely with a sharp nose and slicked-back hair. In general discussions, we all agreed just to stay clear of him, period. He never talked about women except in degrading sexual ways."

ALTHOUGH HE did not communicate well with his co-workers at Kaeser, it did not take long for Evonitz to insert himself into the public dialogue of his new community. The Fredericksburg *Free Lance–Star* published his letter to the editor on February 12, 1993, with a headline reading "Bigotry against gays betrays nation's ideals."

> *To the Editor:*
> *I am deeply troubled by the number of people who have written to express their anger over President Clinton's decision to lift the ban on gays in the military. I would like to believe that, residing in a state so steeped in history, we would have learned something from our past. Discrimination and intolerance are never justified.*
>
> *I am a nine-year Navy veteran. During my career in the military, I served with blacks, Hispanics, Asians and whites. I served with men and women. I served with heterosexuals and also with homosexuals. My fellow service members were highly skilled, hard-working, dedicated professionals. Not once during my career did it ever make a difference what color, race, gender or sexual orientation someone was if he or she could do the job and do it well.*
>
> *Many of the individuals who have written that they are opposed to lifting the ban on gays have provided numerous "good" reasons for continuing to discriminate against their fellow Americans both in the service and out. They have created a veil of rationale which has simply masked the ugliness of bigotry and hatred for those who are different from them.*
>
> *In this country, we supposedly revere the concepts of freedom, justice and equality. Perhaps it is time that we added a new word to the list of concepts that we revere. The word is hypocrisy.*
>
> *Richard M. Evonitz*
> *Spotsylvania*

EVONITZ WAS as uncomfortable at Kaeser as some of his coworkers were with him. He sought and obtained a job at Walter Grinders in Spotsylvania in March of 1995—selling parts and equipment by telephone. The company was a machine tool builder, manufacturing the equipment that cut bits, broaches and other parts. They never actually produced any of those parts themselves except for demonstration purposes. Most of their customers were automotive and aircraft manufacturers. But they also built machines for more exotic purposes—one client was a doctor in Florida who purchased special equipment for use in applications required for hip replacement surgery.

Walter Grinders was a subsidiary of a German conglomerate with sales staff scattered across the country. At their home base of operations in Spotsylvania, they employed nearly fifty people when Evonitz worked there. The staff prided itself on its spirit of teamwork.

Danny Minter was also working at Walter Grinders. Minter had been at the company for a while. He started as a laborer, moved up to the stock room and then to assembly. At the time Evonitz began working there, Minter was responsible for programming two close-tolerance machines that produced parts for building the tool-cutting machines.

Minter's diverse experience at the company made him a valuable resource for Evonitz when trouble-shooting problems or complaints arose from his customers. Their relationship took root on a professional level, but soon sprouted into a friendship.

They socialized outside of work—mostly at Danny's house. They enjoyed sitting around smoking marijuana on occasion, sharing their idealistic visions on how the world should turn, and brainstorming ways to improve existing products.

"We were both inventors at heart," Danny said. Marc struck him as an intelligent, sharp man with a technical mind and a knack for solving mechanical problems. When Danny had an idea for a do-it-yourself homeowners' greenhouse kit, he bounced it off Marc. His friend was enthused by the concept. In no time, he drew up a sketch of the plans and wrote up specs that included the use of the same corrugated clear plastic incorporated by commercial growers in their greenhouses.

From time to time the two men discussed political issues, both agreeing that the system wasn't working and that insurance companies drove the legislative agenda. Marc also entertained Danny with stories of his Navy years. "He was a scheming sucker. He was a single guy with low expenditures and he loan-sharked his money out to other guys. By the time he got out of the Navy, he had thirteen to fourteen thousand dollars put away and used it to buy a [Toyota] MR-2."

Marc had some training in weaponry in the service. "The way he talked, I thought he was a sniper," Minter recalled. He once brought out his 9mm Ruger to show Evonitz. Whenever Minter partially dismantled this weapon for cleaning, it took him about twenty minutes. But a few seconds after handing him the gun, Evonitz shocked Minter by saying, "You can clean it now." There on the table before him was the disassembled gun. Evonitz put it back together in record time, too.

Once when they were talking about Vietnam, Marc told Danny that if he were ever cornered in an impossible situation—like a capture by the Viet Cong—he would not endure the torture. He would grab his gun, stick it in his mouth and pull the trigger.

Chapter 8

Two sisters, an 11-year-old and a 13-year-old, were alone one
day after school in June 1995—safe inside their Spotsylvania
home. They did not hear a sound when Richard Marc Evonitz
broke into their home and breached their security. But there
he was—a gun in one hand and handcuffs in the other.

With threats and shoves, he bullied the 11-year-old into
the bathroom and locked the door. He warned her to be quiet
or else. He restrained the 13-year-old, knocked her to the
floor and raped the innocence from her heart.

When he had finished, he fled the once peaceful home. In
his wake, two young girls had deep, long-lasting scars. The
girls provided an accurate description of their assailant, but
it did not possess enough detail to draw a bead on the man
responsible. Evonitz was untouched and never suspected.

BONNIE AND Marc bounced around from one rental to another, never staying long enough in any one place to get
to know their neighbors, until early in 1996. Late in 1995,
they had purchased a lot, not far from the Spotsylvania
Courthouse, in Massaponax in the South Oaks subdivision,
a neighborhood of $90,000 to $150,000 homes. They hired a

contractor who built their white house with blue shutters to their personal specifications. It sat on South Oak Fork in a cul-de-sac surrounded by houses constructed by enough different builders to mute the cookie-cutter sameness so common in suburban developments.

They moved into the new dwelling in the early spring of 1996. Their next-door neighbors were Kieth and Monica Raba, who had moved into their home six months earlier. Their first social interaction occurred when Monica threw a surprise birthday party for Kieth and invited the Evonitz couple.

The party was the start of a comfortable relationship. The Rabas and Evonitzes invited each other to their homes for dinners and cookouts quite often. Kieth and Monica noticed that Bonnie was an immaculate housekeeper. Marc, however, did not share her intense desire for neatness and cleanliness. One bone of contention between the couple was the disposal of their trash. Marc would take out the garbage from the house to the garage. There it would pile up untouched for weeks. He never seemed to get around to taking it down to the curb for pick-up until Bonnie went ballistic.

Evonitz jumped into the concerns of the community, serving as the president of the South Oaks Homeowners' Association and leading the charge on the protest over a planned rezoning near the subdivision. The neighbors who worked with him on this issue were delighted to have him in the neighborhood. He was an articulate spokesman for their cause. To all outward appearances, life was good for the young couple. Their future looked bright.

Some neighbors reported frequent sightings of Marc sitting on his front porch steps playing the guitar and singing quietly to himself. Others can't recall him ever displaying any musical ability at all. Kids greeted him as they raced by on foot, skateboard or bicycle. Evonitz always had the time to talk to these young residents, but never joined them in their play. If something went wrong with a bike, Evonitz could be counted on to set down his guitar and reconnect the chain or make other minor repairs.

Teresa Lambert, the daughter of one of the neighbors who worked on the zoning concern with Evonitz, thought he was one of the nicest people she had ever met. Nonetheless, she felt a strong sense of instinctual unease when he told her to drop by anytime.

Marc enjoyed socializing with his neighbors on South Oak Fork. Over backyard barbecues, he talked to many folks about his time in the Navy, but, for some reason, never mentioned the subject to Kieth. Kieth didn't even know he had ever been in the service. Marc argued against the death penalty and criticized the harshness and unfairness of the system of criminal justice in this country. Kieth often listened to these and other diatribes, but did not engage in these conversations—he didn't have much interest in politics.

It was reported that Marc had an avid interest in serial killer Ted Bundy. But this obsession never seemed menacing enough to trigger any alarms in the neighborhood.

Marc was considered a lot of fun at gatherings for his wit and his ability to tell hilarious stories. His family knew him for a broad variety of talents in addition to his guitar skills: as a writer of songs, stories and poems, as a sculptor and as a gifted executor of drawings. But his neighbors were unaware of the talents he harbored.

He also enjoyed competitive pursuits—his favorites being video games, chess and pinochle. According to his brother-in-law, he enjoyed beating other people but disliked losing. He had a voracious appetite for science fiction novels—his favorite author was Isaac Asimov. He loved the original *Star Trek* television series and had a tape of every single episode.

When talking about his work and accomplishments, he might have tooted his own horn a bit too much for the tastes of some. Others saw him as a know-it-all. But to most of his neighbors, he was just another guy, not any more peculiar than the rest of them.

Marc had also demonstrated that, like his father before him, he had a serious drinking problem. "He was a silly drunk, to the point of being gross—laughing, making jokes, acting stupid," Jennifer said. "He was not a violent, angry drunk like my dad." Still, his drinking disturbed her, and she confronted him about it on several occasions.

Bonnie was now in her twenties. People on her cul-de-sac thought the slender woman with long brown hair was as nice as she could be. She never hesitated to pause to talk with neighbors and always had a smile of welcome on her face for every one of them.

Interaction with other women and the world at large washed away her blinding ignorance of normal sexuality. At the same time, Evonitz's worsening impotency problems had perverted their sex life even more. In even the best of circumstances, the minds of those who marry too young often get restless for a world they've never known. Bonnie's situation was more complicated. She was weary of being tied in restraints. She developed a distinct distaste for having her pubic area shaved. Now, she knew it was odd that Marc sometimes shaved his as well.

She was certain she would sprout wings and fly before she would be able to negotiate a change in the relationship. She felt used, unloved and lonely. She turned a cold shoulder to Marc and turned her attention to the Internet, where she made virtual friends. Soon, she was having cyber-sex on line. One of her cyber-partners planned to come to Virginia to meet her. When Bonnie announced this development to Marc, a huge argument ensued. Marc swore that he would "meet the guy with a baseball bat" if he came to Spotsylvania.

At the end of August 1996, Bonnie underwent dilatation and curettage, a reproductive health procedure commonly known as a D & C. Shortly after leaving the hospital, she packed her bags for an extended trip to California.

Marc's marriage crumbled before his eyes that fitful summer. Now, he had no outlet for his twisted sexual fantasies of control and domination. By the time September rolled around, he had reached the breaking point. Frustration morphed into rage, and an innocent girl would die on the altar of his anger.

"Predators like Evonitz enjoy the hunt for potential victims as much or more so than committing the crimes themselves. In many interviews with these offenders, a common theme is the thrill of the hunt—and they are constantly on the hunt—so it's not surprising that he had a list of potential victims or people that he had stalked, as just the hunting alone would be exciting or stimulating for Evonitz. Eventually, they reach critical mass and they cross over the line from hunting and stalking potential victims to actually abducting and murdering victims. But it's common for them to have done a lot more hunting than killing."

Greg McCrary, former FBI profiler, on *FredTalk*

Chapter 9

Sofia Silva radiated charisma and compassion. She drew people to her as easily as a traveling preacher draws crowds to his countryside revival tent.

Angie Frantz first met her in 1991 when they joined the Starfires Dance and Drill Team sponsored by the Spotsylvania County Recreation Department. "Since we both were new members, we had to practice on the back row or sit out and watch the others. We spent the time laughing and giggling at other people and the costumes. We would always take our breaks together, and groan when it was time to get back up and practice." Whenever there was a competition, Angie and Sofia would fix each other's hair.

After practice, the two girls would often have their parents pick them up late so they could hang out together at the recreation center. They'd participate in activities there, observe drama groups and other dance teams or just sit back and watch TV. "Sofia was always willing to loan me money for drinks or other stuff in the vending machines if I didn't have any. She was a genuinely nice person who would do anything she could for you," Angie said. "And, she always had a new joke."

In the next academic year, Sofia joined Angie, who was a year older, at Battlefield Middle School. They did not have any classes in common, but when their paths crossed in the halls, they passed notes to each other with those important middle school questions: "What's going on?" or "You gonna be at practice Saturday?" They both shared a love of the color purple and would flash whatever new purple accessory they were wearing that day in acknowledgment of their bond.

Angie and Sofia both went to Courtland High. Again, they had no classes in common but would plan to meet in the hall or to go to lunch together on a regular basis.

Sofia was a vivacious girl with a cascade of long, dark, curly hair framing an expressive face. These beautiful locks once tumbled all the way down her back—they were left uncut until she was 9 years old. Fourteen years later, her mother still cherished a lock of hair preserved from her daughter's first hair trim.

Sofia's warm sepia complexion owed more to the genetic heritage of her father, an immigrant from the Azore Islands off Portugal than it did to the effects of the summer sun. Her easy smile betrayed that, beneath typical teenage angst, there lay a heart filled with a genuine joy for life.

Father and daughter had a constant comic conflict over major league baseball. Dad was a long-time, loyal fan of the Baltimore Orioles. Sofia, on the other hand, rooted for the Atlanta Braves—once telling her dad that she liked the Braves because their players were younger and better-looking.

Sofia had a close relationship with her older sister, Pam. They often borrowed each other's clothing, exchanging outfits as if they were all under joint ownership. On pleasant days, they loved to cruise around town together with the radio on high and the windows rolled low. With barbed big-sister affection, Pam often called her younger sibling "Miss Attitude."

A friend who attended Chancellor High met Sofia through the youth group at Fairview Baptist Church in Fredericksburg. "She was so funny. She always had a smile on her face."

On September 6, 1996, the girls were hanging out at a Pizza Hut playing video games. They teased each other about their rival schools, each bragging that her school would beat the other's in the band competition. They parted that evening expecting to see each other again soon.

ON SEPTEMBER 9, 1996, Evonitz told his supervisor at Walter Grinders that he had a dentist appointment, and left work early.

SOFIA SILVA had started her junior year at Courtland High School in Spotsylvania that month. Sofia was 5'5" but weighed only a hundred pounds. The clothing she wore to school on September 9 flattered her youthful figure—denim shorts, a white ribbed sweater and white-and-blue Nikes. She was seldom seen without the color purple adorning her body, and on this day, she flashed the royal hue on each one of her polished fingernails.

She arrived home from school a bit worn out—not quite accustomed yet to the transition from lazy summer days to the demands of the school year. Despite her momentary weariness, she was excited about the year that lay ahead. She had taken a big step toward defining her future by entering the cosmetology program at the vocational center.

She trudged up the front steps of her home at 3:15 that afternoon. Inside, she shouted hello to her older sister Pam, and acknowledged the exuberant greeting of the family dog, Chase, a German shepherd–Labrador retriever mix. He rolled over on his back and his efforts were rewarded with an affectionate belly rub from Sofia. Chase had joined their family a year before, after he and his littermates were discovered abandoned on a frozen lake in Stafford County.

With Chase plodding behind her, Sofia went to the kitchen

and grabbed a grape soda from the fridge and the phone from its cradle. She went into the living room, popping her can as she walked, and sprawled on the sofa. Chase plopped on the floor beside her.

She called up a girlfriend and exchanged gossip, complaints and commiseration for a short while. Then, the exhausted 16-year-old dozed off for a thirty-minute nap.

She woke with a surge of energy and a strong desire to get her homework out of the way. She took the portable phone to her sister's room, where Pam was listening to music and waiting for a friend to call. She handed her the telephone and said she'd be out on the front porch. With her school papers and her grape soda, she settled on the top step. She tried to concentrate on her work but it was such a glorious day. The oppressive summer heat and humidity was gone and the air held no hint of the chilly days and frigid nights waiting around the corner.

Restless, she got up off the porch and wandered out to the newspaper box on the street. As she reached it, a green Ford Taurus pulled up beside her and a well-groomed thirty-something man popped out of the car asking for directions.

Sofia barely had time to point in the right direction before a rag was forced into her mouth. Her right arm was twisted behind her back. An acrylic fur–lined handcuff snapped around that wrist. She was pushed from the back over to the car and into the back seat. Facedown, her left arm was jerked backward and cuffed.

Hands securely pinned behind her, she still struggled to sit up. She received a hard smack in the head for her efforts and slumped back into the seat. Richard Marc Evonitz slid behind the steering wheel and threw the car into gear. The car jerked away to the driving rhythm of a dance with death.

FORTY-FIVE MINUTES after Sofia handed her the telephone, Pam went out on the front porch to speak to her sister. But Sofia was not there. Her school notes were there. Her drink was there. Pam thought it was odd, but she didn't worry about it. She assumed that Sofia was visiting a friend next door, across the street or down the road.

UNNATURAL HUNGER drove Evonitz. It dominated his thoughts. It dictated his actions. He unleashed it on Sofia Silva. She had done nothing to earn this fate—nothing but cross the line of vision of the wrong man. Richard Marc Evonitz savored her at first sight. He stalked her. He snatched her.

Sofia was scared and confused. Her parents and older sister had loved and protected her all her life. Certainly, she had problems, but they were ordinary problems—the typical teenage traumas of hurt feelings, broken hearts and stark disappointments. No one had ever physically threatened her with serious intent before. No one had subjected her to this level of physical abuse and degradation. Never before had she teetered on the brink of life and death with no control over the outcome.

But Evonitz pulled out the pocket of her safe, sheltered life and dumped its contents on the side of the road as he sped away from her home.

He raced up South Oak Fork, music blaring from the speakers in his car. Kieth Raba was outside in his yard next door when Marc pulled up that afternoon.

Kieth was astonished. He'd never seen his neighbor drive with such reckless abandon in their neighborhood full of children. He'd never heard him play his music with such disregard for his neighbors' ears.

Evonitz braked hard, then swung his car around, backed into his driveway and slid open the garage door. Kieth walked toward Marc's car and signaled that he wanted to speak to him.

Evonitz yelled, "I don't have time to talk. I have something to do." Then he zoomed back into his garage and lowered the door behind him.

Kieth walked back into his yard shaking his head. Another neighbor, Pam Coghill, approached Kieth and asked

him to speak to Marc about the way he was driving before he
hit or killed one of the neighborhood children riding bikes or
playing in the street.

Kieth assumed this mantle of responsibility and went
back over to Marc's house and knocked on the front door.
The door eased open just a crack. Evonitz said, "I don't have
time now," and shut the door in Kieth's face.

Behind that door, Evonitz continued to assault and terrify
his 16-year-old victim. Did she beg? Plead? Cry from her
fear? Did her tormentor take pleasure from her anguish? The
depth of her agony and her total sense of isolation can never
be known—they can only be imagined.

To satisfy his sick primal instincts, he stripped her, then
restrained the naked body of this young, innocent girl on his
bed. He shaved her pubic area. He attempted to rape her. He
shredded the garment of her innocence into tattered rags.

Then, he strangled her, holding her tight until her last
breath was gone—never to return again.

Now he had a dead body on his hands.

He put her outer clothing back on her limp limbs. He did
not bother with her undergarments, socks or shoes. He retrieved a blue quilted moving blanket and a length of rope
from the trunk of his car. He wrapped her securely in it, taking great care to ensure that every strand of hair, each fin-
gertip and every bit of the clothing she wore were securely
concealed, with no hint of Sofia peeking out from inside.
He tied up his bundle using knot-tying techniques he had
learned in the Navy and tossed the package into the trunk of
his car.

Fast asleep in their beds in the wee hours of the night, the
residents of South Oaks, still thought they lived in a safe
community. If the sound of a starting automobile engine pen-
etrated their dreams, they would have never suspected that
the car that passed their homes contained a corpse.

Evonitz pulled out of the subdivision onto Massaponax
Church Road. He turned right on Courthouse Road, State
Route 208, and glided like a ghost past the sheriff's depart-
ment, the courthouse and the office of the state's attorney,

William Neeley. He continued on the deserted road until he reached the Blue and Grey Parkway, State Route 3, in the heart of Fredericksburg. There, he headed southeast. After crossing the Rappahannock River, he entered Stafford County and the road changed its name to King's Highway. The four-lane road with its grassy median was lined with clusters of dense trees broken into large clumps by fields surrounded by white wooden horse fence. After a few miles, he crossed Muddy Creek and entered King George County.

Thirty miles from home and two counties away, Evonitz turned left onto a small road that led to Dominion Growers, a commercial flower producer—past the old, faded red barn on his right and a field on his left that merged into a forest. The road took a gentle curve and the car bearing Sofia Silva was out of view of State Route 3.

Evonitz parked the car on the wooded side of the road and retrieved the dull blue bundle from the trunk of his car. He staggered down the steep embankment to the edge of the woods. There, amidst patches of poison ivy where a marshy spit of water glistened with an eerie green scum, Evonitz discarded the body of Sofia Silva. Did he give a thought to the family who loved her? To the friends who would grieve for her? Did he feel a moment's regret for the woman she would have become?

He washed his hands of the deed and sped off into the night. The next day, he called in sick to work.

He was oblivious to the grave risk he had taken that night. The spot was not as secluded as it seemed. Just a bit farther up the road was a huge iron gate. All night long, on the other side, workers filled semi-trucks with masses of flowers. The cooler overnight temperatures better protected the fragile cargo while it was loaded. Then, one by one, the blossom-filled trucks drove through the automated gate, up the narrow road and out to the state highway. With a small stroke of luck, one of those tractor-trailers could have spotted and reported a suspicious vehicle.

The other danger lurking at this site was in the building of Dominion Growers itself. The owner lived on its second floor. A two-story picture window stretched on its front and overlooked the piece of road where the car was parked and the body concealed. Had the owner glanced out that window at the right moment, the murderous toll of Richard Marc Evonitz could have ended right there. Tragically, he would evade detection to stalk more young victims and bathe yet another family in sorrow.

> *"I cannot begin to imagine how one human being, no matter
> how sick they are, [can] feel they have the right to inflict pain
> and death on anyone, especially a child."*
>
> LE in Hollidaysburg, Pennsylvania, on *FredTalk*

Chapter 10

On the evening of September 9, Phyllis Silva came home
from her job at Mary Washington Hospital in Fredericksburg.
She had to step over Sofia's school papers and an open can of
grape soda on her way inside. Pam greeted her, unaware that
Sofia had not returned. Soon, Humberto Silva, returning from
his construction job in Manassas, joined the two women.

When Pam revealed she had not seen Sofia for more than
an hour, they went to Sofia's bedroom assuming she would
be there. All that was there was her backpack, where she had
slung it atop her bed. Inside her satchel were her house keys,
her makeup and her wallet with eight of the ten dollars her
mother had given her at the beginning of the school week.
Sofia would not have gone anywhere without her keys or her
money or most particularly her makeup. Her mother had re-
stricted the use of it until Sofia reached 16 and, as a result,
she was quite attached to her cosmetics.

Pam was certain something was wrong. Sofia never left
the house without telling her where she was going. They all
thought, though, that there must be an explanation. When
dinner was ready, Phyllis stepped out into the front yard and
called for Sofia. She got no response.

Phyllis grabbed the phone and began calling everyone
Sofia knew within walking distance. No one knew where she
was.

Angie's telephone rang early that evening. The caller, a mutual friend of Angie and Sofia, had received a call from Mrs. Silva. "Have you heard from Sofia?" she asked. "Do you know where she is?"

Angie did not have any answers and was consumed with dread. "I knew she had not run away—she would not leave without her stuff."

The family sat down to an anxious dinner—Sofia's empty chair a stark reminder of her absence. Eyes kept casting that way as if in hopes that she would suddenly appear. After they picked at their meal, they decided to wait one more hour before calling the sheriff. Humberto hit the neighborhood roads, driving up and down the narrow streets in an ever-widening circle.

Oak Grove Terrace was an older subdivision with shoulder-to-shoulder homes sitting close to the asphalt. When he saw anyone he knew, he stopped and asked if they'd seen his daughter. As the sun began to set, the weight of growing fear settled heavier on his chest. He returned home to the expectant, hopeful faces of Pam and Phyllis. When they saw he was alone, their mouths sagged in despair. The two women had not had any luck in discovering what had happened to Sofia, either. They called the Spotsylvania County Sheriff's Department to report her missing.

The Silvas were a religious family who were active at Fairview Baptist Church in Fredericksburg. They raised Sofia under strict moral and ethical guidelines. She had never exhibited any problem behavior. To the family, this pattern meant that Sofia would not run away from home. To investigators, it added up to typical teenage rebellion. The daylight hours and the busy neighborhood made abduction improbable. A neighbor who had been out on his riding lawn mower at the time reported seeing nothing suspicious, reinforcing their skepticism. The fact that she did not take her money or other belongings merely told them that she left her home on a sudden impulse. Nonetheless, they took the precaution of entering her disappearance into NCIC, the National Crime Investigation Center, and sent out bulletins across the state.

On September 10, Richard Marc Evonitz called in sick to work.

Melissa Britt, a cosmetology student with Sofia, was a life-long family friend and distant relative. Often the two girls would baby-sit together to make extra money. She was called out of her classroom and into the hall on September 10. There, Sherry, a mutual friend, told her that Sofia was missing. Melissa knew Sofia well. She knew she was never in trouble. She knew she would not run away. She struggled to breathe as a sense of horror overcame her. Before she could absorb the implications of the disappearance, Melissa's mother, Carol, arrived at the school to take her home. Carol was 40 years old and, because of difficulties with her current pregnancy, the doctor had ordered her to bed. But nothing could keep her in bed at a time like this. "My first thought," Carol remembered, "was, I hope she is a runaway. She didn't seem the type, but it would be the best possibility."

Melissa recalled, "We had class together one day and then she was gone. It was scary. It was weird looking at her picture in the newspaper and on missing person fliers. You really don't look at missing person pictures until it is someone you know. I used to walk a lot from neighborhood to neighborhood all around the area where Sofia lived. And we used to play kickball in her street. I wouldn't **do that** anymore."

Brandi, a student at Spotsylvania High School, wrote of her experience on *FredTalk*, the *Free Lance–Star*'s chatroom. She had arrived home and answered a phone call from her current boyfriend. He told her to look in the newspaper. "It was an article about Sofia's disappearance. The guy I was dating had worked with Humberto, Sofia's father, and he was in complete shock, considering he had just seen her the other day. I remember at school how miserable everyone was over this—at how many people knew her, had gone to school with her, or just over the fact that something like this had happened. I remember inspirational words being spoken to each other—people putting arms around each other's shoulders and offering words of comfort. Tear-streaked faces from frustrated teens, and most of all, the not knowing. At one point, I saw two girls almost get into a fight because one accused the other of saying some horrible things."

Sofia's friend from Chancellor High wrote, "I was at band camp when I heard the news about Sofia. One of my friends came up to me and told me that Sofia was missing. [. . .] I thought they must have some bad information." She added, "After we found out about the prayer service for her, we made sure we were there and we later posted signs all over the school and even wore a purple ribbon every day . . ."

As another day passed, Phyllis stayed riveted to the telephone awaiting a call from Sofia or about Sofia. After work, Humberto once again roamed the streets. Many neighbors joined him in the search, going door-to-door up one block and down the other. Authorities speculated that Sofia had gone off with a friend and now was simply too embarrassed to return home.

Phyllis was not at all pleased with that assessment of events. She bristled at the suggestion that Sofia could be that irresponsible. She called on a personal friend, Martha Smith, the wife of Major Howard Smith of the sheriff's department. Not too long before, Phyllis had thrown a baby shower for Martha and, on this occasion, found her very receptive when she pled her case. Soon, the Major received a call from his distraught spouse, who convinced him of the gravity of the situation.

He conferred with the investigators and soon no longer believed it was just another missing persons case, even though he knew his department handled fifteen to eighteen teenaged runaways every month. He gathered up available resources from around the area.

On September 12, they launched a major search effort complete with search dogs and divers. Doorbells rang up and down the streets of Oak Grove Terrace as police sought anyone who might have seen anything peculiar or any sign of Sofia. The Spotsylvania County Sheriff's Department notified the National Center for Missing and Exploited Children.

This agency, in turn, sent out fax alerts to more than six thousand law enforcement organizations across the United States.

Two divers focused on a nearby pond, going down over and over again—torn between a desire to find her body and bring closure to her family, and the hope that she would be found elsewhere alive and well.

Three search and rescue organizations, DOGS-East, Mid-Atlantic and Blue and Gray, combed the area around the Silva home. Bloodhounds picked up Sofia's scent on the front porch and followed it to the newspaper box out at the street. Then, it was gone.

The teams gathered at a nearby wooded area nearly a square mile in size. The thick woods were west of the Silva home and contained by Leavells, Courthouse and Harrison Roads. The men and dogs combed every inch of the forested land with the help of state troopers on foot and state police helicopters with heat-seeking devices overhead. Near midnight, the search was called off without a single clue pointing in the direction of the missing girl.

As the search proceeded, a crowd of more than three hundred gathered at Fairview Baptist Church for a 7:30 candlelight prayer service. They prayed for Sofia's safety, they prayed for her to be found and they prayed for her family. None of their prayers were answered that night. And the agony escalated in the modest little home on Bounds Street.

FAR AWAY on the southern coast of Massachusetts, the town of New Bedford sits on Buzzards Bay. Once it was the whaling capital of the world and drew immigrants from distant shores. Today, among the descendents of the Portuguese settlers, are members of the Silva family.

Sofia had traveled there often to visit her relatives. If she had run away, it was thought that she might have headed there.

Posters of her smiling face were plastered on telephone poles, storefronts and bare walls. The signs generated many calls to the New Bedford Police Department from people who thought they had seen Sofia around town. Officers checked out every lead, but always came back to the station empty-handed.

SOFIA SILVA first appeared on *America's Most Wanted* on Saturday, September 14, 1996. A short segment showed her picture and gave her description. That evening, before midnight, seven calls came in with reactions to seeing her picture.

Tony Jones from Triangle said that an hour before, he had seen a white female with curly black hair and dark brown eyes, about 5'7" tall, and weighing around 140 pounds at U.S. Inn Hotel on Route 1 in Triangle. She was sitting in the passenger seat of a red Beretta.

Richard Mayfield called in stating he had seen a female matching Sofia's description and wearing jean shorts on the previous Wednesday or Thursday night on Broad Street in Richmond. He said that she was with a white male, about 5'10" or 5'11" with short blonde hair. The man was buying beer at a 7-Eleven.

An unidentified caller claimed to have seen a girl who looked like Sofia on September 13 between 10 P.M. and 3 A.M. at a club called DJ's in Lynwood, Illinois. The Sofia lookalike was in the company of a white female and two white males celebrating a birthday. She was using the name Jeanna and she was quite intoxicated.

From Dallas, Texas, Jennifer Renuso called to report that she had seen a white female with very short cropped-off hair and wearing braces at the tollway Albertson's store on Frankford Road. She appeared to be happy and was accompanied by a forty-something white male wearing dirty blue jeans and a green crop shirt.

Debbie Centron of Claymont, Delaware, said she saw a female matching Sofia's description at 2 P.M. at a gas station. She was with a Mexican man and three other young females. The man bought gas for a maroon new model pick-up truck while the girls, all speaking Spanish, went in the store and bought cigarettes and pretzels.

Douglas Sprow had not seen Sofia, but he wanted authorities to know that she was not missing. She had run away with her boyfriend, whose name he did not know.

Finally, that night, Susan Wall called in from Tucson, Arizona, to inform them that she had seen someone who looked like Sofia hitchhiking on Wednesday, September 11. She was wearing a violet shirt, and got a ride from a Hispanic male in his forties driving a brown car.

Some of these tips may have seemed silly on the surface, but still, every single one of them had to be checked out by the investigators in Spotsylvania County in the hopes one of them contained a nugget of truth.

While leads were checked, rumors that Sofia had been found both alive and dead raced down the streets of Spotsylvania. One story reported that Sofia and her mother had argued because Sofia was seeing an older man, and she left home to be with him. The rumor prompted law enforcement to search this man's home. But family and friends denied that any disagreement had occurred, and insisted that Sofia was not dating anyone at the time.

On September 18, word of Sofia Silva ricocheted through the community. She had been found in a neighboring county, it was claimed, at a local motel with an adult male—a sordid tale, but at least she was alive. The rumor, however, was quickly dashed by reality. Stafford County authorities had found a teenaged runaway at the Days Inn on U.S. 17—but it was a 15-year-old boy. He was found hiding under a bed in the motel, and 27-year-old Robert M. DeShazo II of Falmouth was charged with contributing to the delinquency of a minor. On February 6, 1997, he was found guilty, given a thirty-day sentence, and released for time already served.

Sofia was still missing.

"It was the most horrifying experience of my life. Waiting was the worst part—the not knowing. It was really scary."

Angie Frantz, friend of Sofia

Chapter 11

The thread of hope runs thin with the passage of time, but it possesses a tenacity that allows it to wrap around any strand no matter how unlikely. It was this bulldog determination that brought unusual assistance to the case of the missing teenager.

The producers of *America's Most Wanted* were filming for another program, *Strange Universe*. One segment featured Lyn Buchanan, a self-proclaimed "remote viewer."

Remote viewing is a paranormal technique that proponents believe enables users to experience with all the senses any event, person or place in the past, present or future. The remote viewer sits with a pen or pencil and a piece of paper on which he writes or draws without conscious thought. In this manner he brings back detailed and accurate information on the target of the psychic exercise. Practitioners of this technique contend that it is a skill that anyone can learn, although some psychics have a natural ability. Purportedly, there are 2,000 trained remote viewers in the world today.

At the recommendation of these producers, lead investigator Twyla Demoranville and Detective Robert Jones were enlisted to drive to Mechanicsville, Maryland, and consult with the psychic. The Spotsylvania Sheriff's Department had a healthy skepticism about Buchanan's abilities, but felt that their appearance at the taping of *Strange Universe* would expose a wider audience to the story and photograph of Sofia Silva.

The show's producers constructed a set at Buchanan's home. Demoranville and Jones met him there. Buchanan explained to them that he was not a psychic but a remote viewing practitioner and outlined the differences to them. He expressed a strong desire to help them find Sofia. Demoranville asked him about the location of the missing girl.

Buchanan slipped into the proper frame of mind. He told the detectives that he saw a body. He could not tell if it was Sofia—he could not even ascertain whether the body was male or female. But, he said, it was near or in some type of water. He saw vegetation. He viewed some sort of red material. He claimed the body was near railroad tracks.

Demoranville asked, "Do you see any movement from the body?"

Buchanan shook his head and said, "No."

That was all he could see. He apologized for not being able to provide any additional information.

Buchanan was just one of many offering assistance on the case. Investigators received numerous calls from members of the media, forensic scientists, hypnotists and psychics offering to help in any way they could. At the request of friends of the Silva family, Beverley Newton, a psychic and resident of Fredericksburg became involved in the case. She went to the Silva home and held one of Sofia's dresses. She patted the head of Chase, the family dog, and told the Silvas that he had seen what happened to Sofia.

Other psychics, including one from Bristol, Virginia, called in volunteering information on Sofia's whereabouts. It was suggested that Sofia would be found near a timeworn farmhouse or near a cornfield. It was claimed that the girl had driven off with anywhere from one to three other people. A couple of the psychics believed she'd known her companions. Another one was certain that Sofia had thought she knew the driver until she got close to him, then realized she did not.

Some said she could not leave her current location. Not one claimed to know if Sofia was dead or alive.

• • •

ON THE evening of September 20, a belated response came
in from the airing of the *America's Most Wanted* episode that
displayed Sofia's photograph. A caller who would not identify himself insisted he saw someone resembling her the
night before at the intersection of Route 96 and Ewing Street
in Chicago. She was wearing a black leather jacket, blue
jeans and a black t-shirt. She was all alone, carrying a backpack and hitchhiking.

ON SUNDAY, September 22, tremors of apprehension shook
the Silva household. People out exercising their hunting
dogs stumbled across a brush-covered body near the small
town of Lignum in the nearby county of Culpeper. Beside a
gravel road, a five-foot-wide burned area marked the spot.
The body appeared to be that of a young female, but decomposition and possible fire damage made that conclusion only
an assumption. It would take an autopsy to confirm the gender of the victim.

For two days, the family and their prayer partners at
Fairview Baptist Church sent endless entreaties to the heav-
ens. Finally, authorities announced that it was a woman, but
not 16-year-old Sofia Silva.

The following day the body was identified as 20-year-old
Anne Carolyn McDaniel. On the evening of September 18,
she had wandered off from a group home for the mentally
disabled. It was reported on all the area television stations
that duct tape covered her mouth and bound her hands and
feet. The death certificate indicated that she was dismembered and that the attacker had set her on fire. Hers was the
third female body and the third open murder case in the past
four months.

Sofia Silva was still missing.

> *"Apprehension of the sexual murderer is one of law enforce-ment's most difficult challenges. Because sexual killings of-ten appear motiveless and random, they offer few clues about why the murder occurred or, consequently, about the identity of the murderer. Even the sexual nature of these murders is not always immediately obvious, for conventional evidence of a sexual crime may be absent from the crime scene."*
>
> Robert K. Ressler, Ann W. Burgess and John E. Douglas
> *Sexual Homicide: Patterns and Motives*

Chapter 12

On September 26, Detective Twyla Demoranville received an anonymous phone call. The tipster claimed to have a friend named Carvella Moore who worked at the Four Mile Fork Chevron. This friend had told her that Kenny Fagen, a Holiday Inn South employee, had entered the station and said that Sofia Silva had spent the night of September 9 in room 313 with a male companion.

Demoranville confronted Fagen, who told her his sister was a friend of Sofia. He admitted that he had not seen her, but rumors at the hotel indicated that she had arrived there in a red motor vehicle and spent the night in that room with a young man.

Holiday Inn South management refused to release their room registration records without a warrant. When Demor-anville obtained one, she discovered that no one had stayed in that room on that date—room 313 sat vacant.

The detective also questioned Carvella Moore—whose real name, according to her employer, was Clara Walker. She told Demoranville that sometime around September 9, a teenager with dark curly hair and purple fingernails, wearing a pair of blue jeans, entered the gas station and bought a soda. The investigator whipped out a photograph of Sofia Silva, but Moore/Walker could not identify her.

It was all just another rabbit trail leading to a dead end. But it taught the investigators an important lesson. Having the media on their heels when they were chasing down a futile lead was not comfortable or productive. From that moment on, the detectives requested that the court seal all the search warrants they obtained.

A BAND of tension tightened its grip around the Oak Grove Terrace neighborhood. It was so extreme that residents imagined they could feel it in the air they breathed and in the soles of their feet as they walked the streets. Was Sofia lying dead and undiscovered? Or had she merely run away? What did that mean to the safety of their children? Whose child was next?

The uncertainty made some flinch at shadows. But for Janet Smith, a Justice Department employee, it was a clarion call to action. Recently, many of her neighbors had voiced concern about the increased level of minor vandalism and petty theft swirling around them. Many reported damaged mailboxes, windshields, bottles smashed in their front yards. Others reported tools and other items stolen from the vehicles parked in their driveways. Some had mentioned the Neighborhood Watch program in passing. Years before, an effort to institute a similar program had failed. But, now, spurred on by Janet, it was discussed at length and with determination.

More than forty subdivision residents indicated a willingness to serve on a patrol after Janet delivered Neighborhood Watch surveys to all 300 homes. She was hoping to elicit the cooperation of 100 to 150 families to cover the need for block captains and nighttime patrols. The initial response, however, was sufficient to get the ball rolling. Eighty-five communities in Spotsylvania County had already instituted the program and had seen a reduction of minor crimes as a result. Oak Grove Terrace was ready to become number eighty-six. The first act of the organization was the instigation of daily patrols through the neighborhood at the end of every school day.

At Courtland High, the tension mounted. "School was depressing," Angie Frantz said. "People were upset and scared."

Parents clamped down on freedoms. "I was not allowed to walk out to the mailbox by myself—or do anything by myself anymore," Angie said. "But I was glad to have the restrictions. They made me feel safer."

IN LATE September, two calls came in from the queries spread by the National Center for Missing and Exploited Children. One caller claimed to have spotted Sofia in the early morning hours of September 17 in the Spotsylvania Mall. She said the girl was walking by herself with the hood of a gray sweatshirt pulled tightly over her head.

Another person thought he had seen her at Merrimac Grocery in Culpeper on September 14. Her hair was pulled back and she was with two men, one in his late thirties, the other in his late fifties. They had a dog with them and got into a light blue vehicle with Virginia tags.

On the night of October 2, another television show–generated tip came in to investigators. Glenn Brown from Las Vegas, Nevada, was suspicious about a woman at the Casino Hotel on September 30. She was with an adult Asian woman and she had passed out at the buffet, claiming she had not eaten all day. An ambulance took her from the casino to a nearby hospital. The sightings of the missing teen were endless—each one followed up with escalating desperation.

But Sofia Silva was still missing.

> *"Some dispose of bodies in water because of the practical aspects. They think it will wash off the evidence or will save them from having to dig a grave. For others, it is a psychological issue—the cleansing nature of water."*
>
> Greg McCrary, former FBI profiler

Chapter 13

On October 16, the employees at Dominion Growers tackled a progressively worsening problem on company land. Beavers had erected a dam on Birchwood Creek, causing water to back up and stagnate. This flooding made areas ripe for horticultural development impossible to use. It was not an unusual chore for the workers at Dominion Growers—beaver dams were a perennial problem. What was unusual was what they found.

Maintenance manager Gary Norman and some others were working hard to demolish the dam when he spotted a large blue bundle wrapped in rope. Approaching the unusual object, he could see the distinct outline of an elbow and buttocks under a blue mover's blanket. The stunned crew stopped in its tracks and called in the King George Sheriff's Department at 5:30 P.M.

There was a strong desire to unwrap the bundle in the vain hope that what their eyes told them simply was not true. There were urges to leave the scene and deny what they had found. Nonetheless, all stood vigil, their grim discovery untouched, while they awaited the arrival of the authorities.

Captain Steve Dempsey arrived to process the scene. Taking great care to protect any forensic evidence, he removed a portion of the briars that imprisoned the body. He lifted the edge of the blanket, revealing two feet. On the toes were traces of the telltale purple nail polish that made him suspect they had just found the body of Sofia Silva.

As soon as the body was extricated from its tomb of undergrowth, officers wrapped it in a sheriff's department blanket. Funeral home workers, called to the scene, slipped the bundle into a plastic body bag. Loaded into a General Home Services hearse, it was transported to the state medical examiner's office in Richmond.

As remote viewer Lyn Buchanan had indicated, the body was located in the water. An old, abandoned railroad track did run near the site where she was found. No red material was found anywhere near the scene. But there on the corner of the highway and the small road sat an old barn—beneath its tin roof, the walls were painted red.

That night, Captain Dempsey called Detective Twyla Demoranville at the Spotsylvania County Sheriff's Department, and made her aware of his suspicions.

"There are no magic words to say at a time like this."
Reverend Robert Sizemore, Fairview Baptist Church

Chapter 14

Early the next morning, Major Howard Smith was on the Silvas' front porch again. He told the family that another body had been found in King George County. Police were checking into it, but didn't know anything yet. As soon as he possessed more definitive information, he promised he would come back and let them know.

It was an agonizing day on Bounds Street.

ON THAT same morning, Captain Dempsey and Detectives Karen Barnett and Butch Norris drove down to Richmond. Demoranville and Jones met them at the medical examiner's office with Sofia's dental records. They spent all day there observing the autopsy and aiding in the identification.

Decomposition was so advanced that a cursory examination could not even determine whether it was a male or female body on the table. Further exploration revealed that it was Sofia. She was dressed, but missing her bra, panties, socks and shoes. Her pubic area had been shaved. It was suspected that she had been sexually assaulted, but if she had, advanced decomposition had obliterated the evidence. The cause of death: asphyxiation. The time of death: within forty-eight hours of her disappearance from Bounds Street.

Twyla Demoranville now had the second murder case of her fledgling investigative career. She had thought that the first one had drained her emotions—the shaken baby death of an 8-month-old child—but this case would prove even more demanding.

She had no idea how long Sofia had lain in that exact location, or how often she might have been moved. Investigators combed a huge circumference around the spot where they found her. They looked through every blade of grass and stalk of weed up and down that small road.

The barn at the entrance to the lane was searched and searched again. They looked for any speck of evidence connected to the crime. No possible theory was dismissed without investigation. Had the killer been in the barn? Had Sofia been held there after her abduction? Had she died there? Had her body rested inside it for any period of time? They sought clues in that barn with meticulous attention to detail—but no evidence was ever found.

THE BURDEN of officially informing the family fell on Major Howard Smith. He and Detective Ed Lunsford drove out to Mary Washington Hospital to deliver the news to Phyllis Silva. Riding back to her home in Smith's car, Phyllis suffered in the way that only a mother who has lost a child to violence can. The relief of finally knowing what happened to her daughter after thirty-six days of uncertainty struggled with the horror of knowing that Sofia would never come home again.

When the brown, unmarked police car pulled into the Silva driveway, the news was known and understood before a word had been spoken. Smith and Lunsford helped a distraught Phyllis from the rear seat. A neighbor walked up the drive, embraced her and escorted Phyllis into her home. Smith and Lunsford stood outside. Defeat rounded their shoulders and bowed their heads.

The sheriff's department attempted to contact Humberto Silva before he left work in Manassas, but they were too late. He drove home in his red pick-up truck oblivious to the events of the day until he arrived at his besieged home an hour after Phyllis. A neighbor emerged from his home and hugged him while whispering the news. As they cried together, others joined them and helped the devastated father inside.

Family friend Carol Britt vividly recalled the darkness that descended: "We were very upset when Sofia turned up missing. But all hell broke loose when the body was found. I was always overly protective of my daughter, Melissa, so my treatment of her did not change much. But I did worry a lot more. I tried to hide that from her. We had a very big loss of our sense of security."

"I remember hearing the loud sobs, people crying out and the countless times my phone rang over and over with a friend on the other line needing someone to cry with," Sofia's classmate Brandi said. "I remember thinking, 'This is just us students over here at Spotsylvania High, I can't even imagine the agony of her family.'"

Amidst their own worries for their children and community, family and friends gathered together and formed a cocoon around the Silvas, protecting them from strangers and media as they slid into an abyss of sorrow.

Throughout the community, folks clustered in small groups to talk in quiet voices. Children, too young to understand, rode bicycles up and down the street or shot basketballs through hoops. But the normal boisterous noise of their play was muffled.

Reporters gathered on the fringes of the neighborhood and struggled to maintain a rigid professional demeanor. But the tears welling up in their eyes betrayed their humanity.

TEENAGERS WHO had heard the news straggled with unhappy faces and tear-filled eyes through the halls of Spotsylvania Vocational Center and adjacent Courtland High School. Students unaware of the latest developments noticed the altered ambiance and adopted a subdued demeanor by instinct.

At Courtland High School, Principal C. Hampton Gray called an emergency staff meeting before the start of classes. He gave each teacher a statement to read to the students before beginning instruction. He did not want anyone in the school to learn of Sofia's death through the disembodied voice on the speaker hung in the corner of each classroom.

The crisis intervention team of the Spotsylvania County school system was assigned to help the school's guidance counselors comfort the grieving kids. Those students who were too distressed to go to class could call a parent to take them home.

At the vocational school, twelve of Sofia's fourteen class-mates in cosmetology met with their teacher, Martha B. Maston, and a member of the crisis team. The two other students in Sofia's class had already heard the news and were too overwrought to attend school.

Fliers were posted around both schools verifying what the teenagers had learned from their teachers. Purple ribbons popped up on collars, backpacks and lockers as if by magic.

FAIRVIEW BAPTIST Church conducted their regular Wednesday evening service that night. The Reverend Robert Sizemore offered spiritual comfort to his congregation. On the worshipers' minds, however, one question loomed large: Why did God allow this to happen? To that question, the minister had no easy answer.

"ONE DAY, she closed her eyes and the pain ended. Do not grieve for your friend. She is with God," entoned the Reverend Sizemore at Fairview Baptist Church during the Saturday funeral service.

But more than six hundred people were there to grieve—not a seat was left vacant. Every pew in the sanctuary was packed to capacity, as were the seats in the balcony and the choir loft. The overflow watched the service on a closed circuit television downstairs. Scattered throughout the crowd were the sad faces of students in Courtland High School jackets coming to grips with death long before they had figured out life.

Sofia's relatives traveled from as far away as Massachusetts to bid her farewell and comfort her parents. The youth group, serving as honorary pallbearers, sat together in a special section in the front of the sanctuary.

Sarah Markham, one of Sofia's friends, read a poem written by a 16-year-old who lost a friend to suicide:

> "I know you miss me
> I miss you, too.
> There is nothing I can do."

Sarah struggled to continue to speak, and the mourners ached with her as she read the last lines:

> "Soon we'll be together again.
> Do not forget me.
> I am your friend."

Brandi observed the funeral from the basement of the church. "I remember the words that were spoken and I remember the poem that was read. I remember crying until I could hardly breathe or see through puffy red eyes. Most of all, I remember the hugs and support everyone had for one another."

At the front of the church sat a closed coffin buried in floral arrangements with a preponderance of purple flowers and bows. Outside, the trees lining the street that passed by Fairview Baptist all sported large purple ribbons.

Friends remembered Sofia for her easy smile, her bountiful hugs, her envy-inducing hair. And, of course, they remembered her for purple—the clothes she wore, the nail polish she flashed, the purple Grand Prix she wanted for graduation.

Melissa Britt remembered the Christmases their two families celebrated together. Since the two girls were so close in age, they always automatically exchanged gifts while the others drew names. She made a vow to Sofia on the day of her funeral and kept her promise when Christmas arrived that year. She made a pilgrimage to Sofia's grave to give her a Christmas present—a purple candle.

Promises of heaven are not an instant balm for broken hearts. And they did not stop the tears as the sorrowful group that filled the cemetery chapel tumbled out the doors. Hundreds of mourners formed a funeral procession that converged on Sunset Memorial Gardens to lay Sofia to rest. Reverend Sizemore told Phyllis and Humberto, "They are here because of her. She touched lives and you touched her life."

Major Smith stood in a doorway of the chapel. As Phyllis left for the gravesite, she stopped to wrap her arms around him for a long hug. Then she and Humberto embraced outside before heading up the hill to their daughter's final resting place.

"We were in shock!" said Sofia's Chancellor High friend. "When you're sixteen years old and nothing like this has ever happened in your own world, you tend not to believe things. The funeral was beautiful, and my friends and I would visit the gravesite very often to leave pictures on the grave of things she missed, like prom, graduation and college stuff."

A FEW days after the services, an unknown individual made a pilgrimage to the spot where Sofia's body was found. That person pounded a white wooden cross into the ground. Emblazoned on the cross were four words: "In God's Arms Forever."

ON NOVEMBER 7, the students and faculty of Courtland High congregated to memorialize the truncated life of Sofia Silva. "We gather in this misty morning," said Principal C. Hampton Gray, "to dedicate this tree to her memory."

A maple tree was planted in her honor on a corner to the left of the school. Many of those encircling it were sporting gold angel pins with purple ribbon streamers or bows—the community symbol for Sofia. The strains of "It's a Bright and Beautiful Morning" drifted across the campus as the Courtland Advanced Choir sang with heavy hearts.

Representatives of the Student Council Association tied a big purple ribbon around the girth of the tree and handed a check to Phyllis Silva. "The check comes from the Courtland family and community as a token of our love for you and Sofia," Gray said, "and to defray some of the financial burden you may have experienced."

For a moment, Phyllis' heart was warmed. Knowing how much others loved and cared for her daughter dulled the pain for a short, grateful moment.

But the school community was on tense alert. Parents' calls to the school escalated to overload proportions. They called to make sure an adult was on duty for all after-school activities. They called to ensure that their children did not leave the school with anyone without their express authorization. They called hoping to regain some of the peace and security that had been ripped from their grasp.

"It's the not knowing that's the worst of this," Gray told a *Free Lance–Star* reporter. "No one knows who perpetrated this horrible act. Is it someone in this school? Or someone right off campus in the community?"

"In any given year, most of the thousands of law enforcement jurisdictions in the U.S. will not have a non-family child abduction murder to investigate, and many more homicide investigators will not have one case like this over the course of their careers."

From a nationwide study of child murders
published by the Washington State
Attorney General's Office, May 1997

Chapter 15

Investigators could not stop to grieve. They had work to do. They had forensic evidence—the blue quilted moving pad and rope that wrapped the body, nine fibers of unknown origin on Sofia's sweater, one other fiber on the blanket and, tied into one of the knots on the rope, a hair harboring DNA that did not belong to Sofia—but they did not have a single witness.

To aid them in their search for leads, the local Crime Solvers organization started a reward fund with $1,000. The Spotsylvania County Board of Supervisors, at the instigation of Supervisor Emmitt Marshall, added another $5,000 for information leading to the arrest and conviction of the perpetrator.

The field of possible suspects was huge. It included the ninety employees who worked at Dominion Growers. The grounds were covered step by step. All the buildings were searched from corner to corner. Every truck company that operated any trucks that drove laden with flowers from the facility was contacted. Investigators obtained and scrutinized the logs of every truck. Any trucker in the vicinity while Sofia's whereabouts were unknown was put under the investigators' microscope. All known sexual offenders in the area were tracked down and their alibis validated. And every tip called in to the sheriff's department was examined.

Detectives also searched for links to other recent murders in the area. They looked at the burned and dismembered body of Anne Carolyn McDaniel, discovered in Culpeper County shortly after Sofia's disappearance.

They considered a connection with the case of 74-year-old retired mail carrier and widowed church organist Thelma Scroggins of Lignum. On the evening of July 13, 1996, she was talking on the phone to a friend when she heard a knock at the door. She ended the phone call to answer it.

The next day, Richard Hicks and his wife picked up Frances Brown to take her to church with them. Frances was agitated about her friend Thelma. She said she could not reach her by phone and when she stepped into Thelma's yard, she heard the television on, playing at a very high volume.

After dropping his wife and Frances off at church, Hicks and another male member of Hopewell Methodist Church left for Thelma's house as Sunday school commenced. They hoped to quiet the fears of Frances Brown.

Arriving at the home, they knocked on the door. There was no response. They tried the door, discovered it was unlocked and went inside. Queasiness hit the two men in the gut when they saw a pair of eyeglasses lying at their feet. Their unease grew when they entered the living room—pink hair curlers were scattered across the wood floor and a reddish brown substance dotted its surface. When Hicks reached the bedroom, his disquiet was confirmed—a pair of legs stuck out of the doorway.

Thelma Scroggins had been shot three times on the left side of her head and once in the back of it; all shots were fired from a very close range. She died within minutes of the fourth shot. Thelma's 1994 Ford Ranger pick-up and her purse containing about $20 were missing from the home. At the scene investigators recovered no fingerprints, no DNA evidence, no shell casings and no weapon.

On August 12, Thelma's truck was found in a wooded area about thirteen miles from her home. No traces of blood and no useable prints were found in the vehicle. And although the wooded area and several ponds near the site were extensively searched, no weapon was found.

Spotsylvania County detectives never found a link to the murder of Sofia Silva, but a connection remained a possibility until May 2000. At that time, police arrested 19-year-old Michael Wayne Hash of Mineral, Virginia; 20-year-old Eric Glenn Weakley, of Madison, Virginia; and 22-year-old Jason Lee Kloby from Berwick, Pennsylvania. All three men were charged with capital murder and ultimately found guilty.

Detectives also attempted to find a way to bind together the abduction and murder of Sofia Silva to the death of Alicia Showalter Reynolds. Alicia, a 25-year-old graduate student pursuing her doctorate in pharmacology at Johns Hopkins University, was last seen on March 2, 1996.

She left her Baltimore home that Saturday to meet her mother, Sadie Showalter, in Charlottesville, Virginia, for a shopping excursion at Fashion Square Mall. She allowed a generous amount of time to travel the 150 miles through a rainy and foggy morning to make it to the rendezvous point by 10:30 A.M.

At 11:15 A.M., she still had not arrived. Her mother called Alicia's husband, Mark. Together they decided that the weather must have delayed Alicia and that all was well. These mutual reassurances eroded with each passing minute.

Police were contacted and the search began. At 6 P.M., Alicia's 1993 Mercury Tracer was found on the side of Route 29 near Culpeper, about fifty miles from her destination. A white paper napkin was stuck under her windshield wiper blade indicating car trouble. Authorities thoroughly inspected the vehicle, but found no mechanical problems whatsoever.

A credit card bearing her name was found on a street in Culpeper. Her parka was found in nearby Madison. But there was no sign of Alicia herself.

That Sunday, police set up a roadblock where her car had been abandoned, seeking anyone who remembered anything from the day before. They located three witnesses. Alicia had been seen looking under her hood with a presentable white male wearing a flannel shirt and blue jeans at her side. She was also observed getting into a dark pick-up truck with this same man.

When these reports hit the media, investigators were overwhelmed with similar tales. Twenty women came forward to report that a man in a dark pick-up truck had attempted to stop them along the same stretch of highway. He came up behind them flashing lights or honking his horn. Then, he'd pull up next to their vehicles, gesturing that sparks were flying out of their car or some other trouble was brewing with their vehicles.

The women who refused to pull over stated that he appeared to become angry. He pounded his fists on the steering wheel and his lips scribed quick, tight movements that indicated he was mumbling.

The women who did stop said that he introduced himself as Larry Breeden. He examined the undercarriage of their cars or looked under the hoods. Then, he politely discussed what he thought was wrong and emphasized the danger of continuing to drive the car in that condition.

After that, he offered the women a ride to the nearest telephone booth or to a local mechanic. Two women accepted his offer, and came to no harm. A third woman had an uneasier encounter.

A week before Alicia's disappearance, she was waved over in an adjacent county on State Route 234. After she got into the man's truck, he repeatedly slowed to a crawl, claiming that the bright lights shining through his back window impaired his vision. Her discomfort increased with each deceleration. When he pulled off onto the shoulder, she knew something was wrong and lunged for the door handle. He screamed at her and threatened her with a screwdriver. Then he jumped on her and tried to prevent her from leaving the truck. When she fought back with determination, he gave up and shoved her out the door. As she went flying to the roadside, her arm got tangled up in the shoulder rest. Instead of a simple hard fall, she took a clumsy stumble and broke her ankle.

Culpeper County investigators were now certain they knew what happened to Alicia Showalter Reynolds, but they still did not find her body for more than two months. On May 7, at a logging site near Lignum and State Route 3, twenty miles from where her car was abandoned, a logger noticed buzzards circling overhead. He followed their line of sight and uncovered Alicia's skeletal remains in a makeshift grave.

Although there were many suspicious coincidences, Spotsylvania County found no definitive connection to the Sofia Silva case. Culpeper County investigators followed up 7,800 leads, published a forensic sketch of the 35- to 45-year-old medium-built suspect with light to medium brown hair, but as of 2004, the case had not been solved.

"You can glean some information with just a little bit of knowledge. All you have to do is collect it and it will tell you the story."

Rick Moorer, Western District (Virginia),
medicolegal death investigator,
from *The News & Advance*

Chapter 16

On October 30, 1996, Lieutenant Mike Timms responded to a question from a Fredericksburg *Free Lance–Star* reporter saying that the Spotsylvania County police had a dozen suspects in the Silva abduction and homicide. In no time, those twelve had been whittled down to one prime target—Karl Michael Roush.

Roush was a high school graduate who had received an honorable discharge from the U.S. Marine Corps in 1973. Since then, his life had not been so rosy. His criminal record showed a string of mostly non-violent crimes. On November 3, 1978, he was convicted in Norfolk, Virginia, for possession of stolen goods. In November of the next year, he was found guilty of larceny of an automobile in Towson, Maryland. In September of 1984, Virginia Beach convicted him of driving without a license.

The Norfolk Circuit Court labeled him a habitual traffic offender in October 1986. Then, in December, they found him guilty of trespassing, driving without a permit and frequenting a bawdy place. The last charge is one that relates to being engaged in or soliciting an illicit sex act in a place like a public park, restroom or a house where heterosexual or homosexual prostitution is known to occur.

Norfolk General Court convicted him of "crimes against nature" in December 1987. This offense meant that a perpetrator was in a public place committing any act that violated the sodomy laws of the Commonwealth of Virginia. Most typically, this charge referred to participating in oral sex, but by law, everything but the missionary position is illegal in the state.

In 1990, Virginia Beach authorities nailed him again—this time for indecent exposure and solicitation for immoral purposes. There followed another conviction in Norfolk in 1992—this time for assault and battery—and one more in 1995, for driving under the influence, selling an uninspected vehicle, failure to appear and for being a habitual offender.

In June of 1995, Elizabeth City, North Carolina, found him guilty of two counts of misdemeanor larceny. Then in December, Fredericksburg Circuit Court took their turn, finding Roush guilty of an attempt to possess cocaine. He received a two-year penitentiary sentence with two years suspended. He was awarded five years for good behavior, ordered to pay a fine of $701.50 and released. On August 20, 1996, Fredericksburg court sentenced him to thirty days in jail with twenty-eight days suspended for driving with a revoked license. Throughout his criminal career, he used a variety of aliases: Michael Roush, John Michael Roush, Mark Roush, John M. Rossi, Mark Anthony Roush and John Ross.

He moved to the Fredericksburg area in December of 1994 and had at least five addresses there in less than two years. At the time of Sofia's disappearance, he was renting a basement apartment in a split-level house owned and occupied by Charles and Patti Hudson. His address was 5511 Bounds Street—the same street that the Silvas called home.

ON OCTOBER 21, 1996—a week after Sofia's body was found—Roush was arrested for shoplifting a videocassette recorder from Kmart on Plank Road. He was released from Rappahannock Regional Jail on a $3,500 bond on

November 6. He was scheduled to be in Spotsylvania General District Court on November 14.

SEVEN YEARS before Sofia's murder, the Virginia General Assembly had created the legal option of a special regional jury to help combat the overlapping jurisdictional problems that occurred in many drug trafficking cases. In 1995, the legislative body expanded the powers to include a number of other crimes, including abduction. This grand jury was a powerful tool for the prosecution. Witnesses called were required by law to answer questions presented to them or face contempt of court proceedings—not something a witness would face when being interviewed by police.

Only once before had this regional panel been called up to investigate a homicide, and that was in the murder of Mark Martin, who had been shot during a drug deal. In November 1996, a special regional jury was convened to investigate the death of Sofia Silva. On the panel were members from Spotsylvania, Stafford and King George Counties. Their prime suspect: Karl Michael Roush.

Many suspicious facts about this man emerged during the course of their investigation. At the time of Sofia's disappearance, Roush, a self-employed house painter, was working on a job at a home where piles of blue moving blankets and a lot of rope were stored in the garage. The owner was uncertain if anything was missing. Roush left that job early on September 9 and did not return to work on the tenth.

It was reported by a number of people in the neighborhood that Roush sat in his silver-and-gray 1984 Dodge Caravan watching children boarding the school bus and looking toward the Silva residence. Some had complained that he drove around the neighborhood slowly, stopping to talk to kids.

Landlord Charles Hudson testified that approximately two weeks after the disappearance of Sofia—and months before his lease was up—Roush had moved out without giving notice, and left many of his belongings behind. Hudson also stated that Roush's drinking habits had undergone a dramatic change during the two weeks before he left—he switched from drinking beer to the heavy consumption of Jack Daniel's.

His intoxication, Hudson continued, made him mean, upset and violent. In one of these episodes, Roush told him that he knew how to dispose of a body so that it could not be found.

ON NOVEMBER 14, Karl Michael Roush did not appear in court as scheduled. The court set a new date—November 22—for him to appear and answer charges that he had violated his probation.

The next day, three search warrants were issued in connection with "the unlawful death of Sofia Silva in violation of the Code of Virginia 19.2-32 as amended." One warrant was for Roush himself. It granted authorities the right to obtain twenty-five plucked head hairs and twenty-five plucked pubic hairs, and to draw a 3cc tube of blood. The other two warrants granted authorization to search his Dodge Caravan and his former basement apartment in Oak Grove Terrace. The document specified that officers should seize "human hair, animal hairs, pubic hairs, clothing fibers, carpet fibers, female clothing and shoes consistent with the victim. Also, rope, moving blankets and fingerprints."

A BOLO was issued for the Dodge Caravan and for Roush, who, since he missed his November 22 court date, was wanted on two charges—shoplifting and violation of his probation.

During the search of the apartment on Bounds Street, Charles Hudson pointed out a blue plaid blanket hanging over the back of the sofa. He thought it resembled the one that encased Sofia's body. He also offered up cigarette butts left in the fireplace by his former tenant. The apartment was no testament to neatness—discarded fast food wrappers covered nearly every surface.

The investigators left the residence with a bounty of

evidence for evaluation, including a pair of pink underwear, a blue sock, a gray crate, a chip of wood extracted from the door and a swatch of knotted black cloth.

BONNIE HAD returned from California, but by now her marriage to Marc Evonitz was shattered beyond repair. In the past, no evidence of discord had been displayed to the outside world. Neighbors now heard loud argumentative voices drifting out of the Evonitz home, filling the peaceful night air with tension.

There was a half-hearted attempt at reconciliation. As part of this effort, a false front of domestic tranquility was erected for the holidays. Marc's relatives in the area, Uncle Richard, Aunt Barbara and Cousin Blair and her husband were all invited to a family Thanksgiving dinner at Bonnie and Marc's house. Wednesday night, on the eve of the holiday, Bonnie called them all and informed them that dinner was off. That sparked yet another fight—one that led to physical violence. Bonnie called the police to the house to intervene in the domestic disturbance. No charges were filed. The next day, Bonnie moved to California for good.

Marc fell into a deep depression. He still loved Bonnie, and her absence in his life broke his heart. He put in long hours at Walter Grinders trying to bury his despair under an avalanche of work.

At night, in his home filled with echoes of emptiness, he sat in his bath, a razor blade resting on the rim of the tub—and contemplated slitting his wrists. He wondered if anyone would notice he was gone.

TO THE people living around him, Marc put on a false front of bravado. He became more outgoing and more likely to instigate conversation. He talked to Kieth with great enthusiasm about his new invention. He told him of his plans to start his own business down in Louisa County.

He'd never shown any interest in exercise programs, but

now he joined the local gym. One day, after returning from there, he stopped to talk to Kieth, and described the 18-year-old who had captured his attention at the gym.

"You need to grow up," Kieth told him, "and start dating women your own age."

Marc laughed and said, "I like young girls."

WHILE THE sheriff's department was busy trying to tie Karl Michael Roush to Sofia Silva's murder, their suspect was sunning in Jacksonville, Florida. He vacationed at a Motel 6 with his ex-wife, Sharon Holm.

He returned to the area on Thanksgiving Day. Learning of the outstanding warrant, he turned himself in to the King George Sheriff's Department. On November 28, Captain Steve Dempsey and Detective Ed Lunsford conducted a tape-recorded interview with Roush about the abduction and murder of Sofia Silva.

At the conclusion of the session, Roush agreed to take a polygraph test to verify his truthfulness. Arrangements were made, but as soon as Roush was informed that the examiner was on the way, he changed his mind. He insisted on speaking to an attorney first.

Dempsey and Lunsford informed him that the interview was over and he was under arrest for failure to appear in Spotsylvania General District Court on November 14. They also informed him that they had seized his van and it would be searched for forensic evidence relevant to the Silva case as soon as the warrant arrived.

Roush snapped back, "Whatever you find in that van, you planted there."

*"The beauty of a crime scene is that no matter what happens
there's always some type of evidence."*

Jonathon Pelletier, Lynchburg, Virginia,
police officer, from *The News & Advance*

Chapter 17

The search of the van uncovered hairs, fibers and a purple
flake of unknown material. All was delivered to the Division
of Forensic Science in Richmond, Virginia.

Roush was transferred to Rappahannock Regional Jail to
await the disposition of the shoplifting, failure to appear and
probation charges. In December, he received a five-day sentence for not showing up for his court date the previous
month. Roush had an anxiety-filled Christmas waiting to hear
about the test results from the state forensic lab. He knew the
results should be negative. He feared that he had been framed.

THE SILVA family had no plans to celebrate Christmas this
year. But members of their church brought a small artificial
Christmas tree to their home insisting that Sofia would
want them to have it. Phyllis and Humberto put the purple
ornament–covered tree in Sofia's room and turned on the purple strings of lights. Those lights stayed on twenty-four hours
a day until, months and months later, they finally burned out.

In memory of her daughter, Phyllis bought the car that
Sofia had wanted—a purple Pontiac Grand Prix. She let the
world know where her heart was with license plates that
read: "4 SOFIA."

• • •

IN RICHMOND, Robin McLaughlin was assigned to analyze the fibers in the Sofia Silva murder case. McLaughlin had served as a Virginia state trooper in New Kent and Charles City Counties for three years before coming to work at the state forensic lab. Her husband worked for the New Kent County Sheriff's Department.

Her report about the evidence presented was completed on January 8, 1997. She called the investigators and told them, "You've got him." She wrote that fibers from the carpeting, a rug and a seat cover in Roush's 1984 Dodge Caravan "matched in physical, chemical and optical properties" the fibers found on Sofia's body.

Any doubts authorities may have had were washed away in the face of this seemingly irrefutable evidence. A grand jury was convened.

On January 20, Roush was indicted on the Kmart video-cassette recorder theft, but there was a far worse charge coming the next day. An indictment was handed down charging him with abduction and first-degree homicide.

The good news for Roush was that William Neeley, the Commonwealth's Attorney in Spotsylvania County, declined to pursue the death penalty. Since he had no evidence that Sofia had been tortured before her death, and Roush's criminal record included only one minor violent crime, the ultimate sentence seemed impossible to achieve. The bad news was that Roush now faced two life sentences. No arraignment date was set that day. Judge William H. Ledbetter, Jr., first needed to appoint legal counsel for the accused.

Roush, meanwhile, proclaimed his innocence to anyone within earshot. When pressed for more information, he told reporters for the Fredericksburg *Free Lance–Star* that he would answer all their questions if he could approve any story before it went to print. The newspaper declined his offer.

• • •

In Wheeling, West Virginia, Roush's mother, Elizabeth, was in shock. The charges filed against her son stirred up a tidal wave of painful memories. Elizabeth believed in her son's innocence, but the similarity of this case to the fate of her own daughter, Susie, was almost too much to bear.

Nineteen years before, her 16-year-old daughter went out to a bar one night and never returned home. Weeks later, her body was found in a neighboring county. She had been strangled with a rope. First Sergeant Don Benson, a young trooper at the time, tracked down a legion of suspects, including a psychologist, in his attempts to solve the case. The state forensics lab made his job even more difficult—when the facility underwent reconstruction, much of the evidence in the Susie Roush case was accidentally destroyed. In 2003, Benson continued to be haunted by this unsolved homicide.

On January 22, Charles Hudson was already annoying everyone at the sheriff's department. No matter how many times he was told that the reward was contingent upon the arrest *and conviction* of the perpetrator, he spouted out his demands that they turn over the $30,400 now. He threatened to hire an attorney and sue the county.

Judge Ledbetter appointed Spotsylvania attorney Phillip "Flip" Sasser and a Fredericksburg lawyer and former state legislator, Ben Woodbridge, to represent Karl Michael Roush. On February 4, Ann Harris, a member of the Rappahannock Regional Jail staff, attempted to interview Roush at the jail as part of the procedure to prepare a bond recommendation report. On the advice of Sasser, Roush refused to speak to her.

She submitted the document the next day making no recommendation for release on bond. Her report acknowledged that Roush's lengthy criminal record showed no pattern of violent behavior, but stated, "Subject's current charges are of a violent nature." She noted that he was being held at this time on no bond for Stafford General District Court on a fraud charge for failure to perform promised work. A trial date on that matter was set for February 19. At that proceeding, Roush was found guilty, ordered to pay restitution of $175 and given a thirty-day suspended sentence.

She concluded that his previous conviction on a failure to appear charge and his history of frequent moves and multiple convictions, as well as another pending court appearance, made Roush a flight risk. "Given the seriousness of subject's current charges, it appears subject is a risk of danger to the community."

On the fifteenth of April, all parties in the case stood before Judge Ledbetter. The defense requested more time to prepare for trial. They insisted it was impossible to be prepared for the scheduled date of May 6. Despite prosecutor William Neeley's passionate objections, the judge granted this motion, resetting the trial for September 8.

Ledbetter did deny the defense's other request that the state pay for an independent forensic expert for their client. The attorneys hoped Roush's family could scrape up the money for what they considered a necessary expense.

COMMONWEALTH'S ATTORNEY William Neeley toiled away building a case against the accused. "He acted so guilty," he said, "He jumped bail, fled the area, had a history of sexual deviance misdemeanors and had been acting strangely in the neighborhood—driving around and looking at children." The forensic evidence polished the circumstantial evidence to a high gloss.

ROUSH FIRED off a letter to Judge Ledbetter on April 21 objecting to an incident at the jail:

Dear Judge,

I am writing this letter to your honor to express my concerns over recent developments at the Rappahannock Reg. Jail.

On or about 4-18-97 at approx 1300 hours I was taken from my cell that I occupied for 3½ months by Cpl Dudley, Officer Moore, and Cpl Norris, I was put into solitary confinement by Cpl Dudley at this time. They took my personal things and most important my legal file, containing my entire case that is pending in our court. All I might add confidential. *My attorney Philip Sasser, told me not to show or let out of my possession at any time these documents. Verbally and written letter which I am sending with this letter. I told Cpl Norris about this, he told me to shut up and get into the single cell, so I did, he lock the door and then lock the solid outer door. My legal file with my entire case with every detail was kept from me for 2½ hours. I am deeply concerned about what happened to it during this time.*

I must respectfully inform your honor that I will be asking my attorneys for a motion for mistrial, I don't mean anything disrespectful.

Furthermore your honor, I am being denied hot water in my cell. I have no way to brush my teeth properly and I have no mirror to shave by. I haven't broken any rules your honor. I cannot keep up my personal appearance.

Even more important your honor is my trial coming up in Sept.. I now have to spend the next 4½ to 5 months looking at four walls with no diversion no TV no nothing. I have done nothing to deserve this. I am concerned what my demeanor and physical mental condition will be at that time. When I have to face 12 strangers in a jury.

I didn't want to blurt this out in open court for 2 reasons your honor, I think it would be disrespectful to you and your court 2. I don't think any of us need this in the newspaper, as it tends to print anything and everything.

Therefore your honor I am not asking you to wave a magic wand and solve all my problems at the jail, what I m asking your honor is to request that your honor enter these problems into my court record, for possible future relief.

I come to you as my judge and bring this to your attention. Maybe I am wrong. If I am in any way out of line then I apologize, and will refrain from further communication. Not for one minute would I disrespect you your honor or your honorable court.

> *Thanking You for Your Time and Consideration, I remain,*
> *Respectfully Yours,*
> *Karl Michael Roush.*

His pleas made no apparent impact on the court. But, soon, these potential grounds for a mistrial would be a moot point. Another tragic event in Spotsylvania County would alter the course of Roush's life.

"Oh, earth, you are too wonderful for anybody to realize you. Do any human beings ever realize life while they live it—every, every minute?"

Thornton Wilder, from *Our Town*

Chapter 18

Patti Lisk earned her pre-nursing degree from Mary Washington College in 1974 and received her bachelor's degree in nursing from the University of Virginia in 1976. She followed that with a master's degree from the University of Maryland in 1980.

In the early 80s, Ron Lisk was married to Patti and working in the Office of Safety and Mission Assurance at NASA. January 1, 1982, started a new year and a new way of life for the young couple. On that day, their first daughter, Kristin Michelle, was born. Ron and Patti's second child, Kathryn Nicole "Kati," followed more than two and a half years later on October 12, 1984. They began their family while living in Greenwood Estates, a subdivision on State Route 3.

In addition to his day job, Ron started his own company on the side, Vision Photography, specializing in portraits, weddings and aerials. He operated the business out of his home. Since 1982, he had housed a Piper four-seater at Shannon Airport in Fredericksburg. His pilot's license enabled him to fly and shoot aerial photographs at the same time.

The Lisks bought their home on Block House Road in 1988 for their family of four. It was in a serene neighborhood with a rural feel. There were twenty-seven homes there and most sat well back from the road on three- to five-acre lots.

Only small glimpses of the siding on their house could be seen from the road. Past this cozy cluster of homes, Block House Road narrowed and degraded to a gravel and dirt trail. On most of the length of this portion, trees towered high above on either side of the road and formed a shadowy canopy. Two cars could not pass each other without one pulling over into the shallow ditch by the embankment and stopping as the other vehicle squeezed past. The road abruptly ends when it hits State Route 738.

Vision Photography was a successful enterprise. It was doing so well that in 1993, Ron moved it out of his home into the Fredericksburg Business Park across from the country club. In 1996, he retired from NASA and devoted himself to his business.

The Lisks raised their two cheerful, friendly daughters, Kristin and Kati, with a firm grounding in the scriptures. The family were regular and active members of Goshen Baptist Church.

Both of the girls were good students. Kristin's big love was horses—she took riding lessons at Hazelwild Farm on Thursday afternoons. She was near the end of her ninth grade year. Kati was finishing up her first year at the middle school. In the previous year at Robert E. Lee Elementary School, Kati had drawn a picture of two people with rags and buckets, scrubbing the globe. Her picture was on the cover of that school's calendar for the 1996–97 school year. Kati saw the world as a place where people could make a difference. She was a competitive and enthusiastic player on a recreational basketball team. And she loved to read—her favorites were R. L. Stine's Goosebumps books and the Fear Street mysteries.

The girls were a source of great pride to their parents. Patti and Ron could not have loved them more.

ON THURSDAY, May 1, Richard Marc Evonitz called in to Walter Grinders. He claimed he was sick and took the day off.

. . .

FOURTEEN-YEAR-OLD KRISTIN Lisk darted out of her Block House Road home in Spotsylvania that same morning. With a Pop-Tart in one hand and the strap of her backpack in the other, she slid into the blue Mazda minivan next to her good friend Becca Trigg.

Becca's mother, Dale, smiled as the excited prattle of the two teenagers drifted up from the seat behind her. The girls' friendship dated back to preschool. At the school, Kristin and Becca went to their lockers, then killed time in the band room until they had to go to class.

Kristin's first class was World Geography followed by French II. In third period English, Kristin took her turn reading aloud from *Romeo and Juliet*. Then there was Drama class, where Kristin had established a tradition at the beginning of the year. The class paused at 11:11 to make a wish. Kristin claimed it was the luckiest time of the day, since it was the only time all four numbers were the same.

Kristin attended her Physical Education class next and then went to lunch. As usual, she brown-bagged her meal—pepperoni pizza, chips and a Coke. Before leaving the cafeteria, she made arrangements with a few older friends to get extra coaching before dance squad tryouts.

After lunch, Kristin went to Earth Science class, then on to Geometry—the only class that both challenged and frustrated her. There she had a test. Before crossing the threshold of the classroom, she and Becca Czarnecki kissed their good luck charm, a plastic ladybug that dangled from the zipper on Kristin's book bag. Kristin had a passion for ladybugs—she never went anywhere without one close at hand.

School day over, Becca walked Kristin to her bus stop. As she boarded, Kristin yelled to Becca to call her as soon as she got home.

It was a very typical school day for Kristin, except for the undercurrent that churned up excitement whenever her thoughts wandered. Only one more school day before her trip to Kings Dominion amusement park.

KATI LISK waited at the end of the drive carrying her dark book bag and her clarinet on the morning of May 1. She wanted to wear her Bulldogs Band jacket, but the morning was already too warm. She boarded bus #106 to Spotsylvania Middle School and took her assigned seat in the back.

Her first stop at school was her locker. It was decorated with pictures of her cat Sassy—no pictures of boys, yet.

After homeroom, her first class was Band. There the buzz was all about Saturday's events, a trip to Kings Dominion, followed by a band competition at Patrick Henry High School in Richmond. The seventh and eighth graders would battle for honors that night; but all the sixth graders, like Kati, were going, too, to cheer on the older students. Her other interests included swimming and Girls in Action, a church group that involved kids in visits to local nursing homes and other volunteer activities.

She had two more classes after Band–Physical Education and Language Arts. Then, it was time for lunch. She met her friend Dara in the cafeteria and, like Kristin, had brown-bagged pizza.

After lunch, Kati had three more classes—her favorite subject, Math, followed by Social Studies and Science. She and Dara met again at their lockers, and Kati boarded her bus to go home.

Kenny Foster was very conscious of Kati's presence on the bus. His eyes followed her as she disembarked. He saw her older sister, Kristin, waiting for her halfway up the drive. Kristin was wearing black jeans, black tennis shoes and a white T-shirt printed on the front with "SOLDIERS OF THE CROSS" and on the back "GOSHEN BAPTIST CHURCH."

Kati had reached her bedroom when she thought she heard something not quite right outside. She tossed her book bag on the bed and went out to check with her sister.

She saw a man and a green Ford Taurus. The trunk of the car was up. Where was Kristin? The man spoke to her. She moved toward him. He grabbed her. He bound her.

Then, he tossed her into the trunk with Kristin and slammed the lid. No one heard a sound. No one saw a thing. No hue and cry was raised. The operation was flawless—its stealthy arrogance sealed the girls' fate.

Kristin did not lie still in fear. She struggled to free herself and Kati from their prison. She pushed up hard on the trunk lid, but to no avail.

Marc Evonitz slid his Taurus into the garage at his South Fork home and lowered the door behind him. He brought the girls into his home, where he undressed both of them. Kati was bound and placed in the bathroom on top of a pink rug. Kristin was secured to the bed where he partially shaved her pubic area. The police believe that only his problem with sexual dysfunction spared the two girls from rape. We know the enormity of their fear must have filled the atmosphere of that home with the heaviness of a funnel cloud. We know that their degradation and humiliation passed the bounds of human understanding. But nothing more is known about what happened to those young innocents behind the closed doors of this man's perverted world—their voices were stilled forever.

When he tired of their company, Evonitz asphyxiated the sisters and redressed them—putting one of Kati's socks on inside out on her small, lifeless foot. He carried them, one by one, to the trunk of his car.

> *"Sexual homicide offenders sometimes redress their victims in a feeble attempt to disguise that it was a sexual assault. Leaving them undressed makes it all too obvious. Psychologically, it could be an undoing of the act. It may assuage the subconscious which could be having a small bit of guilt or remorse."*

> Greg McCrary, former FBI profiler

Chapter 19

In the deepest dark of night, Evonitz backed his car down the driveway and headed out of the subdivision, turning right on Massaponax Church Road. At the end of that road, he turned left onto Courthouse Road. At an intersection in Snell, that road merged into State Route 738.

Evonitz drove on with a precious cargo in his trunk—two blameless young girls whom he was about to dump like old, worn-out appliances whose usefulness is long past.

The narrow road zigged and zagged through an unremarkable but lush countryside. Stretches of thick woods alternated with wide-open fields. This late at night, Evonitz could not have noticed the cows sleeping in the pastures or the homes set back off the road, dark in sleep, or the occasional country stores shuttered down till dawn. He may have noticed the most prominent landmark on the road, the modest U.S. Post Office in the tiny town of Partlow. Just past Partlow, he left Spotsylvania County and entered Hanover County. Again and again, State Route 738 came to forks that were not clearly marked even in bright daylight. But somehow Evonitz always managed to stay the course and remain on the winding road even though some of the sharp turns seemed to fold upon themselves.

Finally, he reached Gum Tree Corner, where he crossed U.S. Route 1. He may have encountered traffic as he traversed this major highway. It was the busiest intersection on his route. He continued on 738, now known locally as Old Ridge Road. He drove past the Bear Island Paper Company, across bridges, through wooded areas, past barns and fields. Finally, half a mile from the nearest house, and thirty-five miles from the home of Kristin and Kati Lisk, he stopped his car. One mile beyond this lonely bridge, the paved country lane ended at a road with a thin layer of gravel that meanders its way to U.S. Route 1 in one direction and Route 301 in the other.

The spot he had chosen was menacing even in the daylight. There was a coldness on the bridge that had nothing to do with the weather. It was the nightmare version of the road less traveled.

Trees draped with kudzu and poison ivy loomed over the river like stooped, forbidding hags. The water in the South Anna River slithers downstream like a forsaken and loathed creature of the night. Logjams of fallen trees gang up by the bridge, forming pools of stagnant water iced with a topcoat of alien, repulsive green.

It was in this place of despair and sorrow that Evonitz tossed two lovely young girls into the water. The water splashed high as each one hit the surface. Their bodies tangled in the logs and in each other. No one knows how long he paused to view his handiwork. Odds are he compared this spot to the one where he disposed of Sofia and left convinced that the sisters' bodies would remain undiscovered longer than the thirty-six days his previous victim had waited to be found. Evonitz drove off in a futile attempt to outrace the broken hearts and anxious minds that had been born at the moment of their deaths.

"Death is not the greatest loss in life. The greatest loss is what dies inside while we live."

Norman Cousins

Chapter 20

At 3:10 P.M. on May 1, Ron Lisk called home to check on his daughters. He or his wife Patti would call home every school day if one of the girls had not called first. When he got no answer, he called Patti. "I called home and no one was there."

"Well, you need to get home right away."

Ron was about ready to leave the office anyway. It was the day of the week he was scheduled to take Kristin to the stable for her horseback riding lesson. As he called again and again on his way home without reaching Kati or Kristin, his anxiety level rose. He reached home at 4 and saw Kristin's book bag and Geometry book lying in the front yard by a bush in a very neat pile. The symmetry of the pile was disturbing—neither of his children were known for their neatness.

He went inside and looked for the girls. He knew they had to be there somewhere. He could not find them inside or outside the house. He knew they had been there this afternoon. In addition to Kristin's things out in the front yard, the door was unlocked, the house alarm had been deactivated, Kati's book bag was on her bed and Kristin left a pile of soiled school clothes in her room when she changed. So where were they?

He grabbed the phone and called Patti: "Something is really wrong. The front door is unlocked and wide open."

Patti knew he was right. Her daughters were both very

cautious—safety and security had been emphasized in their home.

"Kristin's books are in the front yard," Ron added.

Ron then discovered a message on the answering machine from Kristin's friend Becca Trigg who had called, as promised, at 3:45. Ron called Becca first. Then he called his neighbor next door. "Have you seen Kristin and Kati?"

When they both responded no, he called every friend in the neighborhood whose number he could remember. Denial roosted on his shoulder—convincing him that somewhere, somehow, there was a logical, innocent explanation.

A close friend dropped by just before 5. After listening to Ron's desperate rationalization and negation of the obvious signs that his daughters were in peril, he said, "Ron, you've got to call 9-1-1."

He took his friend's suggestion and reported his daughters missing.

The Spotsylvania Sheriff's Department set up a road block on Block House Road, questioning all who drove past the Lisk home. They hoped to find someone who had seen something suspicious on Thursday afternoon. And they did.

They received a report that a white pick-up, possibly a Ford F-150, had driven past at approximately 3 P.M. The truck had a camper shell with small oval windows, chrome bumpers and wheels and a blue reflective strip. Soon, the investigators realized that this description matched that of a vehicle involved in an attempted abduction at Longwood College in nearby Farmville just a month ago. A white male asked for directions, pulled a gun and attempted to force a female student into his truck. She screamed and ran away as the prospective kidnapper sped off.

Now police had a solid lead to follow. To track down the white pick-up, they tried to get a list of all of the vehicles matching that description that were registered in the area. They were dismayed to discover that the law did not require the color of a car or truck be listed on the registration. So instead of getting a relatively short list of white trucks in the surrounding counties, they got a never-ending list of all truck owners. This problem was remedied for future investigations when Senator Ed Houck and Delegate Bobby Orrock introduced legislation to change the law in Virginia.

To follow the pick-up lead, there was only one recourse open to the officers. They stopped and identified all the drivers of white trucks. The practice was pervasive in the area— so much so that when Major Howard Smith made a personal stop in a convenience store, the driver of the white pick-up out in the parking lot approached him when he walked through the front doors. Without being asked, he whipped out his driver's license and offered it to Smith—much to the Major's surprise. The driver told the officer that he had been stopped three times in the past two days.

On May 2, Evonitz called in to Walter Grinders and extended his sick leave by one more day.

A MASSIVE search for the girls was also under way. Fifteen hundred people—both professionals and volunteers from the community—combed the woods surrounding the girls' home from Friday through Monday. In all, an area with a twelve-mile radius was scrutinized with extreme attention to detail. Search dogs joined in the hunt starting at the Block House home, but could not track the girls off of the property. Nonetheless, the dog teams soldiered on, joining the others tearing apart the woods in search of Kati and Kristin.

Hundreds of items were collected, bagged and examined during the search, from soda cans to a T-shirt stained with blood. Nothing with any significant connection to the Lisk sisters was ever found.

Churches for miles around bore signs requesting prayers for the two girls. Fliers were posted in fast food restaurants, post offices, convenience stores, gas stations—anywhere and everywhere possible. Every day, a new version replaced the old throughout the community. The first ones were black-and-white. Then fluorescent yellow and red headlines were added. They were followed by larger posters with colored photographs of the girls and their descriptions: Kati Lisk, 5'5", 76–80 pounds, brown hair, brown eyes; Kristin Lisk, 5'8", 90 pounds, brown hair, brown eyes.

At Goshen Baptist Church, where the Lisk family worshiped, an around-the-clock vigil sent up unceasing prayers for the safety of the girls, comfort for the parents and for God's intervention to bring them home. Members of the church passed out yellow fliers asking for a massive moment of prayer every evening at 7:30 P.M. "Turn off the TV, radio, computer and telephone and join us in a quiet time," the missive urged.

A special event had been planned on May 4 at Goshen Baptist long before the girls disappeared. They took time away from their scheduled line-up for the evening to pray for the girls and their parents. Then they released twenty yellow helium balloons one at a time. Tied to each balloon was a prayer.

Down in the basement of the church, hearts broke as members noticed the volunteer sign-up sheet for the Relay for Life. On the top of the list, Kristin Lisk had signed her name.

Piece Goods Shop and Fancy Hats of America donated plastic bags filled with yellow and pink ribbon reels. Soon, this ribbon was tied to trees, mailboxes, lampposts and car antennas throughout the county. At Spotsylvania Middle School, yellow bows adorned school doors, flagpoles and road signs. Homeroom teachers updated students on the search, and guidance counselors stood by to talk with any student who needed them.

Businesses and families donated food at the search center at the Spotsylvania Fire Department's Courthouse Station. So much food arrived for the searchers that two pick-up trucks were needed to haul the leftovers to the Hope House, an organization providing transitional housing and other services for homeless women with children.

Deb Smith did not know any of the members of the Lisk

family, but was moved by their plight. On May 5, she put up hand-made signs along State Route 3 near Five Mile Fork urging people to stop and pray. Her impromptu call brought dozens of cars off the road. People drifted in and out of the grassy field, pausing in their busy days to join hands in a prayer circle for Kristin and Kati Lisk.

A radio station reporter tried to weasel her way up to the Lisk home. She told deputies that she was a minister at the family's church. But the officer spotted her microphone and sent her on her way.

While the girls were missing, more than one thousand tips were called in to the station. Others were gathered as police officers went door to door in the neighborhood canvassing every member of each household.

It was an excruciating week for Ron and Patti. They prayed for the best outcome and they dreaded the worst. The doors to Vision Photography remained locked—the phone calls unanswered. Patti Lisk did not teach a single one of her nursing classes at Germanna Community College. Their lives had come to a total standstill.

Speculation sizzled around them. Ron Lisk said, "People were asking, 'So how can two children be missing unless they've run away from home together?' Believing his daughters did not leave willingly but stuck together under adverse circumstances, he added: "There was an answer in my heart to that, because I knew Kati would defend her sister."

By May 6, the police had uncovered no solid leads. They had received many calls—one reporting a sighting of the girls at a North Carolina shopping center, another on a bridge in Maryland. But all these tips fizzled when probed by detectives. The team now had twenty-two full-time investigators, including agents from the FBI, the Virginia State Police, members of the Spotsylvania County Sheriff's Department and one assigned agent each from King George, Hanover and Stafford Counties. They were all working tirelessly. Major Smith had only managed to get home two nights since the girls were reported missing—and when he did, sleep did not come easy.

• • •

ROAD MAINTENANCE workers from the Virginia Department of Transportation were scheduled to perform routine work on Old Ridge Road on May 6. It was clear and sunny at 2:20 P.M., as the crew unloaded their equipment and got to work. They were enjoying being outdoors on this comfortable spring day until two members of the crew mowing grass on the side of the road spotted something unusual in the water—two submerged bodies floating slightly apart from one another.

Far from the inner city where they might expect such ugly surprises, the discovery stunned them into an awful silence. They stopped work right where they stood, staring at the incredible and unwelcome sight. They could see no marks of violence on the girls' bodies—no apparent reason for their demise. As soon as they could pull themselves out of their trance-like state of disbelief, they called their office to request that Hanover County Sheriff's Department personnel be sent to the scene at once.

Hanover County authorities contacted Spotsylvania County as soon as they heard. Two small bodies in one location might have been a coincidence, but it was far more likely that the road crew might have found the remains of Kati and Kristin Lisk. In a sad irony, the two girls were less than two miles southeast of the spot of their anticipated Saturday field trip, Kings Dominion.

It was only May and the homicide total for 1997 already equaled the total number of murders in Spotsylvania County for all of 1996.

The search for a killer was now under way.

"For offenders like Evonitz, it's the people that are closest to him that may have an idea that there's something sinister going on with that particular individual. The problem is that friends and family members of these offenders tend to get into denial about this. They can't believe the person they know can be capable of such horrific violence. People have to be aware that offenders like Evonitz are not one-dimensional monsters but project the appearance of normalcy and blend in with the rest of society in many ways. But they are living in that community and those closest to the offender have the responsibility of coming forward with their suspicions. In doing so, they may even save themselves from harm as some of these offenders have in the past killed family members as well."

Greg McCrary, former FBI profiler, on *FredTalk*

Chapter 21

On the day the girls' bodies were found, Bonnie Lou Evonitz filed a petition for the dissolution of marriage in the Placer County Superior Court of California in Auburn. She petitioned to return to her original last name of Gower. The reason for the divorce was listed as irreconcilable differences. A summons was issued to Richard Marc Evonitz at 8618 South Fork Court. It was sent by certified mail.

WITHIN AN hour of the discovery of the bodies, Major Howard Smith and an FBI profiler were on the scene. After the girls were removed from their stagnant grave in the waist-deep water, they were transported to Richmond for an autopsy. During the autopsy, a head hair was found on Kati Lisk's sock and another on Kristin's clothing. These two hairs provided a DNA profile that could be compared to future suspects.

Smith searched the area with local officers until 7 P.M., when the encroaching darkness in the thick woods made it impossible to continue.

Some media sources reported that Hanover County did not rope off the area or guard it from trespassers that evening, and that local reporters as well as media from Washington, D.C, and Richmond, Virginia, tramped through the area in the dark. The Hanover County Sheriff's Department dismissed those stories as wild rumors. They insisted that the roads were cordoned off for a half mile in every direction and manned throughout the night. This official version of events gained additional credibility when no personal accounts of midnight ramblings on the crime scene ever emerged in the press.

RON LISK looked out the window on the front of his home when he heard the sound of tires on his gravel drive. A vehicle from the Spotsylvania Sheriff's Department came to a stop and all four doors flew open at once. An officer stepped out of each one. Ron knew right away that his nightmares had come true.

Ron and Patti greeted the investigators on the front porch. Patti turned to Detective Twyla Demoranville and said, "If someone has come and has to tell me that my children have died, would you please do it?"

The detective glanced at the other officials at the scene and nodded her head. The Lisks ushered their grim visitors inside.

In the dining room, Demoranville said, "Patti, I need to talk to you."

Patti, knowing what she was about to hear, responded, "But I don't want to talk to you."

No words needed to be spoken because the new reality in

Ron and Patti's lives was etched across the detectives' faces. But the conversation proceeded with gentle sensitivity. After Demoranville confirmed the Lisks' worst fears, Bill Hagamaier of the FBI assured the grieving parents that their daughters had been found in the river, together, and that they looked peaceful.

"Why they were taken from us makes little sense," Hagamaier said. "Certainly Ron and Patti cried out, 'Why?' I was there. I heard them say it. And I said it, too."

"My girls are safe," Patti whispered. Her rockbed of faith and her firm belief in life eternal blessed Patti with the certainty that her girls no longer suffered.

The next morning, canoes paddled up and down the river looking for clues. State police helicopters hovered overhead seeking out sites that needed to be explored on ground level. FBI agents and police officers on foot from multiple agencies were on the scene sifting through every leaf and twig in search of any sign of evidence that could lead them to whoever had committed this ghastly crime. No possibility was considered irrelevant. Multiple tire-track impressions were taken in a broad radius of the scene. A mile away, a button-down-collar shirt was found on a road leading to Interstate 95. It was bagged and sent to the lab. No connection to the crime was ever found.

Simon and Ann Gore, who lived in the house nearest to the bridge—half a mile away—were questioned extensively and asked, in particular, about a white truck. They could recall nothing suspicious during the six days that the sisters were missing. But, then again, they told the officers, fishermen in pick-ups were a common sight on any rural road and would not set off any mental alarms. The Gores had often enjoyed the one-mile walk down to the bridge and back to their home. That stretch of road would never feel welcoming again.

Back on Block House Road, orange traffic cones, a NO PARKING sign and a Spotsylvania deputy guarded the sanctity of the Lisk home. The neighbors surrounding their property parked their cars near the road to prevent media and curiosity seekers from slipping up their driveways and circumventing the deputy by making an end run through the woods.

AT SPOTSYLVANIA High School, the flag hung at half-mast. A bevy of students gathered beneath it and joined hands in prayer. Many of these kids had no idea that the bodies had been found until they arrived at school that morning.

The school cancelled homeroom to allow the teenagers to spend time together, providing both physical and mental support as the news filtered through the student body. The yellow ribbons worn by kids and faculty alike remained in place—no longer a gesture of hope, but now a message of support to the parents of the two girls.

Sofia's friend Brandi at Spotsylvania High, said that when she heard about the Lisk sisters, she "relived nightmares and pain. It was a horrible *déjà vu.*"

Another friend of Sofia's said, "When the Lisk sisters were taken, we at Chancellor were scared for our lives, thinking, 'They got someone at Courtland and someone at Spotsylvania, they must be targeting Chancellor next'—the only other high school in the county at the time."

Spotsylvania County deputies were posted at the doors of the school to admit only teachers, parents and students. The benefit concert for a child with leukemia scheduled for that day was cancelled. Baseball and softball games scheduled against King George High School were postponed.

Spotsylvania Middle School also lowered their flag to half-mast. In each classroom, teachers read a brief statement and all bowed their heads together in a moment of silence.

IN THE Spotsylvania Courthouse Complex, Commonwealth's Attorney William Neeley was already fielding calls from those who thought the murder of the Lisk girls pointed to the innocence of Karl Michael Roush in the death of Sofia Silva. Authorities still believed in the certainty of Roush's guilt.

• • •

No PLAN was made, no word was spoken, but, one by one, on the evening of May 7, parishioners gathered at Goshen Baptist Church. The young friends of Kati and Kristin dropped down on the steps out front clinging to each other as tears flowed, washing away all remnants of their innocence. Parents whisked the girls inside as the media descended. Members of the press were barred from the sanctuary, where church members remained until after midnight.

AT 9 P.M., media and residents of Spotsylvania congregated outside the sheriff's office for an official announcement about the discovery of the girls' bodies. At this press conference, the FBI profile of the killer was released to the public.

It was the opinion of the experts that before the crime, the guilty person may have experienced some stressful event in his personal life. It could have been a problem with teachers at school; managers or co-workers at his place of employment; with his parents, his spouse or a girlfriend at home; or with law enforcement for some less serious offense.

He would have shown a preoccupation with adolescent girls for quite some time, but would exhibit an awkwardness or lack of success in establishing relationships with them. He would spend his spare time driving around in areas where young girls could be found and may have been seen staring at them. He may also have shown an avid interest in TV shows, movies or magazines featuring young girls, particularly in athletic roles.

In the aftermath of the crime, the suspect could have escalated his use of drugs, alcohol or cigarettes. He might avoid his family, friends and associates. He would skip school or miss work and appointments. His daily activities could show a disruption. He might have left the area for a seemingly plausible reason like a business trip or a visit to a distant relative. He would exhibit a highly nervous, irritable and short-tempered disposition. His normal sleep pattern would be disrupted. He might color his hair, change his hairstyle, grow or remove facial hair or change his physical appearance in other ways. He would be likely to change his vehicle or change the look of his vehicle.

The suspect would have unexplained scratches or bruises and might become physically ill. He would take an unexpected turn toward or away from religion. And, of course, he is likely to demonstrate an intense interest in the status of the investigation of the homicides he committed.

The community was asked to call in their suspicions of anyone meeting the criteria outlined by the FBI. No lead would be considered too small—no suspect too unlikely.

ON MAY 8—exactly one week after the girls were abducted— Spotsylvania deputies were back on Block House Road manning a roadblock. Everyone who traveled the road that day was stopped and questioned about what they saw on the preceding Thursday. Although they were greeted by an abundance of cooperative residents, they gained little new information for their day-long effort.

The investigators questioned school bus drivers about any unusual vehicles or people they may have observed following their buses or loitering near bus stops. The task force encouraged them to call in immediately if they saw anything peculiar.

Pat Stanley drove a school bus that traversed Block House Road every day. Neither one of the Lisk girls rode on her bus, but she had been in that vicinity at the right time to witness an important detail or a suspicious person. She spent many sleepless nights combing through her memories of that afternoon—trying to recall a person, a vehicle, an event that was not right. But she could not shake anything loose. All she could remember was a pleasant spring day.

Caution was the watchword for all the drivers. If they pulled up to a stop and no adult was waiting, they would not let the student—not even one from the high school—disembark.

They would not leave a child with a neighbor without specific, official written permission from the school. Without it, the student would be returned to the school after the bus run was complete.

Volunteers from the community followed every bus, keeping a watch on the children as they disembarked and walked to their homes. Their vigilance often confused the bus drivers, who reported their guardians for suspicious behavior. It created so many false alarms that special signs were printed up and assigned to these volunteers to eliminate confusion and concern.

Delivery people, utility workers and mail carriers who worked in the area were pushed to remember anything they may have seen on May 1. Representatives of the task force traveled out to Hazelwild Farm, the stable where Kristin took riding lessons, and to the high school and middle school, questioning and re-questioning anyone who might possess even a vague tidbit of valuable information.

Since the Spotsylvania County Sheriff's Department did not have a computer-assisted dispatch system, officers had to check the records by hand. They looked through recent area incident reports seeking any cases involving prowlers, indecent exposure, attempted abduction or anything else that had even a remote possibility of leading investigators to a perpetrator.

The influx of media into the small town of Spotsylvania inconvenienced everyone. Workers in the Courthouse Complex complained that the press used up all the parking spaces, making them late for work, and that they could not walk anywhere without tripping over wires.

On May 8, Spotsylvania Middle School delivered large posters covered with cards from the students expressing their support to the Spotsylvania County Sheriff's Department. City businesses and community organizations maintained a constant flow of food into the department. On May 9, the Chancellor Middle School PTO prepared a luncheon in the squad room for the entire staff. On the one hand, the community was united in grief and appreciation for one another.

On the other hand, they were torn apart by paranoia and fear. Parents congregated at school bus stops, eyeballed their neighbors, wrote down license plates of any unfamiliar vehicle—even those of people they knew, if their behavior seemed at all erratic. Door-to-door salesmen were reported to the police. Middle school children begged their parents for Mace.

Children were kept inside after school. All their privacy evaporated as anxious mothers, fathers, grandparents and teachers hovered over their shoulders every moment of the day. No place was safe anymore. Throughout Spotsylvania County, countless families who had moved there to escape the crimes of metropolitan D.C. and to raise their children in a safe environment were now wondering what they had been thinking.

WITHIN DAYS, more FBI agents and an officer from Caroline County were added to the investigative team, bringing the total number to fifty full-time personnel. At the sheriff's department, the high volume of tips surging into the office overloaded their capacity to handle them. A new line was installed with a toll-free number and manned twenty-four hours a day.

Calls reporting abnormal sexual habits were given a top priority. Many times, these calls came from wives in the middle of a separation who were more than willing to reveal the intimate details of the sex lives of estranged husbands. Even Major Smith was taken aback by some of these graphic reports of odd rituals and kinky fantasies in the bedrooms of his neighbors. "I had no idea all of this was going on around me," he said.

By Thursday, calls were coming in from officers in other jurisdictions across the country who saw superficial similarities to open cases in their communities. North Texas police called about the abduction of a 12-year-old girl whose body was found stuffed in a drain pipe.

The National Center for Missing and Exploited Children

The Silva/Lisk Plan

The Silva/Lisk Plan is in memory of 16 year old Sofia Silva and 15 year old Kristin Lisk and her sister, 12 year old Kati Lisk. All three girls were abducted in Spotsylvania County. They were later found murdered. In response to community concern, the local radio and television managers, along with the Sheriff's Office, have adopted the Silva/Lisk Plan to give listeners timely information about area child abductions.

Participating Radio Stations

WFLS 93.3 FM

WYSK 99.3 FM

WBQB 101.5 FM

WJYJ 90.5 FM

Participating TV Stations

Prestige TV
Channel 3

The Silva/Lisk Plan

Questions & Answers

Kristin Lisk

Kati Lisk

Sofia Silva

The Silva/Lisk Plan Activation Criteria:

In deciding to activate the plan, police must consider the following criteria:

1. The child should be 17 years of age younger, or with a proven mental or physical disability and...

2. Police must believe the child is in danger of serious bodily harm or death.

The plan is not intended to be used for runaways. And, while each case must be judged individually; most child custody situations do not qualify.

Does the Silva/Lisk Plan work?

YES. Since a similar effort was begun in 1996 in North Texas police have credited use of a similar plan with assisting in the safe return of several of their children. Listener and viewer participation is the key to success. Since most people listen to the radio while driving, the Silva/Lisk Plan instantly involves thousand of motorists in a giant "neighborhood watch". And, since many people now carry cell phones they can quickly notify the Sheriff's Office with leads and helpful information.

Who activates the Silva/Lisk Plan?

The Spotsylvania Sheriff's Office must decide if the case fits the criteria for activation (see Silva/Lisk Plan Criteria). The radio and TV stations that broadcast the bulletin material do not participate in the decision-making process.

How are Silva/Lisk Plan Bulletins Distributed to Various Radio and TV Stations?

When the Sheriff's Office decides to activate the Silva/Lisk Plan, they send the stations a written description of the child, the suspect, the suspect vehicle, the time and place of the incident, and any other relevant information. The stations quickly verify the activation. Then, using a pre-taped Emergency Activation Message, an audio bulletin containing the police information is sent simultaneously to all participating radio and TV stations in the Spotsylvania area. The bulletin is originated by the Spotsylvania County Sheriff's Office, as they are the "primary" EAM alert plan outlet for the Spotsylvania area. Once the bulletin is received, all Silva/Lisk Plan radio and TV stations break from regular programming and repeatedly broadcast the information to listeners and viewers.

What Does EAM Stand For?

EAM stands for Emergency Activation Message. It is similar to the more commonly know system used for the broadcast of severe weather and other civil emergencies. Each radio and TV station must have a working EAM Plan Agreement with the Sheriff's Office in order to receive the communications and messages.

Is the EAM Always Ready For Use?

YES. Silva/Lisk Plan bulletins go out to all participating radio and TV stations regardless of station format or time of day.

Are Sheriff's Offices or Police Departments Charged a Fee for Silva/Lisk Plan Activation's or Involvement?

NO. Law enforcement participation in Silva/Lisk Plan is free and open to any Department in the Spotsylvania area. Radio and TV station participation is voluntary and is done as a public service without commercial endorsement.

Who Oversees the Silva/Lisk Plan?

A team consisting of law enforcement representatives and media representatives.

What Should You Do If You Witness a Child Abduction or Believe a Child is Missing?

Call 911 immediately, and ask for the law enforcement department that serves your city or town. Then provide them with as much information as you can about the child, the suspect, and suspect vehicle.

The Silva/Lisk Plan was designed before Texas' Amber Alert program went nationwide. It was initiated in May 2001 in Spotsylvania County—the first county in the state of Virginia to institute a missing children's program.

RIGHT: Mug shot after Richard Marc Evonitz's arrest for lewd and lascivious behavior with a child on January 3, 1987 in Orange Park in Clay County, Florida. *(photo by Clay County Sheriff's Department)*

BELOW: The brick rambler of the Silva family on Bounds Street in the Oak Grove Terrace sub-division Spotsylvania County. Sofia was kidnapped from this front yard. *(photo by author)*

Evonitz dragged the body of Sofia Silva down this small hill and dumped her body in the undergrowth. In the background is the gate to Dominion Growers. *(photo by author)*

The marker erected by an unknown person near the spot where Sofia's body was found on October 16, 1996 in King George County, just a few hundred yards from State Route 3. *(photo by author)*

BOTTOM LEFT: The exterior of Courtland High, which Sofia Silva attended. The tree marked with a purple ribbon was planted in Sofia's honor. *(photo by author)*

The Lisk sisters were kidnapped from the front yard of their home on Block House Road in Spotsylvania. *(photo by author)*

LEFT: The location in the sluggish South Anna River where Kati and Kristin Lisk's bodies were found on May 6, 1997. *(photo by the author)*

RIGHT: A memorial to Kati and Kristin Lisk on the bridge where a lonely country road crosses the South Anna River. *(photo by author)*

In Sunset Memorial Gardens. *(photo by author)*

In the small cemetery next to the Goshen Baptist Church.
(photos by the author)

RIGHT: The memorial erected in November 1997 by Commonwealth Council Girl Scouts at the Spotsylvania Community Center in the former Spotsylvania Middle School Building on Courthouse Road.
(photo by author)

Major Howard Smith, Spotsylvania County Sheriff's Department. *(photo courtesy of Spotsylvania Coutny Sheriff's Department)*

LEFT: A 4-year-old Belgian Malinois in the K-9 unit of the Sarasota Police Department. He was involved in the apprehension of Richard Marc Evonitz. *(photo courtesy of the Sarasota Police Department)*

LEFT: The blood-spattered Ford Escort in which Evonitz ended his life—inside the car is the gun he used to commit suicide. *(photo by Sarasota Police Department)*

TOP RIGHT: The stretch of Bayfront Drive in Sarasota, Florida, where the chase of Evonitz ended. Police cars with blown tires are littered along the way. *(photo by Sarasota Police Department)*

Evonitz's body was pulled from his car so his vital signs could be checked. When medics realized resuscitation was impossible, they covered him with a sheet. *(photo by Sarasota Police Department)*

pointed out the likeness to a case in Bowling Green, Kentucky. Seven-year-old Morgan Violi was kidnapped from her apartment complex parking lot the previous July. Her 9-year-old friend broke free from the abductor's grasp and ran away to safety. Morgan's skeletal remains were discovered thirty miles from her home in White House, Tennessee, the following October. As of 2003, the case was still open.

Officials of Lonoke County, Arkansas, called to tell the task force about a man they had in custody. Richard Quinn was charged in the May 16 rape and kidnapping of a 15-year-old girl. She was able to escape when Quinn took her to a Christmas tree farm and got his truck stuck in the mud. The truck led authorities to the man. When his photograph was broadcast on television, he turned himself in. An FBI agent from the Lisk investigative team questioned Quinn. Quinn was convicted and given a twenty-six-year sentence in Arkansas, but he was blameless of the crimes in Virginia.

By the end of the day on May 9, authorities had 1,600 leads to follow. *America's Most Wanted* aired a short piece on the girls at the end of their show the next night. An additional forty leads were added to the list as a result.

Investigators obtained a list of all known sexual offenders in the region—seventeen paroled sex offenders and thirty-four others on probation—and focused serious attention on those men. Surveillance teams followed some of those potential suspects for as much as a week and a half. Richard Marc Evonitz was not on that list. His 1987 offense in Florida preceded the law that would require him to report to local authorities.

His name did pop up on one list—one provided by the Chamber of Commerce detailing all the new business in the area. But there was no record of past sexual offense—no indication that there was anything suspicious about Evonitz at all.

Chapter 22

Eighteen-year-old Jason Talley made some unfortunate decisions in May of 1997. He was on probation at the time for shooting out windows with a friend. He was often in trouble at Spotsylvania High School.

On May 1, the day the Lisk girls disappeared, he skipped school. About a week after the bodies were found, at the encouragement of his father and his girlfriend, he chopped off his shoulder-length hair for the upcoming prom. He added his own personal touch to the transformation by shaving off his eyebrows. The FBI profile warned the public that the killer might change his appearance.

Jason knew the Lisk family well for years. Both families attended Goshen Baptist Church, and Jason and Kristin were in the same youth group. He liked heavy metal music and horror movies. His wardrobe was dominated by clothing in dark purple and black.

In the hypersensitive community of Spotsylvania, these things were enough to start the rumors rolling through town. It was said that Jason had been arrested, that a news conference about his guilt was imminent. Everywhere Jason went, whispers and stares clung to him like a long piece of toilet paper to the bottom of his shoe. The rumors were so widespread that his grandmother heard of his arrest at her home in Panama City, Florida, and called in a panic.

Soon the rumors were reported to the police as facts. He was accused of driving a white pick-up truck that was now painted red. Three teenagers told police that Jason Talley bragged about killing the girls. But Talley insisted he did not hang around with those who made that claim.

Investigators questioned Jason on six separate occasions— even once telling him he was a suspect. Then, Jason took a polygraph test and was eliminated from the list. In the press, Major Smith stated that Talley was interviewed just like many others, but denied that he was a suspect. Still, many of his fellow students believed his arrest was coming soon, and that it was only a matter of time before he was charged with the murders of Kristin and Kati Lisk.

Although he could understand the logic of the police looking at him, Jason could not fathom why so many who knew him could think he was capable of committing such a crime. He winced when girls at school detoured far around him in the hallway. He felt branded. The pall of the past few weeks hung like a shroud over his high school graduation.

WHILE INVESTIGATORS worked the daunting list of leads, the community sought comfort. The funeral for Kati and Kristin was a subdued affair. The Lisks asked for—and were granted—the privacy they needed to say goodbye to their girls. In a private ceremony on Saturday, May 10, they buried the sisters in the cemetery next to Goshen Baptist Church. They requested that in lieu of flowers and other tokens of sympathy, gifts be made to the Kristin and Kati Lisk Memorial Trust Fund, a scholarship program for public and private school students in the greater Fredericksburg area. More than $50,000 poured in from members of the community.

A fellowship service was conducted that afternoon at Spotswood Baptist Church. The public was invited and packed the pews with fear, sorrow and pain. Governor George Allen was in attendance. When he rose to speak, he did so, he said, as a governor, as a father and on behalf of all Virginians.

Scripture readings were scattered through the hour and forty-five minutes of public mourning. Among the readers were representatives of law enforcement: State Police Special Agent Bill Hicks; Bill Hagamaier, chief of the FBI's child abduction and serial killer unit; and Spotsylvania County Detective Twyla Demoranville.

After reading her passage from the Bible, a tearful Demoranville told the congregation, "As a mother, it angers me to know that despite how we care and protect our children, there are still evil monsters among us. Kristin and Kati never knew evil before in their pure and innocent lives."

Throughout the service, two white candles glowed in the front of the church nestled in a bank of yellow roses and flanked by photographs of Kati and Kristin dressed in pink. The Reverend Cliff Reynolds, pastor of Goshen Baptist Church, spoke the last words: "It is not that we forget Kristin and Kati—you have permission to go on. We realize that this great loss of ours is, for Kristin and Kati, a heavenly gate."

The young friends of Kati remembered her as a generous girl who always put others before herself. Kristin's friends recalled an outgoing, active girl who never had a bad word to say about anyone.

The congregation then rose to sing "Amazing Grace." To the melancholy strains of this melody, Reverend Reynolds leaned forward and blew out one candle, then the other.

Ron and Patti Lisk had planned to make a brief stop at the service and then slip out before the others. But when they saw the love and support that emanated from the 1,500 people gathered together to remember their daughters, they stayed long after the service to embrace and thank all those who attended.

MAY 11, 1997, was Mother's Day. For the first time in fourteen years, Patti Lisk did not have a child to mother, or a daughter to hug. It was the first of many broken holidays in Patti's future.

By THE week of May 12, investigators had followed up on five hundred of the leads, but no clear consensus on a suspect had emerged. Camera crews from *America's Most Wanted* descended on Spotsylvania during that week, filming locations and interviews for a lengthier piece scheduled to air that Saturday night.

FBI agents made a return trip to the Hanover County bridge with specialized equipment to record the details of a skid mark seen there, and to search for any additional forensic evidence. By May 13, the tip count had hit 2,600 and the Spotsylvania County Board of Supervisors voted to add $10,000 to the reward fund. The total had reached $150,000 and included two anonymous $25,000 contributions—one from a local donor, another from someone in Maryland. Like the parable of the alms in the Bible, one donation was considered very special. A man reached into his pocket and came up with a total of $2.10. At the sheriff's department, a plaque mounted with two one-dollar bills and a dime hung as a tribute to that man's selflessness and as a symbol of the caring hearts of Spotsylvania County.

When the show featuring the Lisk girls aired on May 16, it generated more than two thousand tips, bringing the total to 4,800. By June 3, that number soared to 5,479—all inputted into the newly enhanced computer system at the Spotsylvania County Sheriff's Department.

FREDERICKSBURG AREA clergy coordinated an interfaith community prayer service at Fredericksburg United Methodist Church on the evening of May 15. Members of many congregations in the area joined to pray for the Lisk family and for the safety and peace of all children.

On that same night, Lieutenant John Burruss met with many area residents at Zion Methodist Church to talk about the Neighborhood Watch program. It was the third night that week he had been out meeting with interested citizens. Since January, Burruss had set up the program in one hundred different neighborhoods and had been overwhelmed by calls from subdivisions across the county since the Lisk girls were abducted. The intense interest was sapping his budget. He found he could not always provide enough handouts to give a copy to everyone in the group.

Safe Neighbors, a non-profit organization based in Vienna, Virginia, encouraged citizens to install an Emergency Beacon Bulb at their front doors. Gerald Walkos, a resident of neighboring Stafford County, invented this special light bulb. It was equipped with software programmed to make the bulb flash non-stop whenever it was turned on and off two times in rapid succession. When done at the time a 9-1-1 call was made, it would guide emergency personnel to the scene.

The bulbs, selling for $5 each, received the endorsement of sheriffs' offices in Stafford and Spotsylvania Counties as well as the National Crime Prevention Council. Walkos donated hundreds of his bulbs at a special community meeting at Spotsylvania High School on May 17.

THE TRAGEDY fueled resentment of the native residents of the county toward more recent arrivals. They blamed the horror on the "come-heres." Roofer Michael J. Williams who lived in the area all of his life told *The Washington Post*, "Maniacs [are] around here, now. Since they came down here from the north and started building these fancy houses, they brought the criminals right along."

The facts showed, however, that the rise in crime had been slight. The population of Spotsylvania County had expanded by 27 percent since 1990, and the incidence of crime had not exceeded that figure by much. In 1990, there were 1.4 violent crimes for every thousand people. In 1995, it rose to 1.8, still below the state norm—Virginia's average was 2.3 violent crimes per one thousand residents.

. . .

BY THE week of May 19, calm crept on cat paws throughout the community. Kristin's locker at Spotsylvania High—adorned with impromptu gifts of yellow ribbons, beaded bracelets and miniature angels—served as a makeshift tribute to the life that was lost. But the overwhelming fear and sorrow that made time stand still slid into the background of everyday concerns. Parents who had insisted on driving their children to and from school now allowed them to ride the school bus once again.

At Spotsylvania Middle School, the younger children were slower to let go of their sense of horror. Nonetheless, a wary sense of normalcy seeped slowly down the halls.

Ron Lisk made a trip to Prince William County to the Potomac Mills Mall on May 20. There, he spoke at the dedication of a kiosk for missing children. As he was introduced, the crowd of reporters was warned that Ron was off limits—he would answer no questions after making his remarks. At the interactive computer display, visitors to the mall could view photographs and the vital statistics of children who had disappeared all across the country.

A silver plate attached to the kiosk read: "This kiosk is dedicated to the memory of Kristin and Kati Lisk and a renewed commitment to deliver our missing children home." At the ceremony, the Mills Corporation, owner of the mall, made a $1,000 donation to the Kristin and Kati Lisk Memorial Trust Fund.

WATER RECOVERED from the lungs of the Lisk girls during autopsy was sent to the Royal Canadian Mounted Police for analysis. They had pioneered new techniques that investigators hoped would help them in this case. Information gained from their work did not aid in the Lisk case, but provided detectives with good data that they could use in any future water-related homicides.

• • •

LIFE SPIRALED downward for Ron and Patti. Thoughts of suicide walked hand-in-hand with Patti down her lonely road of despair. She did not share the darkest depths of her depression with Ron. She did not know that Ron was taking the same journey.

IN LESS than a month, many preconceived notions would be turned upside down, churning up the suppressed emotions of a battered, weary community.

> *"Some offenders are obviously thrilled when someone else
> is charged with a crime they committed because it means
> they've outwitted authorities and can continue to prey on
> other victims. Some want or have a need to be credited with
> committing the crimes but are conflicted because they don't
> want to be identified as the offender. But it's difficult to know
> exactly how Evonitz reacted to the arrest of the wrong sub-
> ject in the Silva case."*
>
> Greg McCrary, former FBI profiler, on *FredTalk*

Chapter 23

Questions about Karl Michael Roush's guilt were popping
up in the minds of a lot of folks in Spotsylvania. At first, investigators and the prosecutor clung with tenacity to their
belief that they had the right man. The fiber evidence rein-
forced that conclusion. Inmates who talked with Roush in
jail were ready to testify for the prosecution. The Commonwealth's Attorney's Office was confident that they had a case
they could win.

Defense attorneys, however, were convinced of their
client's innocence. They hired two private investigators, Al
Baker and Roger D. Goldsberry. These two men logged over
250 hours, presenting a bill to Spotsylvania County for more
than $1,400. Then, using funds raised by the family, Wood-
bridge and Sasser hired Harold Deadman, a retired FBI
forensics expert to review the fiber evidence.

The mustard seed of certainty clutched by the task force
began to crack. The forensic lab reports in the Silva case
tied Roush to Sofia's murder with no room for doubt. But,
the similarities in the Silva and Lisk cases were too blatant

to ignore. All three girls were abducted from their own front yards in broad daylight. All were slender with dark hair. Each body was found clothed and in water. And, most telling of all, both Kristin and Sofia had shaved pubic areas. The review of the events and evidence in the death of the Lisk sisters convinced FBI profilers and lab analysts that Spotsylvania County quite possibly had a serial killer on their hands.

Still believing that Roush's suspicious behavior signaled his guilt as brightly as if a neon sign hung above his head, the investigators decided that they needed to put the rumors—and their growing doubts—to rest once and for all. There are no scientific tests to confirm circumstantial evidence, but there are for fiber and hair. Major Smith drove to the state lab in Richmond and retrieved this evidence. Then, he zipped up Interstate 95 to the experts at the FBI.

The FBI reported their findings on June 2. Their report delivered a blow that left Spotsylvania authorities reeling. None of the fibers matched. None of the conclusions by state forensic analyst Robin McLaughlin were accurate. "We had complete faith in the state crime lab—and still do," said Commonwealth's Attorney Neeley. "They comply with the highest scientific standards and are highly recognized throughout the nation. It was an isolated case where an analyst allowed her desire to connect the suspect to the crime to interfere with the scientific evidence."

Unaware of the activities of the prosecutor and investigation team, the defense sat on the sidelines with a Cheshire Cat grin. Deadman, their hired forensic evidence expert, had reached the same conclusions. The defense was lying in wait with their information, ready to deep-six the prosecution's case in front of a jury.

After reviewing the report from the FBI, Major Smith and Prosecutor Neeley gathered up the paperwork and traveled to Richmond. Experts there studied the FBI analysis and accepted its accuracy without an argument.

On June 9, the State lab in Richmond confirmed the FBI analysis and admitted their mistake to the public. Two days

later, Commonwealth's Attorney William Neeley filed a
motion to nolle prosequi. The document stated:

> 1. The charges against Karl Michael Roush were placed in large
> part due to the forensic evidence which was recovered by the po-
> lice and the medical examiner's office, and which evidence was
> analyzed by the Virginia Division of Forensic Science. A cer-
> tificate of analysis dated January 8, 1997 from the Virginia Di-
> vision of Forensic Science stated, in sum, that a four-way fiber
> match was found by the State's crime lab when it compared
> fibers recovered from Sofia Silva's blanket-wrapped body and
> those found by police in Karl Michael Roush's van. Based in
> large part upon what the Commonwealth believed to be that
> strong forensic evidence, the Commonwealth sought the abduc-
> tion with intent to defile against Roush on January 21, 1997;
> and 2. On June 9, 1997, the Commonwealth's Attorney learned
> for the first time that the Virginia Division of Forensic Science
> had made an error in analyzing the fibers in this case. The fibers
> were re-analyzed by the F.B.I.'s forensic lab and were deter-
> mined not to match. This error has been conceded by the Virginia
> Division of Forensic Science; and 3. While the prosecution still
> has some degree of incriminating evidence against Karl Michael
> Roush, it is the opinion of the Commonwealth's Attorney that he
> lacks sufficient evidence to go forward with this prosecution at
> this time.

This motion would still allow the prosecutors to resume the
case at a later date. "At this point, we still thought Roush
might be involved. We knew we did not have the evidence to
prosecute at this time. We wanted to stay open to the possibility of resuming prosecution if new information surfaced,"
Neeley said.

The defense was not happy. They wanted the case dismissed permanently. But they did not put up much of a fight.
Their relief with the current state of affairs was too strong.

Charges were dropped against Roush on June 16. All scientific and medical reports from the court file were sealed,
on a motion by Neeley. In this document, the prosecutor

officially acknowledged the search for a Lisk–Silva link: "[. . .] the police are investigating any potential similarities between these three abductions and murders [. . .]"

The Sofia Silva case was officially reopened, six months of hard work flushed into the sewer. Detective Ed Lunsford told the Fredericksburg *Free Lance–Star*, "I feel like my guts are coming out. It's like I've been ripped to pieces." He said that he had trusted the examiners, who assured him the fibers did match.

The newspaper erroneously reported that lead Silva investigator, Twyla Demoranville, cried, kicked chairs and banged file cabinets when she heard the news. A reporter who knew the detective on a personal basis had a conversation with her as they left the courtroom. The journalist obviously missed the sarcasm in Demoranville's figurative comments. She was frustrated over the time lost in the investigation, but when she was at work, her professional demeanor never slipped. However intense the emotions suppressed by the detective, they were nothing compared to the shock waves that rocked through the Silva home on Bounds Street.

It was bad news for Roush's landlord, Charles Hudson, too. His dreams of collecting the reward money vanished overnight.

Sheriff Ron Knight and Commonwealth's Attorney William Neeley called a joint press conference. The community at large greeted the news they delivered with shock and disbelief. In retrospect, Neeley said, "There were several months of work to prepare for this case. But it wasn't a waste of time. It was good practice for a capital case I faced down the road."

The finger of blame for this exercise pointed to Richmond, home of the state forensics department. And it demanded retribution. All its demands were met. Forensic examiner Robin McLaughlin was terminated. Her supervisor was demoted. The new head of the forensic lab, Eileen Davis, reviewed every one of the thousand or so cases McLaughlin handled. Her first priority were those analyses involving fiber evidence.

Director of the Virginia State Forensic Lab, Paul B. Ferrara, did not stop there. He ordered new equipment and instituted broad policy changes. Two microspectrophotometers were purchased—one for Richmond and the other for the lab in Roanoke—at a cost of $90,000 apiece. These devices use electronics to measure the color of a fiber, creating results with a higher level of objectivity. For the lab in Richmond, a $35,000 advanced comparison microscope was purchased. It was the latest in technical advancement. It not only allowed the evidence to be viewed side-by-side, but also gave examiners the option of using fluoroscopy to pinpoint the color of a fiber and, with its mounted camera, it provided them with sharp photographs of the evidence.

With a backlog of 3,000 or more cases, creating new policy that would make that list longer did not seem to make sense on the surface. But the error uncovered in the Silva case made it mandatory.

Random reviews were conducted on twenty percent of the cases before June of 1997. Now, one hundred percent of the cases faced an automatic second look. Previously, forensic reports were released to law enforcement to be amended before review. Now nothing can be released until there is a complete review. In the past, notes and reports were reviewed, but not the evidence itself. Now, any time there is a match, it must be inspected under a microscope by a second examiner.

Roush, though cleared on the Silva charges, was still in jail. He had to serve his sentence on the shoplifting charge until October.

IN THE midst of all the confusion about Karl Michael Roush, investigators continued on with their probe into the murders of the Lisk girls. Police followed up on a report out of Boonville, Missouri, about a man in a white pick-up who was stopped for a traffic violation. On the front seat of his truck was a copy of an early May issue of *The Free Lance–Star*.

In Louisa, Virginia, a man driving a white Ford Ranger tried to coax a 15-year-old into his pick-up. Spotsylvania

County authorities determined that he had purchased the vehicle after May 1. They dropped the lead and moved on.

Police obtained a search warrant for an abandoned house on Garrison Lane in the Lake Wilderness subdivision. The document to justify the search read: "The perpetrator involved in the abductions of children or other female victims will often have an abandoned barn, shed or house at his disposal to keep his victims from police detection." Officers left the premises with fiber samples and a chunk of stained carpet.

Eyebrows were raised when it was first revealed that the last person to occupy the house was the twin brother of a former officer of the Spotsylvania County Sheriff's Department. But he had not lived in the house for more than two years.

Tests of the fiber samples and the stains did not reveal any connection to the Lisk girls, nor was there any indication that Kati and Kristin had ever been there. Police would not give details on what led them to this home. They said that it was just one of the thousands of tips pursued by the task force.

> *"Just remember, whoever you are, someday you are going to pay. If it is in this life and you have a family, I will get to see them suffer almost as much as you have caused me to suffer, and my human side will enjoy every second of it."*
>
> Phyllis Silva

Chapter 24

For most of July 1997, investigators refused to comment on a link between the murder of Sofia Silva and the homicides of Kristin and Kati Lisk. Roush remained on their list of suspects in the Silva case. They would not waver while they waited for a definitive response from the federal forensic labs in D.C.

The public, however, suspected that a connection was there. The fires of their conviction were stoked by a tabloid news magazine show, *American Journal*. It aired on the morning of July 16 on a Richmond television station, then again early that evening on WDCB out of Washington. Retired FBI profilers Robert K. Ressler and Greg McCrary were on the show insisting that one man had committed all three murders. Their opinions carried a lot of weight on the street—Ressler pioneered criminal profiling during his stint at the FBI.

One week later, federal, state and local authorities publicly admitted that they were pursuing the possibility of one killer. The theory became the official conclusion on July 30 when the FBI lab delivered their report. Spotsylvania County residents then knew that DNA and fiber evidence tied all three victims together. There was a serial killer in their midst.

Greg McCrary opined about the perpetrator later that day

on *FredTalk*, a chat room on the Internet. He suggested that the perpetrator lived in the area, was gainfully employed and did not appear threatening. He was not a teenager, McCrary believed, but was in his twenties or older. McCrary added that, in all likelihood, the murderer used a ruse to start a conversation and then displayed a weapon to intimidate his chosen victim.

THE LISK–SILVA Taskforce took the investigation in every direction they could imagine. Aerial surveys were performed—possibly at the suggestion of aerial photographer Ron Lisk. Shots were taken of people's houses, cars and places of work in hopes of finding a pattern in the air that was invisible on the ground.

Tensions mounted as the end of August approached and the beginning of another school year rushed toward them. Sheriff Ron Knight asked the county's school bus drivers to be vigilant as they drove their routes. They were urged to look out for strangers and to carry a log book where they could enter any detail that did not appear normal, and write down the license plate number of any vehicle following the bus even if they thought it was a member of the official patrol. Those numbers could be eliminated later. Thoroughness was of paramount importance for the safety of the children.

The school district's transportation department urged their drivers to check for anything unusual at every bus stop before opening the doors and allowing the students to exit. They installed radios in every school bus, providing a direct link to emergency dispatch.

The bus drivers accepted their charge with gravity. Although the school was not responsible, in a technical sense, for children once they got off the bus, drivers would not leave the stop until the student reached the safe confines of home. Their radios crackled non-stop as they called in messages about vehicles parked on the side of the road, white pick-up trucks anywhere in the vicinity of a bus stop or anyone whose behavior was just a bit out of the ordinary.

School buses were a vulnerable target. "We run on a

schedule. If someone wants to follow us, they can be lurking anywhere, out of sight," said bus driver Pat Stanley.

Many neighborhoods designated safe houses where children could congregate until a parent returned home from work. As they approached Sofia's abduction anniversary date, parents dreaded that it would all begin anew.

On September 9, 1997, one week after the start of school, Spotsylvania was stretched as tight as a violin string. Out in King George County, where Sofia's body was found, a hidden camera focused on the spot where her body had lain. Chase vehicles lurked nearby. Deputies hid in the woods and in the red barn. At Sunset Memorial Gardens, officers maintained another vigil around Sofia's grave. All were on high alert in the hope that the killer would return to relive the moment in his mind.

MORE THAN 300 family members and friends, decked in purple ribbons, gathered at Fairview Baptist Church to remember Sofia. They were joined by media representatives from Washington, D.C., and from every corner of Virginia.

The Silvas—Humberto, Phyllis and Pam—sat in the front row, stoic in their pain. In the back row of the church another grieving couple—Ron and Patti Lisk—sat muted in their personal sorrow and in the gravity of the tragedy that forever linked them with the Silva family. Between the two families, an overflowing chalice of emotion passed unseen through the congregation like a sacred rite.

A young woman identified only as Sherri stood to speak, but was overcome with choking sobs. A man rose from the pews, took her prepared comments from her hand and read them to the awaiting crowd.

The first anniversary of Sofia's death left the community drained, and law enforcement frustrated.

JUST DAYS after the memorial, the investigators turned their spotlight on a 39-year-old roofer, Michael A. Jett. He was

being held at the Prince William County Adult Detention
Center on kidnapping and sexual battery charges. Later in
the year, he was convicted. He had snatched a 44-year-old
woman as she was walking on U.S. Route 1 on July 24, and
transported her to Stafford County, where she escaped. During her captivity, she learned his name, his daughter's name
and where he worked. Officers arrested him in record time.

No one would have seen a connection between that crime
and the murders of the three young girls in Spotsylvania except for the comments of another inmate, Joseph Norford.
He told authorities that Jett was fascinated by the Lisk case.
He also said that Jett admitted to enjoying sex with young
girls and had taken some of them to an abandoned house in
Ladysmith, where he shaved the intimate parts of their bodies.

Other inmates confirmed Jett's interest in sex with underage girls. They also reported that Jett had sleep-disrupting
nightmares about the two Lisk sisters.

These statements were all the Taskforce needed to obtain
a search warrant. Jett protested his innocence as authorities
drew his blood and obtained a hair sample. He claimed that
he and Norford had a fight three weeks before, and that these
allegations were the other inmate's revenge. Jett knew that
the DNA testing should exonerate him. But he also knew
about the Roush incident and feared the lab would make a
mistake again.

Officers also obtained a warrant to search his truck and
uncovered a supply of razors. Jett insisted there was a logical explanation. In order to save money to spend on his
daughter, he often lived in his truck.

Meanwhile, officials in Culpeper County were looking
for evidence to tie Jett to the murder of Alicia Showalter
Reynolds. They believed he matched the description of the
suspect given by passing motorists at the time of Alicia's
abduction.

Suspicion around Michael Jett began to fade when it was
confirmed that at 3 P.M. on May 1, he was working up on a
roof in Leesburg and could not have arrived at the Lisk

home in time. It was suspected that the jailhouse informant had fabricated the comments he'd attributed to Jett. Major Smith said that these false statements had built up the community's hope and that it would soon be disappointed. And he was right. The FBI lab test results on the DNA confirmed Jett's innocence of this crime.

An excited community slumped its shoulders at the news. On September 20, the dogged investigators took the case to the public again on *America's Most Wanted*. More than a hundred calls were generated by this broadcast.

A RIPPLE of outrage echoed through the area upon the release of the movie *Kiss the Girls*, based on a novel by James. Patterson. The story line hit too close to home: Seven young women are abducted from their homes throughout the South; the women are held captive and used to satisfy the dark and sadistic pleasures of a man who dubs himself "Casanova." One of the victims in the story was the niece of Patterson's protagonist detective, Alex Cross.

RC Theatres, a movie house chain based in Reisterstown, Maryland, cancelled the scheduled showings in central Virginia. Spotsylvania residents breathed a sigh of relief.

UP IN Quantico, Virginia, a few miles from the FBI Academy, the Child Abduction and Serial Killer Unit, CASKU, was at work providing support to the Lisk–Silva Taskforce. This specialized FBI unit, consisting of fourteen agents, had been created two years earlier by FBI Director Louis J. Freeh to help police across the country solve their most onerous cases.

They have assisted in the murder investigations of Jon-Benét Ramsey and Polly Klaas and aided in the hunt for Andrew Cunanan as he cut a bloody swath through the country. Spotsylvania County requested and CASKU provided an endless stream of advice, information and specialized expertise to aid them in their investigation.

. . .

FRIENDS AND family of Sofia, Kristin and Kati joined a group of Girl Scouts at the Spotsylvania Community Center, housed in the old Spotsylvania Middle School Building on Courthouse Road on November 17. Just outside of the Snow Library entrance at the center, a monument was dedicated in a tiny patch of garden.

Purple pansies and chrysanthemums surrounded a carved piece of green marble in the shape of a leaf, with a bright red ladybug poised on its surface. The design reflected all three girls' love of nature as well as Sofia's penchant for purple and Kristin's love of ladybugs. The stone was engraved with: "Forever Young, Forever in Our Hearts." The three names—Sofia Silva, Kristin Lisk and Kati Lisk—were listed below that. The names were followed by: "They were taken from us too soon."

A few feet from the memorial, a wooden garden bench sat beckoning visitors to sit, rest and contemplate the loss of three lovely lives. Scouts in the Commonwealth Girl Scout Council raised the funds for this tribute and would also be responsible for site maintenance.

TESS RAGIN, now Lorraine Deveaux, continued to visit Perry Deveaux in prison every weekend until the doubts about his innocence began nibbling at the edge of her consciousness. By 1997, her visits were more sporadic.

She had witnessed Deveaux in a rage in the visitors' room. She had seen the look on his face, and in that look she saw a man who was capable of brutal murder. During one visit, he struck her. No guards came to her rescue; no other visitors attempted to intervene. She was frightened and wanted nothing more than to get away.

At last the day came when Tess was convinced of his guilt. He spilled out a detailed confession of the rape and murder of Kathleen Sanderlin. He sanitized the events in the version of the killing he told to her. He claimed that Kathleen had dismounted from her horse and engaged in conversation instead of being jerked down and thrown to the ground. He said that, as he prepared to sexually assault her, Kathleen asked him for $20. Tess was certain that if the young woman did make that request, it was only in a futile attempt to shock Deveaux back to his senses. He also insisted that he had stabbed Kathleen only once—not the twenty-seven times reported in the newspaper. Tess was certain that some of what he told her was self-serving, but it was clear the underlying facts were the stark truth.

Tess attempted to get a divorce on her own. After three hearings, she gave up and hired an attorney. The divorce was final in 1998. Tess resumed the use of her maiden name.

IN JANUARY of 1998, William Showalter, the grandfather of Kati and Kristin, traveled from Earlysville to the State Capitol in Richmond. There he asked legislators to improve the DNA registry in the state.

Virginia is stringent in its collection of samples from criminals, but had not funded enough staff and equipment to process them in an efficient fashion. At this point, the state had collected 160,000 DNA samples from felons, but only 10,000 of those had been processed. On top of that, evidence relating to 700 different crime scenes was backlogged and awaiting analysis. Outgoing Governor George Allen submitted a $7.7 million proposal to add positions, equipment and contract services for outsourcing some of the work to get the state lab back on track. Later that year, the Virginia legislature approved the increased funding for the DNA registry.

At this same legislative session, the Spotsylvania County Sheriff's Department was encouraging state representatives to strengthen privacy protections for autopsy reports. They alleged that details about the autopsies of Sofia Silva and Kristin and Kati Lisk published by the media had hampered their investigations into the murders of the girls.

Many surviving family members of homicide victims backed Spotsylvania authorities in this quest. They claimed that Patricia Cornwell, an author of mystery books who had once worked in the Richmond medical examiner's office, had used actual autopsy records to create her stories. The use of these documents in a piece of fiction, they argued, added to their pain and suffering.

IN MARCH of 1998, the Spotsylvania School Board safety committee presented proposed changes to the community to improve the security of children in the aftermath of the abductions and murders. They recommended that day care be offered before and after school and that more extracurricular programs be offered for the children.

They urged the school board to focus on latch-key children, student assaults and at-risk students in building an effective program. One of their suggestions was "Phone Friends." High school students would be matched with younger latch-key kids. The older ones would assume the responsibility of calling after school to make certain the little guys were okay and to help them with their homework if needed. The committee also wanted to continue hosting "Escape School," an educational seminar that taught children how to escape if they were kidnapped. Over 900 students and parents had already participated in this program. The committee planned to survey parents and start pilot programs where there was the most interest.

At the committee's recommendation, all employees at the schools were issued identification badges and an additional safety officer was hired to work in the schools. At high schools, another assistant principal was hired to handle problems there.

They wrapped up their proposal with these suggestions: 1) train senior citizens to work in the schools; 2) ensure the Neighborhood Watches continue to check on kids boarding and disembarking school buses; 3) expand after-school tutorial programs; 4) have the Parks and Recreation Department offer more after-school activities and promote these to the parents; 5) have the Rappahannock Area Office reproduce and distribute its Youth Services Directory; 6) encourage summer school participation; and 7) perform security audits on all of the schools.

In Fredericksburg, the school district used to provide programs for care of children before and after school at Hugh Mercer Elementary. They dropped them a couple of years before when they were threatened with a lawsuit by a day care company that did not receive the contract. The school board looked at re-instituting these programs.

"No one ever told me that grief felt so like fear."
C. S. Lewis

Chapter 25

The beauty of the Virginia springtime could not warm the chills of dread that shot through Spotsylvania on May 1, 1998. The first anniversary of the abduction of Kati and Kristin hung as heavy as winter's icy mantle on the community on Block House Road. Only a revelation of the identity of their killer could have lifted the pall.

At Goshen Baptist Church, a video camera trained its eye on the girls' gravesite in the tiny churchyard cemetery. Officers from the Spotsylvania County Sheriff's Department hid in the woods and in the church waiting for a killer to pay a sick homage to his victims. Chase vehicles were tucked away out of sight of the wide-open intersection, ready to emerge when given the word.

Deputies hid in the disquieting woods down in Hanover County. There, too, the unblinking lens of a surveillance camera augmented their eyes. They stopped a lot of cars near the bridge that day, but most of them contained friends or schoolmates of one of the Lisk girls making a grim pilgrimage to the site. No one who was stopped at either location stirred any inkling of suspicion.

LATER THAT month, investigators were drawn again to Prince William County by Donald R. Dannemiller, a suspect in the attempted abduction of a 12-year-old girl. Dannemiller had already served six years in jail for murder. He was convicted of killing Taresa Dawn Perry, his 13-year-old stepsister, in 1976.

Now, the 39-year-old was being held on two counts of abduction, two counts of use of a firearm in commission of a felony and one count of possession of a firearm by a convicted felon. These charges were the result of an incident in Manassas.

Dannemiller pulled his blue van to a stop near a group of children at play. He got out of his vehicle and talked to the kids for a while. Then, he snatched a 12-year-old girl and forced her back to his van. He shoved her in and slammed the door shut. While he was going around to the driver's side, the girl jumped out and ran off. Dannemiller pulled a pellet gun and shot her in the side. A man who saw what occurred tried to stop him, but Dannemiller shot him in the head and sped away.

Later that evening, a woman in Warrenton called police to report that someone had shot at her with a pellet gun. She was relating her story to the officer who came to the scene when Dannemiller drove past her again. She pointed him out to the officer and the chase was on. Law enforcement finally nailed him in Fairfax County. In time, Dannemiller was ruled out as a suspect in the Spotsylvania cases. But he received a life sentence for the commission of the Manassas abduction.

IF SOFIA Silva had survived the fall of 1996, she would have graduated from Courtland High School in June 1998. The memory of Sofia still echoed in the halls of the school, and the Class of '98 did not want to graduate without her. She was awarded her diploma along with the rest of her classmates. Her sister, Pam, accepted it on her behalf.

ON THE second anniversary of Sofia's abduction in September, Spotsylvania County officers once again held vigil at her gravesite and at the edge of the woods in King George

County where her body was found. Disappointment became the natural state for investigators—still running down leads that vanished into thin air.

MAJOR HOWARD Smith and Detective Twyla Demoranville attended the Virginia Homicide Investigators Association annual banquet in Williamsburg that October. Demoranville made a case presentation about the Lisk and Silva murders. They hoped one of their peers would have information of a similar crime or a new idea that would move the investigation forward. It was at this event that Major Smith met Charles Pickett, executive director of the National Center for Missing and Exploited Children, an organization that would, down the road, play a pivotal role in the resolution of this case.

Smith also learned about Amber Alert from a visitor from north Texas. The program was created as a legacy to 9-year-old Amber Hagerman. In January 1996, she was riding her bicycle on a Saturday afternoon in Arlington, Texas. A neighbor, hearing a scream, looked outside and saw a man pull Amber off her bike, throw her into the front seat of his pick-up truck and drive away at high speed. Four days later, Amber's body was found in a drainage ditch four miles away, her throat cut. Her kidnapping and murder remain unsolved.

A suggestion that radio stations should repeat news bulletins about abducted children was presented to the Association of Radio Managers in the Dallas/Fort Worth area. They believed in the value of the idea and the Amber Alert program was born.

Smith was inspired to spearhead the effort to introduce the program in his community. On May 1, 2001, Spotsylvania County was the first law enforcement entity in Virginia to institute this missing children's program with the Silva/Lisk Plan. Four local radio stations, WFLS, WYSK, WBQB, WJYJ and the cable system's local public channel were prepared to interrupt the normal broadcasting schedule to air bulletins from the Spotsylvania County Sheriff's Department when a child was deemed to be in danger of serious bodily harm or death.

BY APRIL 1999, tips had slowed to an infinitesimal trickle. To elicit renewed interest and spur public response, Spotsylvania County Sheriff Ron Knight held a news conference. He revealed a piece of evidence that had been concealed for nearly two years. He held up a watch sporting Tweety Bird on its face. He told the media that it was a duplicate of the musical Looney Tunes watch that Kristin Lisk had been wearing when she was abducted. This watch had not been recovered with her body. Investigators suspected that it was now in the possession of the man who killed her.

Knight took advantage of this opportunity with the press to request that they remind the public of the characteristics ascribed to the perpetrator by the FBI. He asked them to call in and report anyone with an intense interest in the case who had changed his appearance or that of his vehicle and whose alcohol or drug habits had worsened.

He also informed them that a small or mid-sized red car and a white van had been seen on Block House Road around the time the Lisk girls disappeared. Investigators were looking for someone who would have owned or had the use of both of those types of vehicles at the time of the kidnapping.

Up to this point, the Taskforce had followed up on ten thousand leads in their attempt to solve these three murders. This press conference beefed up the number of calls coming in to the sheriff's department.

Doug Deedrick, a leading forensic fiber analyst for the FBI, loaded up his equipment and moved it all to Spotsylvania. He set up at the sheriff's office and spent more than a week visiting sites and analyzing evidence from the leads that were called in. On visits to possible scenes, on this and other cases, Deedrick often astonished investigators by knowing right away whether or not the clues pointed to their suspect.

He'd look around and announce, "This is not good for your guy, but take fibers anyway." Deedrick's pronouncements were never wrong.

PLACER COUNTY Court in Auburn, California, formally served Marc with divorce papers for his marriage to Bonnie on June 24, 1998. With Bonnie out of his life, and time on his hands, Evonitz reached out to his father to renew family ties. Joe worked for a company designing signs for businesses, and also still drove a cab. Marc presented him with an entre-preneurial partnership idea—a taxi company that contracted with large businesses. Marc convinced Joe that the demand was there and that he could find the clients.

Father and son soon were building a business together. Joe bought a computer from Marc, who set up the programs and kept the data up-to-date. Before long, Marc's skilled salesmanship racked up enough business that Joe was run-ning three cabs to keep up with the demand.

Evonitz learned the business well at Walter Grinders—enough to try his hand at design improvements for the com-pany's tools. In 1998, he developed his own design for a wheel dresser, a machine tool used at Walter Grinders. This piece of equipment formed the wheel that made the angle on the cutting edge used on other machinery. It was as neces-sary to the business as molds are to a ceramics company. Evonitz invested a lot of personal time in working the kinks out of his invention. He consulted with co-worker and friend Danny Minter about the best drive motor to use—he was un-satisfied with the results he got from the pneumatic air power on his initial prototype. Danny suggested trying hy-draulics oil instead of pneumatics and Marc incorporated that idea into his machine.

According to Minter, it was a "revolutionary design"—the high quality of the dresser exceeding that of the tool be-ing used in the business at that time. The dresser currently in operation had problems in securing the metal that went into the cutter, causing bits to get mangled in the process.

Evonitz's dresser eliminated the problem by lowering the error rate to near zero. "Using his machine would have saved Walter Grinders millions of dollars," Joe Evonitz said.

Walter Grinders, however, did not get as excited about his invention as Marc thought they should. He expressed his indignation by resigning to start KMK Associates with two partners, Kenneth Beck and his wife, Kim—the company name derived from the initials of the three partners. Before he walked out the door, he made copies of many customer files to take to his new firm.

When the new company started soliciting established customers of Walter Grinders, the bit hit the grinder. Evonitz's former employer threatened to sue on two grounds—for the use of the client lists and for ownership of Marc's invention, claiming it as their own, since it was created while he worked for them. Kenneth Beck was supposed to quit his job at Walter Grinders and come work full-time at KMK Associates. When the threats came, Beck panicked and pulled out of the fledgling business.

The threat of a lawsuit, coupled with poor money management, caused a downward spiral that not only destroyed the new company, but cost Evonitz his home. The mortgage lender foreclosed, and his home was auctioned off on the steps of the Spotsylvania County Courthouse in June. Evonitz rented a place down near Lake Anna in neighboring Louisa County for a few months where he struggled alone to reverse the fortunes of KMK Associates.

1999 looked like a very bad year for Richard Marc Evonitz. Along with his business, his marriage, too, was destined to failure. On January 5, after no reply from the respondent, the Superior Court of California entered a judgment of dissolution. The marital status of the parties was terminated and both were returned to the status of unmarried. A "true copy of the Entry of Judgment" was mailed to Evonitz.

In August, Tess, Kristen and Kristen's son, Mattie, came to Virginia to visit Marc. Marc took his family out to breakfast one morning at Aunt Sara's Pancake House at the corner of Route 1 and Massaponax Church Road.

The camaraderie between the diners and their server was instantaneous. Marc asked her out on a date. When she hesitated, Kristen encouraged her, telling her that Marc was a great guy. She still hesitated until she was reassured that he was at the restaurant with his mother, sister and nephew, and not a wife or child. To the table's delight, she then agreed.

The mutual attraction between the couple accelerated to romance in record time. Faith—her name has been changed to protect her privacy—filled the void left in Marc's life when Bonnie moved out of state. Marc smoothed away the rough edges of pain Faith felt from her unhappy childhood. Unaware of the secrets in Marc's past, Faith embraced the shiny prospect of a bright future.

Marc told Joe about how much he loved his new girlfriend. She came up with Marc to visit Joe and Ezghaharia on three different occasions—each one a very stilted event. Faith sat on a chair in their living room. After saying "Hello," she never said a word unless she was asked a direct question. She limited her responses to one word, with "Yes" or "No" being typical. "Strangest girl I ever met," Joe recalled.

Marc's mother, on the other hand, hit if off with Faith from the start. Tess thought she was a very sweet girl who was fun, cute, sometimes quite outspoken—a quality she admired—and, unlike Bonnie, down to earth and not at all egotistical.

Jennifer also took a liking to Faith, although she thought she was too young. "She seemed to have a profound outlook on life and people in general," she said. "She was very intelligent and analyzes things on a deeper level than most people."

Marc and Faith's relationship was going strong by the time Thanksgiving rolled around in 1999. The couple traveled down to Columbia to spend the holiday with Marc's family. Faith told them that she did not like living in Virginia—she hated her new job at a bookcrafters, and Marc's business failure left a bitter taste in her mouth about northern Virginia. In her mind, none of the blame lay with Marc.

Kristen jumped on these revelations and urged the couple

to move to South Carolina. She even offered her home as a temporary residence until they got settled.

On the drive back to Virginia, Marc and Faith talked about nothing else. By the time they returned, their minds were made up. In two weeks, they moved into Kristen's home in Columbia. Marc never warned Joe he was leaving—Joe was left holding the bag on a business he did not want to operate on his own. A few days before Christmas, Marc and Faith were married in a ceremony at Kristen and Jeff's home.

IN PHYSICAL size, South Carolina ranks fortieth in the nation, but in cockiness and determination, history has insured it a spot at the top of the list. It was the first state to secede from the Union in 1860. The Secessionist Convention was held in Columbia in the First Baptist Church, a contemporary city landmark. South Carolina was the state that instigated the onset of the Civil War by firing on Fort Sumter in Charleston Harbor. Columbia, as the state capital, paid dearly for these rebellious actions. It was burned to the ground when General Sherman marched through the South at the end of the war.

In geographic terms, there are three areas in the state, the High Country, the Midlands and the Low Country. Columbia is the heart of the Midlands. The state capital, with a population of more than 116,000, is the largest city in the state—its population about 30 percent black and more than 40 percent Baptist. It was one of the first planned cities in the country. The original streets were more than 100 feet across—built extra wide because of the belief at the time that mosquitoes could not fly without sustenance for more than sixty feet. Thus, by crossing these streets, the pests would die of starvation.

Columbia is home to the fighting Gamecocks of the University of South Carolina, and major international companies, as well as the birthplace of contemporary music sensation Hootie and the Blowfish.

Like Spotsylvania County, Columbia is surrounded and split by rivers. It is just east of the Congaree and just below the junction of the Broad and Saluda Rivers.

The Congaree River leads to the Congaree Swamp National Monument, at 22,200 acres, the largest intact tract of old-growth bottomland hardwood forest in the United States. Swamp forests like this one once stretched from the Chesapeake Bay to East Texas. Congaree is one of the few to survive the onslaught of logging and dam construction.

The stretch of Saluda River extending from the Saluda Dam at Lake Murray down to Columbia is a designated Scenic State River. It flows past the Riverbanks Zoo and Botanical Gardens, named one of the top ten zoological parks in the nation.

The Broad River, the least accessible of the rivers flowing through Columbia, is still popular with residents. Favorite fishing holes are visited regularly and rowers with boats ply their oars across its placid surface.

Downtown Columbia is home to the State Capitol Building and thus is crowded with the government offices and commercial headquarters that are drawn to a state's seat of power. The highlight of a trip downtown is the Federal Land Bank Building. On its side, a local artist, Blue Sky, painted a portrayal of a highway disappearing through a tunnel. Its realism is sufficient to fool more than just Wile E. Coyote.

In this thriving center of government, commerce and gracious Southern hospitality, Faith and Marc made their new home.

THAT JANUARY, Evonitz obtained a position as the Director of Audit Services at Armstrong Compressed Air Services, eighty miles from Columbia in the town of Spartanburg at 110 Corporate Drive. This international company provided solutions for steam, air, water and humidification systems. In his capacity with this company, Evonitz traveled around the country to factories evaluating the efficiency and safety of their compressed air systems.

In April, the couple moved into the Crossroads Apartments complex at 716 Zimalcrest Drive in the St. Andrew's area of Columbia. With 622 units sitting on 45 acres, it was the largest complex in the state. Neighbors viewed Marc as quiet and friendly. He and Faith appeared inseparable. In the rental office, he was known as a professional man who always paid his rent well in advance.

"A new company took over ownership in these apartments in September of 2000," Community Director Yvonne Shelby said. "Before we rent to anyone we run a criminal background check on all potential residents who are eighteen or over. If Evonitz had tried to move in then, we would have seen the sex charge in 1987 in Florida and would not have approved his rental."

When they settled in, Marc had two birds that he had owned since his marriage to Bonnie—a yellow cockatiel and a grey-cheeked parakeet. Faith wanted a bird of her own and bought a gray cockatiel. When Kristen purchased a green-cheeked conure from a pet store, the bird's brother was left in the shop alone. At Tess' urging, Faith added the speckled-headed, wide-bodied bird with a ruby tail to the growing menagerie.

Faith worked at PetSmart and the couple's wild kingdom grew with her frequent acquisitions. She brought home a peach-cheeked conure, two hamsters from the same litter and an assortment of fish and hermit crabs. Kristen had grown tired of caring for Mattie's guinea pig and that creature, too, became a part of the Zimalcrest Zoo.

The growth of the animal population was accompanied by an equally increased development of ties with Marc's family. The couple would often invite Tess to go out with them for dinner and a movie. "I love that girl," Tess said. She thought Marc and Faith had "a great relationship" and that Marc's future looked bright.

ALONG WITH Joseph J. Augustine, an auditor at Armstrong, Evonitz co-authored a magazine article about the importance of cleanliness in pneumatic systems in the food processing industry, titled "Compressed Air: It's What's for Dinner." They were published in *Hydraulics & Pneumatics*, an industry trade journal, in December 2001.

It was a technical piece illustrated with photographs and precise diagrams. At the end, the writers add a subtle sales pitch for their services:

> *If a company's staff feels that it cannot evaluate its compressed air system effectively, then it should consider hiring a skilled, professional compressed air consulting company to perform the evaluation. In addition to improving the compressed air quality and helping to bring the plant into FDA compliance, a skilled consultant may also identify energy savings opportunities, offer system performance improvements, improve process equipment up-time, and reduce process equipment maintenance costs.*
>
> *Most importantly, evaluating the air system can increase awareness of its existence, which overcomes the out-of-sight, out-of-mind attitudes. After all, it's what's for dinner.*

And Evonitz proved to be an expert on out-of-sight, out-of-mind when he lived in Virginia.

> "Common sense is the most important factor in avoiding be-
> coming a victim of a violent offender. It is important to un-
> derstand that a violent sex offender and, in particular, a
> serial killer, views another human being as a mere object for
> his entertainment. These people are sexual psychopaths who
> are great manipulators and born con artists. They will do
> and say anything to get their victim into a position of vul-
> nerability. Young people, male and female alike, must avoid
> trusting people who seem to be offering them something too
> good to be true. This goes for live contacts as well as con-
> tacts on the Internet. You can never trust a person you have
> just met and accompany them to a location you do not know.
> Use your heads and stay alive."
>
> Robert K. Ressler, former FBI profiler, on *FredTalk*.

Chapter 26

Melvin Hogan, a carpet cleaner and father of six, made a
mistake in May 1997, and further complicated it with his
misbehavior in October 1999. At the time the Lisk girls disappeared, Hogan was working just a half mile from their
home and driving a white van.

He was one of fifty men asked to voluntarily provide a
DNA sample in the aftermath of the girls' deaths. He was
one of only ten who refused to comply. If an officer saw any
one of those men go to a restaurant, he would lie in wait for
the uncooperative man to leave. Then, he'd slip in and grab a
straw or a fork used by the person of interest. Police also dug
through the trash of these men, seeking any usable speci-
mens for analysis. They reserved the possibility of getting a
warrant to obtain DNA as a last resort—as much to protect

the privacy of the person involved as to protect the integrity of the investigation itself. Spotsylvania authorities did not have sufficient cause to obtain a warrant against Melvin Hogan, but he missed the opportunity to eliminate himself as a possible perpetrator of the Lisk and Silva abductions.

Then on October 1, 1999, Chrissy Tenheve, a 15-year-old Spotsylvania girl, answered the door of her home on Hickory Ridge Road. Melvin Hogan stood outside her door. He wanted directions to a home where he was supposed to work.

He returned a while later and this time made Chrissy quite uneasy. According to her, Hogan asked if she was alone, and wanted to come inside and use her telephone. He sprinkled in compliments about her good looks while he questioned her about her sexual experience. She was offended by his invasion of her privacy, but she was also very scared. She wanted to end the conversation, but Hogan persisted. Finally, her telephone rang, giving her the excuse she needed to slam the door.

Chrissy then called her father, who rushed home. He parked his car across the end of the driveway where Hogan's van was parked and called the police.

When the police first approached Hogan, they claimed he gave them a false name. He was hauled in for questioning. This time they did have cause to get a search warrant and Hogan was forced to provide a DNA sample. Hogan railed against the authorities for harassing him and endangering his job. When the test results came back negative, investigators insisted that Hogan had backed himself into a corner when he refused to cooperate two years earlier. No criminal charges were filed for his behavior.

MEMBERS OF the Taskforce grasped at another straw—one offered by Scotland Yard. The Investigative Psychology Department at the University of Liverpool had developed "Dragnet," a new program for creating geographic profiles for serial killers, rapists and other felons. It had proven highly effective in the field.

The concept is based on the premise that the locations of crimes are not random no matter how chaotic they may appear. When entering data for analysis, profilers must consider distance, mobility, local demographics and mental maps. A mental map is the cognitive image a perpetrator develops through his experiences, his travel habits, and the places where he works, lives and socializes.

Constructing a profile of the offender's most likely area of residence requires a working knowledge of the case file, crime scene examinations, a study of area maps, a demographic analysis of the abduction sites as well as the body disposal locations, and, finally, a computer analysis of all this data.

A good geographic profile can provide information needed to narrow the area for door-to-door canvassing and police surveillance and help prioritize DNA screening, tips and suspect interrogations. It can be a valuable tool when used in conjunction with a complete investigative package.

Although geographic profiling is based on objective details, it still requires subjective interpretation. To maximize the effectiveness of the interpreter's work, FBI Special Agent John Kuhn of the Lisk–Silva Taskforce traveled to London to provide first-hand accounts. The result of these efforts did not lead to the Lisk–Silva perpetrator. But when they finally identified the murderer, the profile demonstrated an accuracy that was astonishing. As the profiler suggested, Evonitz did, in fact, live in the high probability area within an eight-mile radius of both homes of the victims.

"Nothing inflames law enforcement like the death of a child. It rips right through your fiber. You identify with the families because you have children of your own."

Edward J. Tully, retired FBI agent,
in *The Virginian-Pilot*

Chapter 27

June 1, 2000, the news screamed across the community: It happened again. An 11-year-old girl reported being kidnapped from her school bus stop. Although the girl was alive, a sonic boom of stark terror slapped Spotsylvania once more.

The girl told deputies that a man forced her into his black pick-up truck with Florida license plates. After her escape, she said she hid in the woods for a few hours before walking more than two miles back to her home.

She worked with police to create a composite of a white man in his early forties. His hair was brown, flecked with gray. He had a prominent scar on his right cheek and his moustache curled up on the ends.

This news stirred interest far past Virginia. Down in Florida, Detective Mike Nelson of the Hernando County Sheriff's Office heard about the Florida tags and perked up at the news. He had been investigating a series of abductions, including the kidnapping of 12-year-old Jennifer Odom. She was snatched after disembarking from her school bus in February 1993. Six days later, Jennifer's body was found in a grove of orange trees.

On July 15, Detective Nelson turned his eyes away and Sheriff Ron Knight asked that all composite posters be destroyed. The little girl had lied.

Investigators hunting the perpetrator stumbled over a number of inconsistencies in the girl's story. Then, a man told police that he had been at that bus stop watching his child wait for the bus. The other little girl was never there that morning. Because of the girl's age, no criminal charges were filed against her.

For the moment, Spotsylvania returned to an uneasy peace.

In April 2001, John Tyler Community College on the outskirts of Richmond conducted an anti-violence conference. The focal point of the event was the marketing of murder through television shows, music and video games. The conference was dedicated to the memory of Kati and Kristin Lisk. Patti Lisk attended and spoke with reserved optimism that one day the killer of her daughters would be identified.

An FBI computer, linked to the DNA databases in forty-six states, had compared genetic evidence from crime scenes to known felons since 1998. Six hundred cold cases are now closed because of the help of this technology.

By the time the fourth anniversary of the disappearance of Kati and Kristin Lisk rolled around in May of 2001, the FBI had compared the evidence to the DNA profiles of 400,000 felons in all of those states. They did not get a single hit.

The FBI had also compared DNA and other forensic evidence from the Spotsylvania County slayings to evidence found at more than 20,000 crime scenes from coast to coast. And they had examined another ten thousand samples of hair, fiber and fingerprints.

The multi-county and FBI Taskforce still met weekly to report on any new findings and to brainstorm next steps. Eleven thousand leads were entered into the computer databases at the Spotsylvania County Sheriff's Department, but the end was not in sight.

• • •

ON THE first day of the 2001 school year—just days before
the fifth anniversary of Sofia Silva's disappearance—a 12-
year-old Spotsylvania County girl got the scare of her
young life. She got off her school bus and sat down on the
front porch of her home. A man with straight black hair and
olive skin pulled up in front of her house in a boxy light
brown car.

He asked her if she would like to get into his car. When she
said no, he drove away. Police asked that anyone seeing a man
meeting this description should call them immediately. The
Spotsylvania County Sheriff's Department wanted to know
who he was and what he'd been doing there. No stone was
ever left unturned.

As THE fifth anniversary of Sofia's death rolled around, life
in the Silva home was still mired in the past. Her bedroom
walls still were covered with photos of her friends. Her bed
still sat in the same spot, ready for Sofia to slide between the
sheets. All of the mementoes of Sofia's life still remained
where she'd left them. A few new things had been added to
the room—a portrait of the teenager painted by a sympathetic stranger hung above her bed, a handmade quilt sewn in
Sofia's memory stretched across its foot, angels of all shapes
and sizes filled empty spaces.

The Silvas often replayed videos of Sofia to recapture the
moments of a vibrant young girl's life. The family became
avid viewers of true crime documentaries on TV. As they
watched cases being solved on the thinnest thread of evidence, they yearned for the day that a small trace of forensic
proof would rise up and doom Sofia's killer to an unforgiving abyss of justice.

FOR THE third time, the focus of the detectives was drawn to
Prince William County. Forty-eight-year-old Franklin Todd

Ritenour pulled his white pick-up truck up to three girls, ages 10 to 14, at about 5 P.M. on January 5, 2002, in Manassas. He asked them to look at his map and help him with directions. The girls approached, but noticed that his "map" was blank. They backed away and told him they would have to get their parents to help him. As he drove off, one girl memorized his license plate number and called police.

At 7 P.M., on Streamwalk Lane, a 9-year-old girl was playing soccer with her two younger sisters. Ritenour snatched the girl, forced her into his truck and raced off. The sisters gave police a description of the pick-up and the connection was made.

When officers spotted and tried to stop Ritenour's vehicle on Ashton Avenue, he slowed down and shoved the girl out of his truck. He killed his lights and zoomed off in the darkness. Police maintained pursuit and saw him abandon his truck and run into the woods. Helicopters and search dogs were brought in to hunt down the fugitive. Ritenour used his cell phone to call his daughter and ask her to come pick him up.

She did not know why her father was on the run, but she came to his rescue. When her car was spotted in the area, the tags were quickly traced to Ritenour's home address. She was stopped, and First Sergeant Wheeler convinced her to cooperate. Wheeler put the young woman's overcoat on over her uniform and slid behind the wheel of her car.

When Ritenour saw the car, he came running, waving his arms to get the driver's attention. Instead of escaping with his daughter's help, he was under arrest. He was charged with abduction, intent to defile and attempted rape.

Now Spotsylvania investigators were tracing his whereabouts since 1996, pursuing his connection to the Lake Anna area, where the Lisk girls were found, and awaiting the results from the testing of his DNA at the state lab.

He was exonerated on the Spotsylvania murders, but convicted on two counts of abduction and one count of sexual penetration in Manassas. On the first kidnapping charge, he was sentenced to ten years in the penitentiary with five years suspended and seven years' probation. On the second charge, he was given thirty years with fifteen years suspended and seven years of probation. On the third charge, he received twenty-five years with twelve suspended and five years' probation.

ON JANUARY 9, 2002, at 8 A.M., 12-year-old Ashley Pond said "I love you" to her mother and left her Newell Creek Village apartment in Oregon City, Oregon, to go to her school bus stop. She never made it there. She simply disappeared.

Initially, police suspected she had run away, and the case was treated as a missing persons investigation. But she left without taking any spare clothing and she never called any of her friends. By the end of the month, authorities considered her to be missing under suspicious circumstances and quite probably in serious danger.

Miranda Gaddis, a 13-year-old friend and classmate of Ashley, was very concerned. She discussed the disappearance often, searching for answers. In March, her dance team was preparing for a benefit performance. They would donate the proceeds to Ashley's reward fund. At 7:30 A.M. on March 8, in the same apartment complex, Miranda's mother said goodbye to her as her daughter stood in the kitchen in a gray terry robe with a towel draped around her freshly shampooed hair. Her mother never saw her again.

The story reverberated in faraway Spotsylvania County. Because of the similarities in the geographically disparate crimes, an FBI investigator from the Lisk–Silva Taskforce flew across the country to look for connections between the murders in Virginia and the disappearances on the West Coast. He came back empty-handed, hoping that more would be known when the two Oregon girls were found.

The remains of Miranda Gaddis were found in a backyard shed on August 24. The next day, Ashley Pond's body was found on the same property under a concrete slab. Ward Weaver was charged with aggravated murder, abduction, rape, sexual abuse and abuse of a corpse. At the time of this writing, Ward Weaver has not had his day in court. There was no connection to the deaths of Sofia, Kristin and Kati.

IN THE spring of 2002, Darrell David Rice, a 34-year-old computer programmer, was serving a 136-month sentence in the Petersburg Federal Correctional Institute south of Richmond, Virginia. He was behind bars for a July 9, 1997, incident in the Shenandoah National Park.

Yvonne Malbasha, a single mother from Canada, was bicycling in the mountainous wilderness area with a friend. She was an athletic woman who had competed in a number of demanding triathlons. She was clearly up to the challenge of biking the length of Skyline Drive. When the trail she and her friend were following forked, the two went in separate directions.

Yvonne was riding alone when Rice passed her in his blue pick-up truck. She didn't give him a second thought. Then, he came back past her again—this time without any license plates on his vehicle. She had a moment to register the rage on his face and then she was being pushed off the road. He jerked his truck to a stop and came at her.

He screamed that he was going to get her and threw a soda can in her direction. He grabbed at her chest and demanded that she expose her breasts. He tried to manhandle her into his truck, but he had more than met his match in this well-conditioned woman. She threw her heavy water bottle at his head and managed to get her bike in between them. He grabbed her bike, tossed it aside and jumped back into his truck.

For a split second, Yvonne thought it was over, then Rice aimed his truck and gunned it in her direction. She grabbed her bicycle and jumped behind a fallen log. He backed up and tried to get to her four times until another vehicle approached.

Hearing Yvonne scream, the driver—a park ranger—

asked her if she was okay. When she said she was not, he got a description of the truck and its occupant and broadcast it over his mobile radio.

Meanwhile, Rice put the Maryland tags back on his truck and changed into another set of clothes. But there's no place in the middle of a national park to get a quick paint job, so his blue pick-up was soon spotted and Rice was under arrest.

When his truck was searched, authorities found the type of cable ties that police use for disposable plastic handcuffs, along with a length of nylon rope, maps of Culpeper and central Virginia and a tarp big enough to be used to conceal a body. After finding these suspicious items in his truck, park rangers discovered that this was not the first time they had encountered Rice. In May 1996, when they were searching for two missing hikers, Rice was in the park. They had interviewed him and noted that his knuckles were scraped. Rice was now a suspect in the murders of 24-year-old Julianne Marie Williams and 26-year-old Laura "Lollie" S. Winans.

Rice pled guilty to the attempted abduction of Yvonne Malbasha. He served his time while investigators pursued his connections to the slaying of lesbian lovers Julianne and Lollie the year before.

The couple, along with Taj, Lollie's golden retriever–Lab mix, arrived at Shenandoah National Park on Sunday, May 19, 1996. They'd planned to hike and camp in the park through Memorial Day, May 27.

When they had not returned on May 30, Julianne's roommate was worried. She called Julianne's parents in Minnesota, who in turn contacted the park rangers.

On June 1, 1996, Taj was found wandering around Skyland Lodge. Soon, the rangers discovered the campsite of the women about half a mile away. They were both bound and gagged. Both of their throats were slit.

On April 9, 2002, a federal grand jury handed down an indictment on Darrell David Rice, charging him with two counts of capital murder and two counts of committing a hate crime, stating that he "intentionally selected" Julianne and Lollie because of their "actual or perceived gender or sexual orientation."

Attorney General John Ashcroft read a prepared statement the next day. In it, he said that the hate crime charges were based on statements made by Rice. Ashcroft said, "Rice had stated on several occasions that he enjoys assaulting women because they are, in his words, quote, 'more vulnerable' close quote, than men. The government's notice sets forth numerous incidents in which Rice acted in a hostile and violent manner toward women solely because they were women. In addition, the government's notice describes evidence of Rice's hatred for homosexuals, including his statement that Julianne Williams and Laura Winans deserved to die because he believed they were homosexual."

As soon as these indictments had been made public, two sets of investigators drew a bead on Darrell David Rice. In Prince William and Culpeper Counties, investigators saw a remarkable resemblance to the composite sketch of the suspect they had in the twenty-nine stalker cases that included the murder of Alicia Showalter Reynolds. The dark pick-up truck enticed them even more.

In Spotsylvania County, they saw a potential trail of murder, including their three unsolved cases—a trail of murder that abruptly ceased when Rice went to prison. Major Howard Smith immediately contacted the FBI lab and asked them to run a comparison on Rice's DNA to the profiles extracted from the hairs found with Sofia, Kati and Kristin. It would be more than a year before other suspicions about Darrell David Rice were questioned in the light of new evidence.

Two weeks later, they had their answer. There was no match—Darrell David Rice was just one more step on the ladder of 12,000 fruitless leads. "Being in this investigation was like being in an amusement park," Major Smith said. "It was one non-stop roller coaster ride."

DETECTIVE JOE Chagnina of the Spotsylvania Sheriff's Department and Special Agent David Riley of the Virginia State

Police were assigned as cold case investigators. They would start from the beginning, probing the files and looking once again at all of the thousands of leads.

THE NATIONAL Bloodhound Training Institute, founded in Fredericksburg in 1999, announced the first Sofia Silva Award on June 17, 2002. This non-profit organization is dedicated to assisting bloodhound teams and other qualified K-9s throughout the nation.

The Sofia Silva Award was created to bring honor to the Silva family and to Sofia's memory. It is given in recognition of individuals who have performed with a determined sense of duty and responsibility by assisting in saving the life of a lost or missing person.

Phyllis and Humberto Silva presented the first award to Detective Mark Holmes of Port Arthur, Texas. On April 13, the detective was dispatched on a call for a despondent woman. Authorities found three suicide notes at her home. The trail was nineteen and a half hours old when Holmes and his dog, Bo, set out to find her. In four and a half hours, they covered more than seven miles. They were certain the woman was near. Holmes called in the ground search team. One hundred yards from the spot where Holmes and Bo stopped, the team found the woman, overdosed on drugs and suffering from heat exposure and insect bites. She had fallen into a coma, but after extensive medical care, she recovered.

Just ten days after the presentation of this award, the Silvas would welcome the news of another manhunt with a dramatically different outcome.

"We're going to keep knocking on your doors, we're going to keep stopping your cars, we'll keep walking through the river, crawling through the mud. We'll do whatever it takes to bring justice."

Supervisor Bill Hagamaier, FBI

Chapter 28

Mattie Weyand, Kristen's 7-year-old son, was exploding with excitement on Sunday, June 23, 2002. He was flying to Orlando with his grandmother Tess and his aunt Faith, to explore Disney World. They planned to return on Thursday. Evonitz was left home alone and, as far as the women knew, he would be going to work. Instead, he had vacation plans of his own.

Evonitz was feeling stressed out that June. He was upset that his sister Kristen was considering leaving her husband and child to live with a man whom the whole family distrusted. He was also worried about Faith. Her multiple sclerosis made him extra-protective even in normal times. But in recent days, Faith had had sudden attacks of dizziness that caused her to pass out. And, as the past has shown, Evonitz did not cope well with life's anxieties. His outlet for stress relief often involved the creation of a new victim. This time was no exception.

MONDAY AFTERNOON, Evonitz took a large, beige Rubbermaid container out into the parking lot of his apartment complex. Soon he realized that cramming it into his Ford Taurus or his Escort was not a good idea—particularly not when he had another option right at hand. His plans would best be served using his mother's 1998 green Pontiac Firebird.

He stowed the container neatly in the back seat of her car and hit the road. He drove out of Columbia in Richland County and over to West Columbia in Lexington County. He turned onto Old Barnwell Road and into the Dove Trace sub-division.

TEENAGERS KARA and Heather were the best of friends. Kara spent the night at Heather's house. The next morning, Heather's mother, Cindy, paused in the living room on her way out to the car. Kara was asleep on the love seat and her younger daughter, Jessica, was on the sofa. She looked down on them for a while, savoring the look of innocence and sweetness that bathed their faces in repose. Then she left for work without a moment's concern for the day that lay ahead.

Kara and Heather slept late and awoke excited about their plans to spend the afternoon together at the lake. Before they could go, Heather had to fulfill her mother's demand that she water the flowers, and she had to take a shower. Kara took over the watering to speed up their departure. Heather went into the house to get ready to go.

Kara was lost in thought as she performed the mundane chore. She noticed a green Pontiac Firebird drive past and it appeared to be leaving the neighborhood. She was pulled out of her reverie when the same car returned and pulled into Heather's driveway. Kara thought it was one of Heather's mother's friends coming to visit.

Evonitz sat in the car for a minute, then hopped out with samples and a binder in his hand. "Is there someone here I could give pamphlets to?"

Kara said, "It's not my house. It's my friend's house and she's inside. She's taking a shower."

"Are her parents here?"

"No."

He started flipping through the papers and said, "Okay. I'm just going to give you these samples."

He held them toward her and Kara leafed through his binder filled with magazine samples. She paused when one caught her attention. They exchanged smiles and meaningless comments as she perused his selection of wares. Unbeknownst to Kara, beneath the binder, Evonitz held a .25-caliber semi-automatic handgun, and it was pointed at her midsection.

Without a telltale sign of evil intent, he stepped around to her right side, threw his arm around her shoulders and whipped his pistol up to her throat. He made it clear: He wanted her in the car. Now.

"Why don't you just come with me?" he said, giving her a nudge.

"Stop," Kara responded.

"No. You just need to come with me." He trundled her over to the driver's side of the car, opened the door and pushed up the front seat. "Get in."

Kara saw the large Rubbermaid container filling up the back seat. "Where am I supposed to go?"

He pulled the lid off the container and said, "Get in."

Kara bundled up her fear and stuffed it inside her full satchel of common sense. With forced calm, she clambered into the container in the back seat as she was instructed. He closed the lid on top of her.

The car pulled away from Heather's home. Although she knew what his intentions were from the start, *This isn't really happening* repeated in her head. She asked more than once where they were going and what he wanted. She got no response.

Then she asked, "Is there any way you can just contact my mom and let her know I'm okay? I know everybody's so worried about me."

"I guess they'll have to worry for a couple of days," he replied.

The car came to a stop about ten minutes later in a more deserted area filled with the ubiquitous loblolly pines surrounding a sandy, unpaved road. Evonitz lifted off the lid. From her confinement, Kara could see nothing but the sky and treetops out the back window. Evonitz snapped a pair of furry handcuffs around her wrists. He grabbed a wad of paper towels and rammed them into her mouth. Her jaw was further stretched when he forced a rubber ball into her mouth to hold the towels in place. He tied a length of fabric around her neck, then fastened the loose end to her handcuffs. He pushed the lid tight on top of the container, forcing her into a more constricted ball inside her plastic prison. Inside, where he could not see, Kara allowed her fear to scratch lines across her face, and tears of anxiety to roll from her eyes.

As they drove off again, she concentrated on visualizing where they traveled. She remembered crossing railroad tracks whose bumps jostled her, sending pain shooting up her spine. She thought they entered a highway when she heard the sound of sudden acceleration. The hum of the tires changed and it sounded as if they crossed a concrete bridge. She had no idea where she was, but maybe it would make sense later. There were other things to think about now—the car was coming to a stop.

HEATHER EMERGED from the shower and dressed for the trip to the lake. When she was all ready to go, she stopped outside to call Kara, but her friend was not there. She walked out to where the hose was lying on the ground. It was still running. She went through the house, room by room, calling her friend's name. She got no response. Kara was nowhere to be found.

She went next door to her neighbor, Gordon Shaw. He told her that Kara had gotten into a car with a man who looked like her father. Heather knew Kara's father was out of town.

She picked up the phone and called her mother, Cindy. When she told her she could not find Kara, Cindy said, "I'm sure she's around the house."

"No, you don't understand. She's not here," she said and reported what the neighbor had said.

"Maybe she's gone for a ride down the street," Cindy suggested.

But Heather was insistent and her worry was infectious.

"Lock the door. Don't let anybody in," Cindy ordered.

Cindy hung up and called Kara's mother, Debra. She relayed her neighbor's description of the man and the car. When neither were at all familiar to Debra, Cindy said, "I think Kara's been abducted."

Debra flew out of her office and raced to the place where her daughter was last seen. Cindy dialed 9-1-1 and was connected to the Lexington County Sheriff's Department at 2:30. She reported the possible abduction. Then, she, too, headed for the house.

Waiting for the arrival of the police and the two mothers, Heather searched and re-searched the house. She peered out windows looking for her friend in the yard. She could not find Kara anywhere. She called other friends who were equally clueless.

KARA FELT a hard jerk as Evonitz lifted her container out of the back seat. She banged around inside with each footstep he took as he carried her across the parking lot. Then they went up stairs. *One, two, three, four*, Kara counted in her head, *five, six, seven*.

He thumped the container down on the top concrete step, jarring the young girl inside. She heard the jingling of keys as the right one found purchase in the lock. She was jerked upward in her portable jail and then moved forward a few steps. The sound of the slamming door sent a charge of panic across her skin. She banged down on the floor again. A deadbolt lock slammed home.

She squeezed her eyes tight as she listened as intently as possible to undecipherable sounds of scraping and shoving. Then she heard something she recognized—the twittering and cooing of birds. The lid whisked off her plastic prison. Fear began to clutch her, and then she felt the air—fresh air, cool air. She wanted to gulp it in with huge hungry swallows, but all she could do was flare her nostrils and inhale it deep into her lungs. She looked around and saw a room filled with birds, animals and fish.

Aquariums sat on shelves and on the floor. Cages of all sizes were scattered everywhere. Cedar shavings tumbled to the floor around the edges of the small rodent cages. Food and medications for these creatures as well as pet periodicals piled up on the tops of shelves, counters and stacked boxes. Dropped morsels of pet food were scattered around on the carpet. Mixed in amongst these products on every surface was the detritus of everyday life—candles, a box of envelopes, a glass jar two-thirds full of collected pennies, restaurant fliers, pencils, pens and scissors.

Kara's mind raced—evaluating and re-evaluating her situation. Somehow, at her young age, she knew by instinct that her life rested in her own hands. She decided that a strategy of cooperation was her best weapon in this fight for her life. She knew, with patience, it would lead to an opportunity for escape. She may have been "freaking out on the inside," but she hid it well.

She rose but did not leave the container until permission was granted. A shiver went down her spine as she spotted a stack of large plastic containers, like the one that had served as her temporary prison, stacked against one wall.

Evonitz led her to his bedroom. He untied the fabric that held her hands up to her neck. He unfastened the handcuffs. She felt a jubilant swell of freedom, but it was squashed as he forced her to undress. She gritted her teeth to suppress the trembling in her hands.

He then attached her to a homemade wooden restraining apparatus on the bed—her legs pulled spread-eagle. He raped her as she willed herself not to struggle. When he was through, he removed the ball and wad of towels from her mouth. She forced a tiny smile of gratitude she did not feel. When she asked for some water, he ordered her to call him "Daddy" and to say "please."

"Daddy." The word was a painful lump in Kara's throat. "Daddy, may I have a drink of water, please?"

He held her glass to her lips and she gulped with greed. Then he was on her again, penetrating her for his pleasure.

DEBRA AND the police arrived at Dove Trace Court at 2:45 P.M. Cindy pulled up a few minutes later. Gordon Shaw reported seeing the Firebird, which he incorrectly identified as a Trans Am, pull up in front of the house. He saw a white male wearing a plaid shirt, blue jeans and a baseball cap step out of the car. The man had blonde hair, was about 5'11" and weighed about 230 pounds. Shaw saw the man speak with Kara, but nothing appeared unusual in their encounter. Kara seemed to get in the car and to leave with the man on her own accord. That eyewitness account convinced the two officers that Kara had run off.

Kara's mother, Debra, told the officer that her daughter had no history of running away. She insisted that Kara was not unhappy at home. Heather concurred with her assessment and said that Kara had never once mentioned any desire to run away. Neither Debra nor Heather could think of anyone they knew who owned a vehicle matching the one described by the witness.

The two pointed out that Kara's shoes were still there. Kara's purse was still there. It didn't make sense that she left without them. The officers insisted that Kara must have gone off with a friend. "She's just a runaway," one of them said.

"No," Debra fired back.

The police turned to Heather. "Are you lying for Kara?" they asked.

The young woman denied the accusation. Cindy told the officers, "My daughter is worried about Kara—we all are— and she would tell you if she knew anything."

"She's just acting like a teenager," the officer said. "She's holding back. She knows something she's not telling."

Both Debra and Cindy repeated that they were certain Kara had been abducted. The officers told Debra to just go home and wait. Kara was listed on the incident report as a runaway.

Later, Debra recalled, "They had no compassion. They didn't care. It was just horrible."

Police were then dispatched to the home of Kara's boyfriend, Chris, looking for Kara or the reported Trans Am there, but without success.

Debra called Kara's father, her ex-husband Ron. "Kara's gone."

"What do you mean, gone?" he asked.

"She's missing from Heather's house. Her purse is there. Her shoes are there. The water was left running."

Ron felt as if he were sinking into a large, black hole.

HER FRIENDLINESS to him and the calm façade she forced on her face led her captor to ask, "Are you scared?"

"Yeah, I'm scared."

"Why are you so scared?"

Kara looked him dead in the eye. "Because I don't want to die."

Together, Kara and Evonitz watched the news to see if there was any word of her abduction. There was no mention of her disappearance at all. At this time, the police had no idea whether she was a runaway or a kidnapping victim, or if she had just left with another friend for the afternoon.

After the news, Evonitz forced his captive to watch pornographic videos from his extensive collection. He paused them from time to time, to sexually assault her again. Over and over, he told her he would not hurt her. But Kara knew his promises were as hollow as the tennis balls that bounced in the court next door.

Temporarily sated, he rose from bed to go to the kitchen to wash the dishes. Kara offered to help in an attempt to gain his trust and lower his vigilance. "Is there anything you want me to do?" she asked.

"No."

"Are you sure? I'd like to help."

"Well, if you want to sweep the kitchen floor, you can."

He unfastened her from the device on the bed so that she

could. When the bizarre domestic scene ended, they returned to the bedroom.

Kara knew she had to use the bathroom before she was bound again. After prompting from Evonitz, she got the phrase just right: "Daddy, I have to go pee pee."

Permission was granted. Behind closed doors, she allowed herself to cry. She would not allow that to happen in front of her tormenter. She refused to allow him to see her fear. She washed the damage to her face in the sink and emerged from the bathroom with a tense smile and said, "Thank you, Daddy."

RON HEADED home without a moment's hesitation—business could wait. With his flashers on all the way, he made the four-hour trip from Georgia in under three hours.

When he arrived, he called the contact officer at the Lexington County Sheriff's Department. Two hours later, the officer returned Ron's call and explained what they were trying to do.

Ron snapped at the man. "First thing you need to do is list her as being abducted, not as a runaway—not wait twenty-four hours."

IT WAS a rough evening for Heather and Cindy—both were drowning in guilt. Heather blamed herself for asking Kara to water the flowers. She should have done it herself—she should have been the one dragged off by some unknown stranger.

"I felt so much responsibility because she was here—at my home. I was supposed to take care of them," Cindy said.

But Cindy was also angry—the intensity of anger increased with every passing moment. She finally decided she had to do something about it. She snatched up the phone and called a detective she knew at the Lexington County Sheriff's Department. She explained that she was not happy with the initial officers. They did not see it as a

serious incident and she, on the other hand, feared that
Kara had been abducted.

That investigator and one other detective arrived at
Cindy's home a short while later. They asked to speak with
Heather in private. Since her daughter seemed comfortable
with the idea, Cindy granted her permission.

The two detectives also questioned others in the neighborhood that night. They answered all of Cindy's questions
and told her they had received one call from someone who
reported seeing Kara. They assured her that Kara would be
entered in the NCIC database. When they left, they said they
were going over to Debra's house. Cindy now had the com-
forting belief that they were concerned and were convinced
that there was more to the story than just another sad tale of
a teenaged runaway.

KARA'S PLAN was working. Her abuser now trusted her
enough to risk going to sleep.

"It's time to go to sleep. We're going to sleep," he told
her.

"Okay," Kara agreed.

He put the handcuffs back on her wrists and shackled
her ankles to the wooden board. He pulled up the rope tied
to the headboard. It had a C-clamp on it and he fastened that
to her hand restraints, pulling her hands up to the left side of
her head. He attached another rope from the footboard to the
device around her legs.

Kara drowsed. When she awoke, she kept her eyes closed
until Evonitz's loud snores assured her he was still asleep.
With the stealthiest moves possible, she worked loose the C-
clamp attached to her handcuffs. Every time her captor
shifted in his sleep, she froze and waited for his snores to resume. Slow deliberation and infinite patience were her guid-
ing lights as she plucked at the knot tying her to the footboard.
At last, the knot worked loose. Her fettered hands flew toward
her mouth to muffle her involuntary gasp of relief.

Evonitz's snores stopped mid-breath. He rolled over on

his side. Kara held her breath. She knew if he saw her now, she would be in deep trouble. The handcuffs were still attached and the leg restraint was still fastened to her left leg. But she was not tied down anymore. Her heart seemed to stop until his snoring resumed.

Kara exerted exquisite caution as she eased herself up inch-by-inch. She crept so slow, slow, slow to the end of the bed and slid as silently as a teardrop over the footboard. She pulled on her shorts. Her handcuffs prevented her from putting on her shirt right. She gritted her teeth as she compressed her hand, ignored the pain and forced one hand out of the cuff. She then slid her shirt over her head.

She eased one foot before the other, fighting the adrenaline-induced urge to flee. At the door, a pile of obstacles blocked her way. She tried to be as quiet as the passage of time as she moved one thing after another to the side. When one item clattered to the floor, she heard the snoring from the other room snort to a stop again. Noise no longer mattered. Frenzied, she pushed everything out of the way, threw open the door and flew down the stairs.

Evonitz was awakened by the dissonance from the other room. He knew trouble was on the way. He made his preparations to run.

Chapter 29

Sixteen-year-old Irmo High School student Kenya Spry got into the car of his uncle, Cory Thompson, in the parking lot of the Crossroads Apartments complex. Kenya worked during the summer with his uncle in his grandfather's construction business. Before they could pull away, a young woman came running right at them. She was wearing shorts and a top. Kenya saw a dangling chain and, when she got closer, realized it was attached to a furry handcuff clamped to one of her wrists. She was breathless and, to the teenager's eye, appeared to be in shock.

She clutched the side of the car and begged, "Please take me to the police department."

Cory agreed without question—he had no doubt of her sincerity as Kara told them she had been kidnapped and raped. Kara turned and pointed to apartment 301 and said, "You'll have to remember which apartment it is, because I don't know where I am at."

Kenya was too shocked to speak. They rushed her just around the corner to the Region 4 headquarters of the Richland County Sheriff's Department and escorted her inside.

Kara was now able to drop the façade of calm she forced herself to wear while she was captive. She trembled all over and her voice quavered as she related her abduction, rape and escape to Corporal K. L. Pate.

Major Howell "Holly" Siniard ran Kara's name through

NCIC twice. He could not find her. Although he did not know it at the time, Lexington County had never put her name in the computer, despite their assurances to her mother that they had. Cindy's detective acquaintance swore that he had called in three times to make sure Kara was listed. And three times he was told that she was in the system.

Since, to Siniard's knowledge, no missing persons report had been filed on this child, he expected to encounter a woman who did not notice—or did not care—that her daughter was not at home. "Hello, ma'am. I'm Holly Siniard with the Richland County Sheriff's Department. Do you know where your daughter is?"

"No. I reported her missing yesterday in Lexington County."

"We have your daughter."

"You have her?" Debra's hands were shaking. Tears filled her eyes, blurring her vision.

"Yeah," Holly Siniard grinned. "She's right here."

"Can I talk to her?"

"Sure," Siniard said and handed Kara the phone.

Debra repeatedly asked Kara if she was okay. When Kara had reassured her enough times that Debra really believed her daughter was safe and sound, she hung up and rushed to the station.

Kara and her parents then went to the hospital where medical personnel obtained a rape kit and gave Kara an overall examination.

THE RICHLAND County Sheriff's Department dispatched officers to the apartments off Bush River Road. Eight patrol cars raced to the scene, securing all three entrances. They stopped first in the business office, where they questioned the staff to pin down the apartment they wanted. When they arrived at 716 Zimalcrest, no one was home. But now they knew the name of their suspect: Richard Marc Evonitz.

The South Carolina State Law Enforcement Division prepared a line-up of drivers' license I.D.'s. Investigator Scottie

Frier of the Lexington County Sheriff's Department picked up the line-up from the state police and took the six-pack of photos to the hospital. He laid the array in front of Kara. She identified Evonitz without hesitation. The pictorial line-up was then given to Columbia lead investigator Holly Siniard, who placed it into evidence at the Richland County Sheriff's Department.

Lexington County's mobile command center rolled into the Crossroads Apartments parking lot and set up shop. The thirty-four-foot-long unit provided a base of operation, giving the officers privacy and a source of communications. It was equipped with a radio and phone and fax lines. Investigators from both counties used this 1990 Holiday Rambler to keep headquarters apprised of every development, to coordinate strategy and to make decisions about what could and should be released to the public.

All the commotion caused a few residents to call the business office at the apartment complex to find out what was going on in their neighborhood. The staff, however, was surprised at the small number of calls they received.

WITH THE help of Kristen, the older of his two sisters, Evonitz spent two nights at a Days Inn in Orangeburg. On June 25, at 11:15 A.M., as Evonitz holed up in the motel, Captain Jim Stewart of the Richland County Sheriff's Department called the Columbia branch office of the National Center for Missing and Exploited Children to report the incident and request assistance in gathering information about their suspect. Charlotte Foster took the call and relayed the information to national headquarters in Old Town Alexandria and to the desk of Cathy Nahirney, supervisor of the case analysis and support division. Cathy had been an administrative support person for businesses and non-profits throughout the 80s when she took an extended temp assignment at the center. When that job was completed, she took a full-time job elsewhere, but it was too late—she had already left her heart at the national center.

When she could stand it no longer, she called up and begged them to hire her in some capacity—any capacity. She was willing to take a drastic cut in pay to get back to the work she found so fulfilling at that non-profit agency.

As luck would have it, the organization was ready to start up a new department for analysis. She read the proposal for it and was hooked. She created the division from scratch after she walked in the door in July 1990. Cathy felt she found her calling. The behind-the-scenes nature of the work suited her temperament. And, as a life-long lover of jigsaw puzzles, she was in a perfect position to spend her days putting the pieces together. But behind all that, this work held her heart—her commitment to the job was a living, breathing reality. "I do not have any children of my own. But all these children we work so hard to find are my kids. I have a very large family," she said.

Cathy logged on to the agency's database of public records to do her research. Her fingers flew on the keyboard as fast as a frog's tongue slaps a bug, typing in Richard Marc Evonitz's name, birthdate and Social Security number. She had a doctor's appointment and was anxious to get the job done and get out the door.

She printed out the pages of data and, as is her habit, she was counting them to make sure they were all there as they rolled out into the tray. When the list of previous addresses for Evonitz spewed out, an alarm went off in Nahirney's head—Spotsylvania and Fredericksburg were on the list. She went back into the computer to verify the dates that Sofia Silva and the Lisk sisters were reported missing. Her initial intuitive response was right—Evonitz had lived in Spotsylvania County at the same time. "When I saw that, I had a physical, visceral reaction," she said. Her stomach tensed, her heart raced.

Cathy was quite familiar with these cases—they had haunted her heart for years. The similarities with the current case were so blatant, she was surprised she needed the help of the computer to make the link. In both states, you had a bold abduction of young girls in broad daylight—whisked away from front yards in quiet neighborhoods.

When she had finished digging and printing, she had sixty pages of data on Evonitz. She monopolized the fax machines on several floors of the building sending the pages down to Captain Stewart. Then she called his desk and left a voicemail message to inform him of the possible link she had found to the murders in Spotsylvania. She didn't want Stewart to be surprised if the investigators in Virginia gave him a call.

When she finished faxing, she shuffled the pages together and took them to Charles Pickett, case manager for Lisk and Silva. She told him, "I think this is the guy who abducted and murdered the Spotsylvania girls. Please get this information to your best contact down there right away." Then she raced out the door to see her doctor.

Pickett called Major Smith and told him about the information they had uncovered at the center. He gave him all the details he knew about the case two states away.

In Evonitz's apartment, Richland County authorities were startled by their latest discovery—a front-page clipping from the May 2, 1997, edition of the Fredericksburg *Free Lance–Star*. The headline read: "Spotsylvania girls missing: Sisters disappeared yesterday." Beneath the banner was the story, complete with photographs of Kristin and Kati Lisk.

"A chill came over all of us," Sheriff Leon Lott said. "We knew we had a monster worse than we could imagine."

Ten minutes after the first call, Pickett called Smith again to inform him of what had been uncovered in the apartment. It sounded like a good lead—perhaps the best in years—but Smith tempered his excitement. He'd been down too many dead end roads.

The Richland County Sheriff's Department requested that the FBI establish a pen registry on Evonitz's cell phone. This registry allows the investigators to target a given number.

The computer will then record any incoming and outgoing numbers from that target.

The sheriff's department also contacted Armstrong Compressed Air, which owned the Nextel phone in Evonitz's possession, and they consented to have the phone monitored. Whenever he placed or received a call, authorities knew Evonitz's approximate location because the signal would hit the nearest cell phone tower. Each time he made a call, they knew he was within a one-mile radius of a particular tower.

ON JUNE 25, at 2 P.M., Investigator Scott Faust of the Richland County Sheriff's Department stood before Magistrate Judge Valerie Stroman-Boyd and signed arrest warrants on Evonitz—one for kidnapping, the other for criminal sexual conduct in the first degree.

"Sometimes people closest to the offender get into denial about the possibility that the person they know or in this case would be married to would be capable of such violence. However, I would speculate that there may have been some deep-seeded [sic] suspicion in the mind of a wife or especially someone with intimate contact with Evonitz. I think his sexual deviancy could not have been totally hidden from people with whom he had intimate relations. And that may have given rise to some suspicions, but they may have lapsed into denial not wanting to admit the worst possibility."

Greg McCrary, former FBI profiler, on *FredTalk*

Chapter 30

Kristen went to her vacationing mother's home to pick up the mail and carry it inside. When she approached the mailbox, she was surrounded by police demanding to know, "Who are you?"

Once Kristen's identity was established, the officers informed her that her brother was on the run. She did not believe them when they told her that Marc had abducted and raped a young teenager. She thought it must have been a consensual relationship and afterward, the girl cried rape. Or else the police had identified the wrong suspect. There was no way, she thought, that her brother Marc committed that crime.

Kristen called and left a message for her mother at the hotel where she was staying with Faith and Mattie. When the vacationing trio arrived back at their room that evening, Tess returned Kristen's call.

"Mom," Kristen asked, "could you come home early?"

"No," Tess replied. "Why should we?"

"Marc is in trouble."

"What's wrong?"

"It's bad, Mom."

"Is he all right?" Tess asked.

"You need to come home, Mom."

"Why, Kristen?"

"Marc kidnapped a girl and raped her at gunpoint."

"That's ridiculous."

"No, Mom. I'm serious."

"You can't be." To Tess, it was all sounding like a sick practical joke.

"He did it, Mom."

"He couldn't have."

"It said on the news that he was a registered sex offender in Florida."

"No way," Marc's mom denied it, entrenched in her belief that this was impossible. This was not her son.

"They said it's true, Mom," Kristen insisted. "I'm serious."

"Okay. I believe you. But I don't believe he did this. We'll be home as soon as we can."

Tess hung up the phone and turned to Faith and Mattie. She was confused and disoriented, but she slapped a mask of calm over her face. "We have to go home. Kristen doesn't want me to tell you why right now."

Tess called the airlines and arranged for a flight out the next day. She called the front desk of the hotel, informed them of their early checkout and set up transportation to the airport.

As Tess settled down for the night, her eyes refused to close. She stared into the darkness trying to comprehend the incomprehensible.

IN THE morning, Tess pulled Faith aside and explained the reason for their early departure. Faith shared the same total disbelief as her mother-in-law—the police might suspect Marc, but none of these charges could be true. From the hotel and from the airport, she tried again and again to reach Marc on his cell phone. But he had turned the phone off to avoid being traced and she could not get through.

At the Columbia Metropolitan Airport, two separate couples awaited the arrival of the trio from Orlando: Kristen and Jeffrey Weyand and Nick Lawrence and Laura Rushing. Nick and Laura were close friends of Marc and Faith. Marc was to serve as the best man at their wedding in October. Neither pair was aware that the other one was there till the arrival of Tess, Faith and Mattie. After pained greetings, the stunned group of seven made their way to the Weyand home. Faith and Tess spent the night there. At the request of the Richland County Sheriff's Department, Jeff drove Marc's mother and wife in for questioning at 9 A.M. After a couple of hours, the two women left the sheriff's office and went to the apartment at 716 Zimalcrest.

The phone rang. A despairing mother talked to her son. "I love you, Marc."

"I love you, too, Mom."

Tess choked on the tears that threatened to take her voice away. "I'm so sorry."

"No, Mom, I'm sorry." Marc's voice cracked as he cried.

"I'm sorry I didn't protect you."

"It's not your fault, Mom. You couldn't have done anything."

Tess handed the phone to her daughter-in-law and slumped lifeless in a chair.

After the call, Faith and Tess wandered through the apartment distracted and disturbed. They didn't know what to do. They didn't know what to believe. They were lost in the familiar surroundings of home. They went back and forth from the apartment to Tess' home to Kristen's house—in constant motion, as if they could find the answer to their misery if they could reach the right place at the right time.

Because they feared the phones were tapped, Faith and Marc set a time for him to call her at a pay phone. Faith and Tess waited beside the phone, but it never rang—they had forgotten when their plans were made that most pay phones do not ring through any longer.

While they were out on their fool's errand, Marc called the apartment and left a message: "There's nothing anyone could have done. I am utterly alone. I do not know how this is going to end."

The two returned to the apartment and cried over his message, sobbed over the despair in his voice.

The next day, Marc called again. Using coded phrases, husband and wife attempted to arrange a location where they could meet. Tess sensed that Marc did not really believe the two could get together, but continued the charade to give comfort to Faith. When Faith translated the real meaning of his plans, she realized he wanted to go to Bradenton, Florida. She said, "No. Don't. It's too obvious."

The monitor caught the activity on the cell phone—they had a hit in Orangeburg, but they did not know whether it was a stationary or moving target.

On the morning of June 27, the burden of protecting her brother bore down on Kristen Weyand with the crushing intensity of a collapsed roof. The guilt of her silence weighed on her mind. With regret and relief, she admitted what she had done. She told authorities she put her brother up at the Days Inn in Orangeburg, near the intersection of Interstate 26 and Route 301, in room 142.

Richland County Chief Deputy Dave Wilson called the Orangeburg County Sheriff's Department to request assistance. He then gathered an investigative team—Captain Jim Stewart, Lieutenant Stan Smith and Investigators Kevin Baker, Dave McRoberts, Shawn McDaniels, John Lutz and Norris Macon—and drove forty miles south.

While law enforcement raced toward him, Evonitz left the Days Inn. He ignored Faith's advice and headed south to Florida to the home of his younger sister Jennifer.

Chief Wilson's team was still en route when Investigators Todd Williams, Gerald Carter, Toni Powell and Lieutenant Rhonda Bamberg set up surveillance near the motel. From monitoring Evonitz's cell phone, they doubted that he was still inside the room. They were aware, however, that he could return.

When the Richland County officers arrived on the scene, personnel from both sheriffs' departments descended on the motel. The staff, although concerned about the company's policy on patron privacy, did not hesitate to cooperate with law enforcement after they were made aware of the seriousness of the charges against their temporary tenant. The manager turned over the key to room 142. The investigators unlocked the door. Guns drawn, they took cover behind the doorsill waiting for any sound of movement inside the room. They entered, guns out front, scanning every corner—searching each potential place of concealment and ambush. They threw the bathroom door wide open and slammed their backs against the frame. They jerked open the closet door and stood like rigid sentinels on either side until they were certain the room was secure. All was clear. Their prey had fled—possibly warned by his sister Kristen.

Captain Stewart and Lieutenant Smith from Richland County and Investigator Carter from Orangeburg County searched the room for clues. They dug in the bathroom trashcan and pulled out two razors containing hair. From the top of the dresser, they nabbed a Gatorade bottle. They also recovered a navy blue jacket with the initials "RM" on the chest, several cigarette butts and an empty box labeled "Handiworks Tool Sex." But the most menacing item of all was an envelope. On it, Evonitz had jotted down directions to a neighborhood in Lexington County—it was a different subdivision, but one near where he had abducted Kara. The note also contained the description of a young girl—yet another potential victim who had been caught in the crosshairs of Evonitz's perversion. After the room was searched, Orangeburg County law enforcement remained on the scene, staking out the room, guarding against the suspect's return.

Authorities then hoped information about his current whereabouts would come in from monitoring the movement of his cell phone. The pen registry was not yet in operation. The last cell phone call hit a tower near Jacksonville, Florida. The phone rang in Bradenton, Florida.

"Marc, did you do what they are saying you did?" Jennifer asked.

"What are they saying I did?"

"You know what they are saying."

"Yeah, I did it," Marc admitted.

"How long have you been doing this?"

"Years."

"How many states have you done this in?"

"A couple."

"Where?"

"Different states."

"Who?"

"I'll tell you when I meet you," Marc insisted.

JENNIFER WAS torn between family loyalty and doing the right thing. The abduction and rape of the teenager in South Carolina weighed heavy on her conscience. Marc's vague confessions to other crimes convinced her she had to act. She picked up the phone and called the Sarasota office of the FBI.

A call then went out to the Manatee County Sheriff's Department reporting that Evonitz was eating at an IHOP. He was not in the restaurant or its parking lot when the officers arrived. They fanned out in the surrounding area, looking behind buildings and around corners.

Tormented by her betrayal, Jennifer hoped to meet her brother and explain and urge him to turn himself in to authorities, but she arrived at the IHOP a few minutes late. Her heart raced in anticipation and dread. She scanned the parking lot but saw no sign of her brother. She went inside and looked in every booth. He was not there. She made a quick trip to the restroom and then went back outside to wait in her car.

She was torn with indecisiveness. Should she stay here and wait for him or go home in case he calls again? She saw police cars across the street, but she had called the FBI, not the sheriff's department, and did not make the connection. Finally, dazed and confused, she headed back home.

The Manatee County personnel spotted Evonitz and the chase was on. Once that department stopped their pursuit, the Sarasota Police Department was on his tail. Word of the chase traveled north. The Orangeburg County Sheriff's Department now knew Evonitz would not return to the Days Inn there. The day-long surveillance was terminated.

While running from the law, Evonitz called his wife, Faith, leaving messages on her answering machine. The desperation in his voice escalated with each successive call. He confessed that he had committed murder and said that he had been "involved in more crimes than I can remember." Tess said that Marc had never alluded to any murder in any state when he talked to her. All she knew about was the abduction and assault of Kara in South Carolina. And that was enough to numb her with horror.

After stop sticks blew out his tires, his car mired down in the dirt when he leaped a curve. Evonitz was cornered in the ritzy Bayfront area of Sarasota.

THE SARASOTA Police Department's K-9 unit members were all gathered together for their weekly training session at the Robarts facility. When they got the word, dogs and handlers descended on the waterfront en masse.

Lieutenant Sutton ordered Evonitz to exit from his vehicle with his hands outside the window. Evonitz stuck his empty left hand out the window. In his right hand, he held a gun—and he held it to his mouth. The order was given again.

This time, Evonitz put his left hand on the outside handle of the car and swung the door open. But he did not move and the gun remained in his mouth. He was ordered to drop the gun and step out of his vehicle. He still did not move.

Officer Thurow stepped out from behind a palm tree with his AR-15 rifle to provide cover for Officer Alan Devaney—he and his leashed K-9, a 4-year-old Belgian malinois named Matt, approached the driver's side of the Ford Escort. Thurow kept his weapon trained on the subject in the car as the duo approached Evonitz.

Matt sunk his teeth into the suspect's left leg right above the ankle and tried to pull him from the car. When that did not achieve the desired result, Matt released the leg and clamped down on the elbow of his prey. Then, he wrapped his mouth around the softer tissue of Evonitz's forearm. Evonitz did not budge—the gun stayed wedged between his teeth. Officer Devaney commanded the K-9 to cease and they both crept back away from the car.

Sutton repeated his command to drop the weapon. Evonitz shoved the barrel of his gun deeper into his mouth. Sutton shouted his order again. Hopelessness descended on Evonitz like darkness in a desert. He made a small movement. One finger tightened its grip on the trigger. He increased the pressure, pulling the trigger back toward the barrel. At the point of no return, a blast of detonation rocked the air. The gun delivered a bullet into his mouth that raced to his brain. Before anyone had time to react, Evonitz slumped over the console and into the passenger seat.

While others covered him with drawn weapons, Officer Gilbert approached the suspect, handcuffed him and moved him from the car to the roadway. Emergency medical technicians from the Sarasota City Fire Department rushed in to provide aid. They attached electrocardiogram patches on his chest and abdomen. They attempted to establish an emergency airway using a technique called needle cricothyrotomy. An introducer needle attached to a special catheter pierced the cricothyroid membrane in the neck to aspirate air. It was to no avail. Richard Marc Evonitz was pronounced dead at the scene from a self-inflicted gunshot wound to the head.

By this time, there were enough law enforcement personnel on hand to have a convention. Sarasota officers, detectives and traffic units were joined by FBI Special Agents David Street and Lynn Billings; Manatee County Sheriff's Department Deputy Hartman, the lead man in the original pursuit; and even the police department's public information officer, Jay Frank, was on hand. They knew it was only a matter of time before the media descended like a plague of locusts.

"This is a psychopathic offender. They commit suicide for reasons not typical in most suicides. People normally commit this act out of guilt, remorse, shame. He may have not wanted to face a trial and the public humiliation. But when trapped and they commit suicide, it is usually a control issue. They are not going to submit to authorities or society—he will not allow us to have that victory."

Greg McCrary, former FBI profiler

Chapter 31

Someone was at the front door. At this hour, on this night, Jennifer knew no one would come calling with good tidings of great joy. She peered outside and spotted three people—two of them FBI agents—standing like vultures of doom on her doorstep.

She welcomed them in, assuming that they had come to ask her questions about her brother. She had no suspicion of their real mission. They did not come to get information, but to share it. The two agents identified themselves and flashed their badges, and then introduced the victim's advocate who accompanied them. A numbness formed in Jennifer's fingertips and toes and crept up her limbs until it engulfed her whole body as the advocate informed her of her brother's demise. Guilt gnawed at the edges of her consciousness as she weighed her level of responsibility for his death. The agents gave her the option of calling Tess or having them send someone to her mother's home.

Although it was not the easiest option for her, Jennifer elected to call her mother herself—she knew Tess would rather hear the news from her. She located her at Kristen and Jeff's house. First, she explained the situation to her brother-in-law. He listened and then put Tess on the phone. After a painful recitation of Marc's suicide, Jennifer exposed a deep regret: "I didn't tell him I loved him, Mom. I should have told him before I hung up the last time."

As Jennifer talked to her mother, Jeff delivered the bad news to Kristen. At 2 A.M., the phone rang in the home of Joe and Ezghaharia Evonitz. On the other end of the line was Joe's son-in-law, Jeff Weyand.

After identifying himself, Jeff said, "Marc is dead."

The fog of sleep embracing Marc's father in these wee hours of the night vanished in a flash. His imagination raced through accident scenarios and sudden fatal illnesses. Until this call, he was unaware of anything that had happened in his son's life in the last three fateful days.

"What happened?" Joe asked. He did not expect to hear suicide. And he certainly did not anticipate the series of events that precipitated it.

MAJOR HOWARD SMITH of the Spotsylvania County Sheriff's Department had made all the necessary arrangements to travel to Columbia first thing in the morning. He would meet Captain Steve Dempsey of the King George County Sheriff's Department and Doug Deedrick and Melissa Branner of the FBI at a small local airport, and they would fly down together in a Virginia State Police aircraft. They wanted to examine Evonitz's apartment and car first-hand.

Smith was sliding under the sheets, hoping to get a decent night's sleep for tomorrow's demanding day. His eyes had just enough time to droop to a close when the telephone rang. It was Charles Pickett once again. This time he told the Major that Evonitz had been found. And he was dead.

WHEN DANNY MINTER awoke the next morning, he had no premonition that anything extraordinary would happen. The phone rang, his son answered it and no bells went off in Minter's head to warn him of what was to come.

He did not pay much attention to the boy's conversation, but did notice his tone of voice sounded a bit more agitated than usual when he talked to his grandmother. As soon as he hung up the phone, he turned to his dad. Excitement and disbelief etched in his face as he relayed the news of Richard Marc Evonitz's death. Minter thought, "No. It's got to be another guy."

He raced behind his son to the computer and watched as the story came up on the Internet. "It can't be" repeated like a mantra through his mind as the story unfolded on the monitor. Then, a picture of Richard Marc Evonitz scrolled up on the screen. It was true. It was the man who worked with him, smoked pot with him, brainstormed with him. It was the man he had invited into his home. Retrospective fear raced through his body, spiking his adrenaline and sending surges of chills across the surface of his skin. Evonitz could have come into his home at any time. He could have harmed his children—his daughter. He could have done anything. "How could I have known someone like that and not realize it?" Minter moaned.

He thought back to the time when the news of the murders swept through the county. As fear and unease ate away at him and his neighbors, he never once looked at Evonitz and thought it could be him. He heard FBI profilers talk about the perpetrator using a ruse to lure victims close to him, but he never once thought about the consummate sales skills of his co-worker. While the whole town was abuzz with conjecture about the murders of Sofia, Kristin and Kati, he and Evonitz had not spoken about the crimes on any occasion. It did not bother him in the least bit at the time. But now Marc's muteness had a sinister explanation.

THE FIRST order of business in Columbia was an appearance before a Richland County judge. In minutes, Major Smith walked out of that encounter with a search warrant for the apartment and another for the Ford Taurus.

He went straight from the courtroom to 716 Zimalcrest Drive in the Crossroads Apartments complex, a cluster of more than six hundred units in wood-clad two-story buildings shaded by tall pine trees. The unit housing Evonitz's home was next to the community's swimming pool and tennis courts. Inside the apartment was Faith's miniature zoo, a collection of birds, fish, hermit crabs and hamsters.

The chaos in Evonitz's mind was reflected in the chaos of his apartment. In addition to the mountain of clutter created by the creatures and the supplies connected with their care and entertainment, an upheaval of miscellany ruled the crowded space.

Bottles of prescription drugs popped up everywhere. A check with the local CVS/Pharmacy revealed a long list of prescriptions on file for Evonitz: Clidinium/CDP and Prevacid 30 mg for stomach disorders; Sulindac 150 mg and Naproxen 500 mg to treat pain and reduce inflammation; Ultram 50 mg, Hydrocodone/APAP and Propoxy-N/APAP to relieve moderate to severe pain; Prednisone 10 mg, a corticosteroid to reduce swelling; two antibiotics, Cipro 500 mg and Ceftin 250 mg; Zyrtec 10 mg, an antihistamine; and Viagra, to treat male sexual dysfunction.

Candles, bowls and bottles of vitamins and over-the-counter pain relievers overpowered the counter space in the kitchen. A glass bowl overflowed with an assortment of odds and ends—a pack of basil seeds, an Armstrong Compressed Air employee I.D. tag, a lock, film canisters and envelopes with ripped ends.

Next to the kitchen, the dining table was covered with a sheet of plastic the color of dark green garbage bags. Sitting atop the makeshift tablecloth were computer equipment, bird magazines, CDs, costume jewelry and piles of papers. The area beneath the table was packed with cardboard boxes. The wall next to it was piled high with even more boxes, computer equipment, framed pictures and pet toys and food.

Between the dining and living areas, an ironing board formed a barrier separating the rooms, next to a stereo system covered with a disheveled stack of CDs. Cages crowded around an immaculate set of black leather furniture arranged in an L shape in the living room. The only object on the leather upholstery was a clear purple plastic roll-around exercise ball for the guinea pig. On the coffee table centered in front of the sofa and love seat sat an ashtray full of butts, a remote control, a sheet of postage stamps and yet another animal cage.

The chaos continued in the bedroom. Overfull laundry baskets disgorged their contents of clothing onto the floor. The surfaces of the nightstands flanking the bed were gray with ground-in cigarette ash. On the floor surrounding them, discarded cigarette butts, covered elastic hair bands, fast food drink cups, coffee mugs and candy wrappers lay scattered like archeological remnants of a past civilization in a maze of extension cords.

The top of one dresser was piled high with Beanie Babies, Barbie dolls, a computer monitor and a stack of boxes, papers and computer manuals. Concealed between the open bedroom door and the wall was a wealth of belts, framed artwork, a guitar, a long bamboo pole and a wooden board mounted with two large eye hooks with a frayed piece of rope attached to each one.

With infinite patience, the officers and agents picked over every inch of the apartment. In the top drawer of one of the nightstands, beneath a sheet of paper, officers uncovered a revolver, ammunition and a spray bottle of tanning oil.

Smith examined the contents of the footlocker where the newspaper clipping had been found. It also contained a note with a general description of the location of Block House Road where the Lisk family lived. Another note had vague directions that led to the spot where the remains of Alicia Showalter Reynolds were discovered.

But that was not all—there were more ominous comments about other young girls whom Evonitz was stalking. Some were notes from when he lived in Virginia—including comments about a handful of girls in the Fredericksburg/ Spotsylvania area, and two in Culpeper. One note detailed directions to an "old farmhouse" and gave a four-digit street address. It talked about a 12- or 13-year-old brunette who was home alone from 3:30 until 4 in the afternoon every school day. Investigators traced that trail to Laurel Thomas, now 17 years old, living with her family in a century-old farmhouse. The address on his note matched the last four numbers of their five-digit address.

Another note contained a street address that led the Task-force to 16-year-old Katherine Howard, who was described as being a 10- to 12-year-old blonde. Also jotted down was the fact that her brother would be in the house.

Other scribblings were current—girls he'd stalked in the Columbia area. He had jotted down the physical descriptions of the objects of his attention as well as habits, like jogging, and the location of their homes.

Smith also found an abundance of pornographic videos and magazines. When they finished their search, they found a total of more than 300 videos and hundreds of magazines—material on shaving, bondage and sex with children. Many of the dresser drawers were so filled with these pornographic materials that no space was left for the couple's clothing.

The investigators discovered enough sex toys in the apartment to open their own X-rated shop. They found a variety of restraining devices in addition to the homemade board found behind the bedroom door—cuffs, collars, leashes and ties. A collection of dildos—battery operated and manual—along with attachable tips in different textures designed to create a host of sensations, were uncovered. Penile rings, clamps, clothespins, lubricants and rub-on stimulants were also discovered stowed away throughout the room. One of the oddest items found was a complete Evenflo breast pump kit—the kind often used by young mothers to extract breast milk so that others could feed the baby in their absence.

The footlocker also contained a treasure trove of women's panties and bras, some quite small and none belonging to Evonitz's wife, Faith. The thought that each piece of underwear could represent a victim sent a ripple of apprehension and dread through the room.

Captain Dempsey was down on the floor on his hands and knees going through the items stored in the closet. He excavated the contents of a cardboard box. Beneath a stack of about twenty smutty magazines, he located a pink bathroom rug. He stopped and called over to Deedrick. A grim smile crossed the FBI analyst's face when he saw the rug. "Yeah, I like that." They had found a match to the mysterious pink fibers discovered on Kati.

A handmade afghan also caught Deedrick's interest as a possible fiber match. At first, Faith objected when they wanted to take it in for testing. However, when she was informed that Evonitz's first wife, Bonnie, had made that coverlet, she could not get rid of it quickly enough. Authorities also seized computer disks, letters and canisters of film from the apartment.

The discovery of a prescription for Viagra answered a lot of questions, like why they'd found no semen in the Spotsylvania cases, and why the latest victim was raped so often in such a short period of time. When asked about it, Faith admitted that her husband had had problems with impotence, and as soon as he had heard about the new drug, he'd hurried to the doctor.

When asked about the contents of the footlocker, she said she had no idea what was inside. Marc had guarded it, keeping it secured with a padlock, and threatened dire consequences if she ever attempted to force it open.

Next, the investigators tackled the Ford Taurus. They vacuumed it to retrieve every fiber, hair or other microscopic trace of Kati, Kristin and Sofia. They cut out chunks of carpet and bagged them for comparison with the fibers found on the girls.

Then Dempsey climbed into the trunk and lay down on his back. He dusted the lid for fingerprints. He did not expect to find anything useful after all these years. But he did. When the shadow of prints began to rise from the dust of the powder, a powerful jolt of adrenaline took his breath away. There, above his head were prints—a fingerprint and a handprint of a child. And by the position on the lid, he knew there was only one way that those prints could have gotten there. The lid had to have been touched by the hand of someone inside attempting to push the trunk upward. He was certain these prints belonged to either Kristin or Kati Lisk.

Dempsey climbed out so that photographs of the prints could be taken and preserved for future reference. Then he laid the thick fingerprint tape across the evidence to lift it and place it on the card. But when he pulled back the tape, nothing was there. He got out fresh tape and tried again. And again. And again. Smith took a crack at it. He, too, had no success. The prints would not lift.

A close inspection revealed to the seasoned officers a sight that neither one of them had ever seen before. With the passage of time, the heat from the sun beating down on the lid had fried the prints into the paint. Dempsey and Smith looked at each other.

Smith asked, "What do we do now?"

Dempsey shrugged and shook his head.

Then, they looked at each other with widened eyes and went for some tools. Together they removed the trunk lid from the car and took the whole thing to the FBI lab in Washington, D.C.

In all, two hundred pieces of evidence were retrieved from the apartment and the car and delivered up north for analysis.

IN FLORIDA, an ambulance transported Evonitz's body from where he had died to the medical examiner's office on Hawthorne Street. The cause of death, gunshot wound to the head, and the manner of death, suicide, were apparent from a cursory examination of the body and reports from the scene. Nonetheless, a complete autopsy was performed as mandated by state law.

In addition to a thorough external examination of the body, the medical examiner conducted a complete survey of the internal structure. The body cavity, cardiovascular system, organs, glands and the musculoskeletal system were described, weighed and analyzed. Numerous slides and Polaroid identification photographs were taken and radiographs of the head and body obtained.

The examination revealed that Evonitz had moderate to severe fatty liver metamorphosis, active hepatitis, early cirrhosis and some arterial stenosis or hardening of the arteries. The medical examiner removed and bagged a scissored blue T-shirt, brown woven leather belt, blue denim jeans, white socks, white tennis shoes and white briefs. He extracted a "fully jacketed, somewhat deformed small caliber lead projectile" and associated fragments from the fatty soft tissue of Evonitz's scalp at the spot across and slightly to the left of the entry wound.

He turned over the clothing and bullet fragments, along with fingernail clippings from both hands, blood, pulled head hairs and pulled pubic hairs, to the Sarasota Police Department.

The medical examiner also sent blood and urine samples to the University of Florida Toxicology Laboratory for a comprehensive drug screen. That analysis disclosed the recent ingestion of a decongestant, an antihistamine, marijuana, Valium, an anti-anxiety drug, and Serex, a pharmaceutical used both for the treatment of anxiety and the alleviation of symptoms induced by alcohol withdrawal.

FOR THE next two and a half days, Smith and Dempsey conducted a series of interviews with Faith. Dragging information out of her was as difficult as herding cats. She was still in love with Evonitz. Her grief over his death was intense, her loyalty to her husband intractable. She told investigators that if she could have done so, she would have joined him without a moment's hesitation and participated in a murder/suicide or double suicide pact. She forgave him for everything and anything he had done.

With reluctance, she admitted that Evonitz often shaved her and sometimes shaved his own pubic area. She told them that bondage was a recurring theme in their sexual relationship. She had been bound to the restraining apparatus on the bed on a regular basis. And the wire-enforced furry handcuffs fastened to Kara's wrists had been fastened to hers more times than she could remember.

· · ·

NEXT, THE invasion of the South Oaks subdivision in Massaponax kicked into gear. Officers from the sheriff's departments in Spotsylvania and King George Counties, state troopers and FBI agents went door-to-door interviewing the surprised former neighbors of Richard Marc Evonitz.

Two FBI agents knocked on the front door of the Raba home. Kieth explained that he and his wife had a newborn baby. He did not want to invite them in just now because Monica was feeding their child at this time. Kieth joined them outside and talked with the agents in his yard.

Kieth's feelings surpassed shock when they told him about the abduction of 15-year-old Kara in Columbia, South Carolina. They asked Kieth about Bonnie, telling him they were unable to locate her and were concerned for her safety. Kieth repeated what Marc had told him—Bonnie met someone on the Internet and moved to California.

Kieth listened in stunned and bewildered silence as he learned that Evonitz was suspected of more than just the abduction in South Carolina. The FBI revealed the 1987 sexual indecency incident in Florida and told him they were also investigating Evonitz for the murders of Sofia Silva and Kristin and Kati Lisk.

"I thought I was friends with Marc. Instead I was friends with a serial killer," Kieth said. "I did not doubt what they told me for a minute. What they said started to make sense out of a lot of things."

The most surprised of all were Christopher and Elissa Parks, current residents of the white house on South Fork Court that was home to Evonitz from 1996 though 1999. They granted permission for law enforcement to search without a warrant. Forensic experts used specialized filtering vacuums to gather trace evidence. Among the items seized were carpet fibers from the computer room, living room and bedroom and other dark red acrylic fibers.

The home Evonitz rented near Lake Anna just before he

left the Spotsylvania area was searched, too. Nothing useful was extracted from that location.

IN FREDERICKSBURG, sparks were flying in the frenzied environs of *The Free Lance–Star*. Rose Ann Robertson, a journalism professor from American University, was working at the paper that summer. She recalled the electricity generated by the breaking news. "This is a community newspaper and it was a community event. Reporters in the newsroom felt this was not three strange girls they were writing about. These wounds went deep.

"As good as they were about being objective, they were concerned about opening old wounds for the families. They were concerned and discussed often how much of the old stuff they needed to dig up."

The people like Rose Ann who were responsible for driving traffic to the Web site worked to keep the page as fresh as possible. "The community was captivated," she said. "Anything new on the Web site would get thousands of hits."

The urgency of the Web site staff put it in conflict with the reporters' proprietary instincts. They wanted to break news on the front page of the paper. They feared that anything published on the Web site could be scooped by *The Washington Post* or by any of the television stations covering the story. The two conflicting groups reached a wary peace. The news staff passed along most of the new information to the Web crew. The online staff accepted it when a piece of information was just too hot to release before the newspaper hit the stands.

MONICA RABA was home alone with her baby; Kieth was at work. When the doorbell rang, she swung the front door open with her infant daughter in her arms. She was greeted with flashing lights and snapping shutters. She slammed the door shut as soon as she could, but it was too late—she and her child stared out from the front page of the newspaper the next day.

Monica was terrified. She feared that a member of Evonitz's family would exact revenge on her and her baby. She worried that other criminals hearing of Evonitz's crimes would copy them and this exposure made her a target. From that day on, she refused to answer the front door when she was home alone.

NEXT DOOR in Spotsylvania, Detective Twyla Demoranville was assigned the responsibility of informing the Silva and Lisk families about the latest developments. Ron Lisk told her that the next time she came back, he wanted her to have all the i's dotted and all the t's crossed. He did not want to know any more until they could tell him with a certainty that Richard Marc Evonitz was the man who murdered his daughters.

WITH EACH passing day, the staff at Crossroads Apartments in Columbia grew more concerned about the animals left in the Evonitz apartment. They retrieved the abandoned pets under the watchful eyes of officers—taking them to the business office where they could make sure they got enough food and water. It was not an unusual act for this group. There were never any feral cats raiding the Dumpsters in their complex. Staff adopted every abandoned animal on the property until they could find it a good home.

Faith Evonitz, however, did not appreciate their concern and compassion. She voiced her displeasure at their actions in no uncertain terms when she collected her pets a couple of weeks later.

IN ARLINGTON, Joe Evonitz responded to calls from the media with an angry tirade. He accused the press of trying his son in the newspaper based on innuendo rather than evidence. Then he would slam the phone down on their ears without answering any questions.

"The progression would indicate that he is transitioning from flashing to sexual homicide. There is a good possibility that there are other crimes. Some sexual offenders plateau off at nuisance crimes that include no physical assault. But offenders like Evonitz transition through to rape. Evonitz continues to escalate to homicide. Stability in his life can mitigate against him acting out. But this was too prolonged a period of time. It is difficult for me to believe he remained crime free."

Greg McCrary, former FBI profiler

Chapter 32

On July 2, the Fredericksburg *Free Lance–Star* published an editorial about the surprising developments in South Carolina and Florida:

> *As the shocked former Massaponax neighbors of Evonitz discovered, we had a possible serial killer living in our midst—working here, going to barbecues here, getting into (surprise!) anti–death penalty discussions here. We don't want to believe that monsters masquerading as humans live in our midst. But this community has awakened to that reality [. . .]*

They concluded their piece with a cry for action:

> *Clearly, the procedure on the management of sex offenders needs a major overhaul. Evonitz apparently had other things on his mind—like plotting kidnappings, rapes and murders—to bother registering, and would hardly want to put a big*

*target on his back for police. Yet if Evonitz's name had been
in a national databank, perhaps he wouldn't have had the
opportunity to leave Virginia and show his monstrous face to
more victims. We'll never know for sure. But a national system of registering sex offenders might make the capture of
sick, murderous predators like Richard M. Evonitz less a
matter of luck.*

THAT SAME day, the shocked Silva family wrote a note and
attached it to their front door:

> *The Silva family appreciates your concern during this emo-
> tional time. We would greatly appreciate your understanding
> of our need for privacy. We will not be available for any
> comments.*

WITH FURIOUS intensity, the Lisk–Silva Taskforce toiled
round the clock to dot all those i's and cross every t. For a
large part, it was a waiting game—waiting for the FBI lab
to match DNA, match fibers and identify fingerprints, or to
eliminate Evonitz as a suspect. The director of the FBI laboratory wanted to speed up the process as much as possible by
adding personnel. He started with one full-time forensic examiner, but soon built a squad of twelve specialists with an
exclusive focus on the Evonitz case. Background research on
their target, however, kept them all occupied during the wait.

They interviewed everyone they could find whose paths
had ever crossed the life of Evonitz. In discussing these
encounters, Major Smith said, "Every woman we talked to
thought he was creepy. They couldn't tell me why, but he
made them uncomfortable."

They worked to reconstruct every step of Evonitz's days
from his birth to his death. It was not an easy task. His family moved a lot as he was growing up. Then, service in the
Navy continued the nomad pattern as he was transferred
from base to base. To complicate matters further, he'd had

job-related travel, both for training while in the service and with his civilian jobs afterward.

Investigators in Culpeper were also interested in Evonitz. They searched for a link to the death of Alicia Showalter Reynolds. Other than the vague notes found in Evonitz's apartment, no connection was ever found. But no evidence conclusively eliminated him either. Investigators involved with the case do not think he is their man.

DETECTIVE JIM Stone of the Arlington County police had a series of gunpoint rapes in his community in the late 1980s. The cases had never been solved. But they did have the DNA of their suspect. Evonitz fit the description of the rapist, and his father lived in Arlington at the time.

There were enough coincidences for Stone to run with it. He might, at last, put these cases to rest. However, when the DNA analysis came back from the FBI, Stone scratched Evonitz off his list.

IN FLORIDA, Lieutenant Joe Paez of the Hernando County Sheriff's Office was looking for answers in the 1993 Jennifer Odom case. The 12-year-old girl had disappeared from her Pasco County bus stop. Her body was found six days later in the southeast section of the same county. When Evonitz was stationed in Florida at Naval Station Mayport, he was 180 miles northeast of Hernando County. It was a bit of a distance, but it was still worth a shot.

The fate of Jennifer Odom was the main focus of the sheriff's department's cold case unit. Unfortunately, they had no DNA evidence to compare with Evonitz. They worked with the FBI to determine the whereabouts of the suspect at the time the 12-year-old girl disappeared. Their exhaustive timeline work ruled out Evonitz—he was not in Florida at that time. Detective Mike Nelson's cold case crew continued to follow up leads in this decade-old murder.

• • •

CAPTAIN DWAYNE Courtney with the Aiken, South Carolina, Police Department wondered if Evonitz was responsible for the death of 17-year-old Jessica Carpenter, an Aiken High School student. On the afternoon of August 4, 2000, Jessica's mother returned home from work and discovered her daughter's lifeless body. She had been raped and strangled, and her throat was cut. Her death had a dramatic effect on the small community, located forty-five miles from Columbia. There are only a couple of homicides a year in Aiken, and Jessica was the only teenaged victim in memory. Evonitz was eliminated here, too—this time by DNA evidence. Aiken law enforcement later linked the DNA to another suspect who was soon awaiting trial for the crime.

IN DUVAL County, Florida, on Sunday, November 4, 2001, Jennifer Medernoch, a 14-year-old Joseph Stilwell Middle School student, left her home in the Woodland Estates mobile home park. She was ticked off at her mother at the time. They had a spat on Friday evening about the messiness of her bedroom. Then, she was forced to spend her whole Saturday with her mother cleaning it up.

When Jennifer did not return home that evening, her mother, Angie Medernoch, assumed she was spending the night with a friend in the neighborhood. The next day, however, she was not in school. Angie reported her daughter as a missing person. She would be missing for days.

Two teenaged boys in the adjoining Clay County went fishing off the bridge over Long Branch Creek on November 8. Down in the water, they saw what appeared to be a body lying facedown. They were not sure if it really was a person or just a leftover Halloween prank.

One of the boys brought his father up to the bridge, who then called the police. The naked 5'2" body had brown eyes and long brown hair. It was covered with blood. On

November 12, Clay County authorities identified the victim as Jennifer Medernoch.

When Richard Marc Evonitz came to the attention of Clay County authorities after his death, Jennifer's homicide was still an open case. Her age, physical description and the fact that she was dumped in a small body of water made him a person of interest in their investigation. Unfortunately, they had no DNA evidence from Jennifer's body to attempt a match with the suspect. As of early 2003, Clay County law enforcement and the FBI were working together to try to place Evonitz in that area at that time.

IN NORTH Carolina, 23-year-old high tech employee Stephanie Renee Bennett, was found raped and strangled in her North Raleigh apartment on the afternoon of May 21, 2002. In July, Lieutenant Chris Morgan investigated the possibility that Evonitz was the man he sought in that murder. DNA analysis reports from the FBI eliminated Evonitz as a suspect. Lieutenant Morgan said that the search for Stephanie's killer remained a daily occupation in Raleigh.

THE TASKFORCE discovered that Evonitz had attended Navy classes in Norfolk, Virginia, in June 1986 and January 1988. Authorities in Virginia Beach, Suffolk, Portsmouth, Norfolk and Chesapeake reviewed all unsolved cases in those time frames.

In Maine, Lt. Ted Ross of the Portland Police Department and the Maine State Police Department searched the files in 1988 and 1989 when Evonitz was stationed there at the Bath Iron Works.

The Maine State Police cast a suspicious eye at an abduction in July 1989, along the Maine Turnpike. A concert at the Old Orchard Beach had just disgorged its audience, crowding the highway with vehicles heading home. A young woman's pick-up truck developed a flat tire, leaving her stranded on the side of the road. Someone stopped, but instead of assisting her, abducted her from the scene. The skeletal remains of the young woman were found a couple of weeks later in New Hampshire.

It had been an exceptionally hot July that year in New England. Hot weather is always accompanied by a dramatic increase in the insect population. The swarms rushed to her abandoned body. Other wildlife roaming the area assaulted her as well. Because of this damage, the manner of death could not be ascertained—and the case has never been solved. Neither the state police nor the Portland police found any other open cases of murder or abduction in that time period.

Law enforcement agencies in South Carolina, Florida, Illinois and California dusted off their cold case files, too, and looked for any connection they could find. The job was easy for those with DNA evidence. But in cases where there was none, the research into the Evonitz timeline continued.

CHARLES PICKETT and Cathy Nahirney at the National Center for Missing and Exploited Children spent every day that week doing nothing more than fielding calls from the media. One constant question in every interview was: "Do you think he did it?"

Cathy hoped it was Evonitz. She had a strong feeling it was Evonitz. But to the press, she simply said, "I don't know." She'd been down this road many times before in her twelve and a half years with the center. She was not about to start second-guessing the investigation and the forensic evidence now.

WALTER GRINDERS was overwhelmed by attention from reporters, and appalled that their company was connected to these horrific crimes. They issued a press release that read:

Richard Marc Evonitz worked here at Walter Grinders, Inc. from March 1995 to January 1999, selling machine tool parts via telephone. He left to pursue his own business. During his employment, he gave us no reason to suspect that he had any involvement with the unspeakable crimes of which he is now accused. We are cooperating fully with law enforcement officials. As always, our thoughts and prayers go out to the victims and their families.

After the company issued that document, all inquiries from the media were answered with that press release. No further questions were entertained.

IN RICHLAND County, South Carolina, officials contemplated charging Evonitz's sister Kristen with aiding her brother in his attempted escape from justice. Had Evonitz kidnapped or assaulted someone else after he talked to Kristen, charges would have been filed. Since he did not, the idea was dropped.

THE FUNERAL for Richard Marc Evonitz was a low-keyed affair. His family gathered at the Dunbar Funeral Home in Irmo, South Carolina, to comfort one another. Marc's remains were cremated—the family did not want a gravesite, fearing it would be desecrated.

"At this stage of the investigation, Evonitz is the best possible suspect period. Everything about him that is known to date places him into the category of a serial and sexual killer. His patterns and motives demonstrated in the South Carolina case combined with his lifestyle and age are very characteristic of a person that would do the type of crimes we've seen here in the Spotsylvania area. Since Evonitz killed himself in Florida, it is highly unlikely he will flee from law enforcement nor will anything said by police interfere with his 'prosecution.' Therefore, I think that the police could be a little more candid on what they're finding on a timely basis rather than waiting and keeping everyone waiting for the grand announcement which is bound to come soon."

Robert K. Ressler, former FBI profiler

Chapter 33

The twelve-person FBI forensic team continued to work full-time analyzing the more than 600 pieces of evidence gathered in the Silva/Lisk investigation. It was an amazing allocation of resources for an agency that was overburdened by the demands of terrorist-related work stemming from the tragic events of 9-11.

They compared the fingerprints from the trunk to those on cards the Lisks possessed. They ran a DNA profile to match with the sequence on the hairs recovered from the crime scenes. And fiber comparisons were a big part of their work here, too.

Reports from the FBI lab arrived in Spotsylvania the week of July 9. Despite cries from the media and the public, law enforcement would not divulge any of the results from this first round of tests. "I called the lab every day asking, 'Did you find anything?'" Major Smith said. "I was sitting on the edge of my seat just like everybody else." Most residents of Spotsylvania viewed this comment with extreme skepticism.

While the community held its breath, *America's Most Wanted* was back in town filming again. Their seventh episode with information on the Silva and Lisk murders aired on Saturday, July 13. The highlight of the show was the first media interview with Kara, the abductee in South Carolina. At the time, Sheriff Lott said it was the first and only media interview the victim would do, and that she only agreed to this one in the hopes that she could help other victims by sharing her experiences. Although her face was shrouded in darkness, her voice spoke loud and clear about her eighteen hours of torment at the hands of Richard Marc Evonitz.

The FBI hoped that viewers would call in and help them fill in the blanks in Evonitz's life. They wanted to hear from people who knew him in various parts of the country who could provide new information for the timeline. They also thought it possible that a victim might recognize Evonitz as the perpetrator. They were rewarded with twenty-five fresh leads; among these were a number of women who claimed they spotted Evonitz following them in the past.

The following Monday, the Taskforce called a meeting to brief agencies throughout the region. Investigators from Fauquier, Caroline, Orange, Culpeper, King George, Prince William, Fairfax, Arlington, Alexandria and Louisa Counties in Virginia, Charles County in Maryland and Virginia State Police received a complete rundown of Evonitz's life and crimes. They returned to their jurisdictions to see if any piece of information about his method of operation would match unsolved cases in their files. Also present at the meeting were two new members of the Taskforce from the Naval Criminal Investigative Service—one from Quantico Marine Corps Base, the other from the Naval Surface Warfare Center in

Dahlgren. They would track Evonitz's movements during his nine years in the Navy.

AUTHORITIES RELEASED Evonitz's Columbia apartment near the end of July. Just a few days before the kidnapping of Kara, Marc had visited the business office and signed a renewal on his lease. The new commitment had not yet gone into effect and management released Faith Evonitz from that obligation. They also filed a formal eviction notice to ensure that she did, in fact, vacate the premises.

When Faith turned in her keys, apartment management discovered she had abandoned some personal property—among them the bed where her husband had restrained and raped 15-year-old Kara. After contacting their former tenant to make sure she wanted none of the items, the staff disposed of all that remained.

ON AUGUST 8, Major Howard Smith bowed to public pressure and went on *FredTalk*, an online chatroom on the Web site of the Fredericksburg *Free Lance–Star*. He made his reluctant appearance burdened with the concern that participants would raise many questions that he would not be free to answer. And he was right. He got a lot of flak from participants about not releasing the information that was now known. He insisted that he would not do so at the request of the two families of the victims who did not want details coming out piecemeal.

A participant identified as "Grandma" asked, "Why has it taken so long to get the DNA back? When the guy in California was caught, they had the DNA back in a number of days."

"The task force never said they didn't have the DNA test results back," Major Smith responded. "We have said we have some of the forensic evidence that has been tested and completed. But we are waiting until all the evidence has been examined before releasing anything."

Then, "Mike" joined the chatroom to state his concerns. "Major Smith, I have read where Richard Evonitz was a possible suspect in the Lisk–Silva murders or, at least, someone that was looked at while he was a resident of Spotsylvania. Please explain what investigation was done regarding him prior to excluding him from the suspect list. I have also read where if you had known about his prior sexual conviction in Florida that it would have brought greater scrutiny upon him. Based on what we know now, and hindsight is always 20/20, why didn't investigators at that time check with his employer to see if he was at work the day of the disappearances? That would seem like it would be standard police work. The employer would have immediately provided details that he was not only absent both days the girls were missing but he had called in sick the day after each. That would be a serious red flag, wouldn't it, sir? I can understand maybe not catching it at first but since all the man hours spent on this case over the years, I am puzzled that if he was on a list that no one would have checked him out."

"First of all, he never came up as a suspect," Smith said. "His name was on a permit to apply for a business license in the county. But he never came up as a suspect or an individual we wanted to look at in this case." Smith shared much of the community's frustration over the length of the investigation but, try as he might, he could not see what more they could have done. "We knew nothing about Evonitz until the case broke in Columbia. Also as far as Evonitz's conviction in Florida, at that time, he was not required to register as a sex offender in Virginia, so, therefore, his name was not on the sex offender list we had. So we had no reason to suspect Evonitz or look at Evonitz until he was reported by the Center for Missing Children in the South Carolina case."

In talking about the problems encountered during the investigation, he said, "Another road block that obviously has come up is the fact that with the sex registry, right now, we have the law that requires the individual convicted of the crime to come to law enforcement to register. And, obviously, these are people who have committed serious crimes and we expect them to be truthful and faithful and come to us on their own. And that's something that has to be changed. I think it should be mandatory that when people are convicted of sexual crimes they should be registered right then and it should be put in a criminal database where every law enforcement agency in the country has access to it. If we had had that—I'm not saying it would have made a difference in this case—Evonitz's name certainly would have surfaced very early in this case if we had that information and we would have been able to look at him."

Smith also discussed the impact this case had on his personal life. "Having a small child, I am much more cautious now about where he goes and who he's with. I've put an alarm system on my home. He's not allowed to stay at home by himself. I think that has not only changed my life, it has changed the whole community and the way we live. I guess it's kind of taken away our innocence. I think we were a community that considered ourself a small community where things like this did not happen. And this has shown that no one is exempt from having a tragedy like this in their community."

Patti White asked, "How is it possible that not one witness has seen anything near these precious children's homes when these horrible crimes took place?"

"I think history has told us about cases like this that people who are serial killers are [. . .] very intelligent, they're very bold, they're very cunning," Smith answered. "They're often referred to as a person who could sell anything. They are able to blend into the general public. They look like the guy next door. These cases would be easy if serial killers all looked like these three-headed monsters you see in the movies. That's why it is so important to get the public involved and to get the public to call in no matter how trivial they think their information might be."

The major continued to dodge questions about the culpability of Evonitz. "Out of the 12,000 leads that this task force has investigated, Evonitz is by far the strongest lead we've looked at." He also said, "I think we need to be aware that even if Evonitz is the person responsible, there certainly are other sex offenders and other predators in our society and we should not let our guard down."

"Jesse" asked, "Major, in general, would you agree with the proposition that monsters like Evonitz nearly always foreshadow their evil deeds by leaving signals of aberrant behavior, even as children? And that the major problem is that parents, teachers, coaches, clergy, etc. either refuse or are incapable of reading these signals?"

"Yes, I would agree that people like this from early behavior start showing some type of indication that there is a problem," Smith stated. "And a lot of times it is not recognized by parents or other people who have contact with them. Or sometimes it's overlooked. As with most investigations, when you start looking at people that are involved in serial killings or rapes, sexual predators, there's always a past there that started at a young age."

Before he closed, he promised a full disclosure of all the evidence within a couple of weeks. In the ninety-minute chat, one hundred people asked questions. Smith answered fifty-one of them before his time was up.

IT DID not take a couple of weeks, however. The answers the community desired were revealed. Four days later, Major Howard Smith stood on the doorstep of the home of Ron and Patti Lisk. When the door opened, he said, "All the i's are dotted. All the t's are crossed. Richard Marc Evonitz is responsible for the death of your daughters."

"When your child is murdered, closure comes when the lid of your casket is shut."

Patricia Sarti, mother of a murdered child

Chapter 34

Media representatives gathered at Spotsylvania County's Holbert Building in the Board of Supervisors' meeting room for the 3 P.M. news conference on August 13, 2002. The event was broadcast on two local cable channels in the area.

Spotsylvania County Sheriff Ronald T. Knight stood back from the microphone and podium set up on the stage. Behind him were the solemn faces of Major Smith, King George County Sheriff Clarence W. "Moose" Dobson, Spotsylvania County Commonwealth's Attorney William Neeley, Lieutenant Rick Jenkins of the Virginia State Police, FBI Special Agent Donald W. Thompson from Richmond, and Dr. Dwight E. Adams, director of the FBI Laboratory. Stretched across the back of the room were all the other members of the Lisk–Silva Taskforce.

Sparks of anticipation crackled through the media, family, friends and onlookers in the room. Cathy Nahirney and Charles Pickett slid into the first seats available. Cathy had never been present at a press conference before. This day was the highlight of her career—the culminating point of all the work they had done.

The families of Sofia Silva and the Lisk sisters clustered together for comfort and strength. Their blanket of sorrow smothered any outward display of excitement.

When Sheriff Knight stepped forward to the microphones

to speak, the room turned as still and heavy as the air before
an impending storm.

> *"Five years and eleven months ago, life in Spotsylvania
> County, and in this entire region of Virginia, changed forever.
> Spotsylvania County suffered the most horrible of crimes.
> The abduction and murder of children is the most abhorrent
> crime in civilized society; one that not only devastates the
> families and friends of the victims but traumatizes the entire
> community as well. We have now experienced these crimes,
> and they overwhelmed our community with a sense of grief,
> fear and uncertainty, much of which still lingers to this day.*
>
> *[. . .] "Investigation by the task force quickly determined
> that all three of these murders were linked by common foren-
> sic evidence and were perpetrated by a serial killer driven by
> his strong sexual obsessions. Expert criminologists agree that
> the most difficult crimes to solve are those committed by the
> psychopathic, serial offenders. These people are usually very
> intelligent and show no outward signs of criminality. They ap-
> pear normal to most people with whom they come in contact;
> they hold jobs, live in nice neighborhoods, blend in among
> people around them, and become a regular part of the com-
> munity. They also use careful planning to commit their crimes
> and go to great lengths to avoid detection. They make serious
> efforts to not leave or to cover up any forensic evidence. All of
> these factors were present in these three murders.*
>
> *[. . .] "Among the most compelling pieces of forensic evi-
> dence in this investigation are two fingerprints from Kristin
> Lisk found inside the trunk of Evonitz's 1992 Ford Taurus.
> This vehicle was operated by Evonitz during the time period
> of both the Lisk and Silva cases. In addition, a head hair was
> found inside the clothing of Kati Lisk, which was recovered
> along with her body. The mitochondrial sequence of this head
> hair is identical to that of Richard Marc Evonitz. Another hair
> found in the clothing of Kristin Lisk has been microscopically
> identified as belonging to Evonitz. One hair found entwined in
> the rope used to bind the body of Sofia Silva has been micro-
> scopically identified as belonging to Evonitz.*

"Additionally, overwhelming fiber evidence supports the conclusion that Richard Marc Evonitz was responsible for all three murders. This fiber evidence not only links all three victims together, but also links the victims back to Evonitz's property, his residence in Spotsylvania, his current residence in South Carolina and to his vehicles. The fiber evidence collected is especially overwhelming because of the great number of fibers found on all three victims which have been determined to have come from various carpets and other material found in Evonitz's residences and vehicles. In addition, several sources of fibers from Evonitz's vehicle and residences were found on each of the three victims individually. We believe the overwhelming amount of fiber evidence found on all three victims and linked back to Evonitz meets the threshold for a criminal conviction.

"In addition to this overwhelming and powerful forensic evidence, the task force has uncovered other significant information that confirms that Evonitz had both the opportunity and wherewithal to commit these crimes. In the recent abduction and assault of the girl in South Carolina, investigation determined that Evonitz abducted his victim, placed her in his vehicle, brought her to his residence and assaulted her there. Luckily for that brave little girl, she was able to escape and lead investigators to her captor. Investigation has determined in South Carolina, Evonitz chose the day of his abduction and assault on a day in which he took off from work and his wife had left the state on an extended trip. Task force investigators determined in Spotsylvania County that on the day Sofia Silva was abducted, Evonitz left work early and then took off sick the following day. In addition, investigation determined that during the Silva abduction, Evonitz's then-wife had recently left the state on an extended trip. Like the South Carolina abduction, no one else was home in the Evonitz residence during the Silva abduction time period. Investigation has also revealed that on the day of the Lisk sisters' abductions, Evonitz had already been separated from his former wife for several months and was living alone in his residence. Like both other abductions, Evonitz did not go to work on the

Lisk abduction day of May 1, 1997, or the day after, and did not return to work until May 5, 1997. These absences from work and the departure of his wife on each occasion gave Evonitz ample time and opportunity to commit the Silva and Lisk abductions and bring them back to his residence, while transporting them in his vehicles. This activity is consistent with the fiber evidence later found on all three victims.

"Sexually obsessed serial offenders often display a signature aspect in their crimes and frequently employ the same technique and utilize the same devices with each victim. Evidence discovered in this investigation has demonstrated that there are many such similarities, not only in the Silva and Lisk murders, but also with the more recent abduction in South Carolina. All the girls shared common physical characteristics, such as age, hair color, and size. All three Spotsylvania girls are believed to have been abducted in a similar manner and at approximately the same time of day.

[. . .] "Another striking example of all of Evonitz's victims is that the fibers found on the handcuff restraining devices Evonitz used in his South Carolina abduction were also found on all three victims in Spotsylvania County."

The emotions of this investigation welled up in the sheriff's chest. He paused to suppress the constriction in his throat and the tears in his eyes.

"The powerful evidence and other information developed since June 26, 2002, have led this task force, the FBI Laboratory experts, and the Commonwealth Attorney's Office to conclude that Richard Marc Evonitz is responsible for the abductions and murders of Sofia Silva and Kati and Kristin Lisk. The purpose of this press announcement today is to help bring some comfort, and provide some answers to the Silva and Lisk families. We also hope the identification of a now deceased perpetrator of these horrible crimes will bring some sense of relief to the community at large.

[. . .] "Serial offenders, like Evonitz, often commit crimes

*in different jurisdictions. We are pursuing every possible av-
enue to determine if Evonitz might have been responsible for
any other crimes."*

Knight choked as he wrapped up his presentation—the
tracks of tears visible to all.

> *"I would like to end this proceeding with a statement to the
> families of Sofia Silva and Kristin and Kati Lisk: You have
> suffered an unspeakable and senseless tragedy which we know
> has greatly affected you and everyone near you. The entire
> community shares your pain. We know that today's announce-
> ment can never fully heal the pain and sorrow you have and
> continue to experience. Our hope today is that this announce-
> ment gives you some answers to your many questions and that
> it may bring you some small amount of closure and comfort in
> knowing that the individual responsible has been identified
> and is no longer in a position to harm anyone else.*
>
> *"To the families of Sofia Silva and Kristin and Kati Lisk,
> we offer our condolences, our prayers and our best wishes
> for the future. Thank you."*

Many in the audience, like Cathy Nahirney, struggled and
failed to hold back tears. Each one of the men flanking the
sheriff stepped up to the microphone to make a statement.
The final one in the group to come forward was Dr. Adams.
He detailed the evidence scrutinized by his lab that brought
them to this day and this conclusion.

The wealth of fiber evidence alone was astonishing—
particularly considering that the bodies had been moved and
were left in water for days or weeks. All three girls had fibers
from the same blue fuzzy handcuffs that bound Kara in
South Carolina. Dark red acrylic fibers found in Evonitz's
Spotsylvania apartment and on his possessions in Columbia
were found on all three girls. Light red acrylic fibers from a
pocket of Evonitz's shirt matched fibers on each victim.
Carpet fibers from three different rooms of his home in Virginia were found on all three. Pink fibers from the bathroom

rug found under pornographic magazines in a box in the closet of the South Carolina apartment were the same as fibers found on Kati Lisk. Fibers from an afghan made by Evonitz's first wife, Bonnie, were discovered on the bodies of Sofia and Kati. Fibers from the trunk of his Ford Taurus were matched to fibers on all three girls. There were even fibers linked to the computer mouse pad in his apartment.

Then, there was head hair. The mitrochondrial DNA analysis matched the hairs found on the victims to Evonitz: one inside the sock of Kati Lisk and another wrapped in the rope that bound Sofia in the moving blanket.

Most miraculous of all the evidence was the fingerprint and palm print of Kristin Lisk on the trunk lid of Evonitz's car. Children's prints are always more difficult to lift than those of adults because juveniles leave fewer oils behind. That difficulty combined with the passage of so much time created minuscule odds of finding a useable print. But the prints were there and, fortunately, the Lisks had recorded their daughters' prints when they were younger.

Fiber, hair with DNA, and latent prints—each element on its own was powerful. Added together, the evidence was overwhelming.

The most heart-rending portion of the press conference was now under way. The families approached the microphones. The first to speak was Ron Lisk, father of Kati and Kristin. His tear-stained eyes cast about the room gathering strength from the faces of family friends and neighbors scattered among the media. "Patti and I were robbed of our children. And the community was robbed of our trust of our fellow man."

He acknowledged his gratitude to 15-year-old Kara, who had escaped from Evonitz. "We want to express our sorrow to the young lady in South Carolina for all she had to endure, but at the same time thank her for her courage and her bravery."

Many in the community expressed outrage that Evonitz took the easy way out by committing suicide. Melissa Britt, a friend of Sofia, said, "I felt a little bit of closure with Evonitz's death, but I think he got off too easy. He needed to suffer more. To feel some pain. Maybe then he would feel remorse."

Many in law enforcement are certain that Evonitz left behind a legacy of crimes that will forever remain unsolved. Ron Lisk had a different perspective: "We, as a family, are relieved that we won't be subjected to a long trial."

He then expressed a strong desire that other parents would learn from his pain. "While this announcement will bring closure to many, our grief is ongoing and will last throughout our lives as we know them on earth. Please, please don't let your guard down. There are others out there fully capable of heinous acts. Please hang on tight to your children. Love them every day. Treasure each moment with them. Give them a hug every day."

Phyllis Silva, in a pale purple dress to honor Sofia, thanked a multitude of investigators for all they had done. She reserved a special thank you for Detective Twyla Demoranville, the lead investigator in the Silva case since the day she disappeared. Demoranville became the principal contact between both families and the task force. She was a strong and steady source of information and emotional support. "You will always be with us," Phyllis told her.

She acknowledged the faith that helped her family through these tragic times. "God has walked with us every step of the way. He carried us when we could not carry ourselves."

Phyllis then turned her gratitude to the public. "There's no way to thank this community and the people who prayed for us in the last five years and eleven months. Many of you who sent cards or gifts, we've never met. But you are in our thoughts."

Phyllis then spoke to the family of Richard Marc Evonitz with gracious compassion. "I know that this is a trying and sorrowful time for you. You have lost a loved one. You loved him. You cared about him. But you can find peace with God."

Sofia's sister, Pam, expressed her outrage at the killer and his fate. "I've heard the comment that Evonitz took the coward's way out. But our family feels that he is facing a much higher judge and receiving a much harsher punishment than he would ever receive here on earth."

When they had finished their comments, officers escorted the shaken family members out of the building and drove them home. In the Holbert Building, the Taskforce responded to a barrage of inquiries from the press. In trying to explain to reporters how an awarded Navy man who was so charming and friendly could possibly hide such a dark secret, Major Smith said, "That's why these people are so hard to catch. They aren't these two-headed monsters. They don't draw suspicion to themselves."

Sofia's Chancellor High School friend expressed the relief shared by many in the community. "Years went by and nothing was ever said. I thought they would never solve the crime, but I am so thankful for the girl who was able to get away from him and let everyone in Spotsy rest a little more at ease knowing the madman who took our friends away can't hurt anyone else. I know that we should not let our guard down because there are more people out there with a mind just as sick as his was, but I hope this is closure. I know, almost six years later, it is for me and my friends."

Brandi echoed her remarks. "I'll always remember now. I'll always remember a brave young girl. I'll always remember the tears of relief that one of the world's monsters is gone."

Angie Frantz expressed bitterness at the outcome. "I'm glad they found out who it was, but no one got justice. He was such a coward, but because he killed himself, you can never find out why—Why Sofia?"

Kieth Raba, Evonitz's former neighbor, had mixed feelings. "I believe in the death penalty. Because of his suicide, there is no closure for the families, particularly for the unknown victims. But he did save a lot of taxpayer dollars."

WHEN THE draining yet gratifying conference was completed, Sheriff Knight walked across the Spotsylvania County government complex to his office. With flint in his eyes and justice in his heart, Knight summed up the feelings of many that day: "I hope that son of a bitch is burning in hell."

"Never leave them mad. Always tell them you love them. Keep them as close as you can. But never leave them mad— you never know."

Kara's mother, Debra

Chapter 35

The Spotsylvania Crime Solvers Board of Directors met the day after the announcement of Evonitz's responsibility for the deaths of Sofia Silva and Kristin and Kati Lisk. Major Smith made a brief presentation about the case. As soon as the last word passed through his lips, a motion was made to give the $150,000 reward money to Kara, his final victim.

Sheriff Moose Dobson of King George County asked his board of supervisors to donate $5,000 to the reward fund. He informed them that Spotsylvania County had contributed $10,000 and Stafford County and the city of Fredericksburg had each contributed $5,000 to the fund. The board agreed, and some of the money they allocated was used to pay for the transportation and hotel expenses to bring Kara and her family to Spotsylvania for the reward ceremony.

THAT SAME day, Major Smith again appeared in the *FredTalk* chatroom. One of the participants asked, "Is there any part of you that wishes you could have taken Evonitz alive so you could face down the man you've been chasing for so long? And so that he would have to face the community he tormented?"

"I have mixed feelings about that," Smith replied. "I would have liked to have had the opportunity to interview Evonitz and find the answers to a lot of these questions that

I'll never have. I would have liked to have been able to interview him and learn something about his MO to share with other law enforcement officers when working cases like this, but there is another side of me that feels that this is the best ending for the families here in Spotsylvania and for the little girl in South Carolina. The families won't have to go through a court hearing and the girl in South Carolina won't have to go to court and talk about what happened to her there."

Commonwealth's Attorney William Neeley shared a similar sentiment. "The circumstantial and forensic evidence was overwhelming and compelling. We would not have hesitated to prosecute this case." He added that the Lisk case was the stronger of the two because of the presence of Kristin's finger- and palm-prints. "One side of me would have loved to prosecute this case," he continued. "Life in prison is a long and miserable existence. But he saved the taxpayers' dollars and he saved anguish for the families."

KARA, WITH her parents and her best friend, Heather, came to town for the event on August 26 at the Wytestone Suites hotel. The families of Sofia Silva and Kristin and Kati Lisk were eager to meet the young hero and express their appreciation.

Richland County Sheriff Leon Lott, Officer Alan DeVaney and Matt, the police dog, from Sarasota also traveled to Spotsylvania to attend the ceremony. And, of course, a large contingent of the Lisk–Silva Taskforce gathered there as well. The event was closed to the public. The identity of Evonitz's final victim was a guarded secret.

The Spotsylvania Crime Solvers Board prepared the obligatory oversized copy of the check. Ron and Patti Lisk and Phyllis and Pam Silva presented it to the girl whose resourcefulness brought a serial killer's career to an abrupt end. The gratitude of the community was scrawled across the memo line: "Thank You. Heroism and Courage. Spotsylvania Cherishes You."

Ron Lisk spoke for the members of both families when he said, "I want to sincerely thank you for your amazing internal strength. You will always be in my thoughts and prayers. Thank you."

Joy and grief commingled in the room, creating an emotional stew where no one knew from one moment to the next whether to laugh or cry. K-9 Matt, present at Kara's request, wagged a little levity into the day—begging for belly rubs from anyone with a free hand. Light-hearted jokes raised questions about his viciousness. The Spotsylvania County Sheriff's Department presented him with a basket filled with dog biscuits and a dog tag engraved "Our Hero Matt." Ron and Patti Lisk gave him a bulletproof vest.

Kara's parents said she would be allowed to use some of the money to fix up her car and to spend on herself when she took a trip to New York in the near future. The bulk of the money, however, would be held in a trust fund until Kara was 25.

Kara announced her own plans for the future, which she formulated in the hospital after her escape from Evonitz. "I want to be a doctor, in the emergency room. It just came to me, that's what I'm meant to do. It's how I'm meant to help other people. And it came to be because of all this." She had proven in her encounter with Evonitz that she had a strong enough will to get what she wanted. With a 3.8 GPA, she had also shown that she possessed the ability and intelligence to make her dream come true.

About this young hero, retired FBI profiler John Douglas wrote, "I'm amazed by her bravery, and my thoughts are with her as she tries to survive the emotional burden that monster has left her with. I've worked with a large number of victims and their families, and the horror certainly does not stop when the attack is over. I hope she receives the support and compassion she unconditionally deserves."

Again, Ron Lisk echoed the sentiments of many in that room. "I pray something good will come from all this. I pray in the future that law enforcement and the courts will have no patience for child molesters and murderers."

• • •

To THE great surprise of the detectives on the Lisk–Silva Taskforce who had done all they could to conceal her identity, Kara revealed herself to the public on *The John Walsh Show* on September 23. As the show opened, John Walsh said that he was going to introduce everyone to a girl who was "a real hero" to him.

Sixteen-year-old Kara stepped out onto the set with an air of confidence that belied her years. She was lean and graceful, with a bountiful abundance of dark, wavy hair. Her heart-shaped face was home to dark blue eyes, a rounded nose and a cupid-bow mouth with full lips. When she smiled, it reflected a radiance over every inch of her face.

Walsh told her, "I know it took a lot to come here, and I think your courage in being here will set an example for young women all over the country."

After a break, the show shifted emphasis to the ordeal of Ron and Patti Lisk. As Ron spoke of his daughters, a small smile of pleasant memories crossed his face. "Kristin was bright. She did great in school. She was a sweetheart. She was very popular. She had so much to look forward to, so much to give the world eventually. Kati, I called 'the tenderheart.' "

Next it was Pam and Phyllis' turn in the spotlight. Phyllis held Pam's hand as she talked about Sofia. "She was just so full of life. So bubbly—so happy—would do anything to please. People at church said she always had a smile—she was always smiling when she came into church. She would always say 'Hello.' She was just so sensitive—so caring."

After Kara's friend, Heather, told her story, Kara returned to the stage to share hers. She was greeted with rocking hugs from the family members of the victims. When Kara finished her recitation, her mother, Debra, read a statement to the victims' families from the father of Richard Marc Evonitz:

> *"I want to apologize to the families on today's show. I feel sorry—sorry—for the deaths of Sofia Silva, Kristin Lisk and Kati Lisk. I feel sorry for what he did to the young girl in South Carolina.*

"I am shocked at my son's actions and am in disbelief at the unspeakable crimes of rape and murder on those innocent girls. I have conversations with my son in my own head and I ask myself, 'Why did you do this, Marc? Why?' And I can't get an answer.

"I cannot comprehend and will never comprehend the monster he became. I will never be able to forgive him for his actions.

"My heart goes out to the families on today's show and the only thing I can say is I am deeply and truly sorry for my son's actions."

When Debra reached the end, her voice choked—Pam and Phyllis fought back tears. Then Kara was showered with appreciation from the other guests. Ron Lisk said, "Kara, I hear your story now and you're a whale of a person. I want to say thank you. There's so many people—lives you have touched by what you did. And I want to say thank you on behalf of all those families in our community that suffered with us. I want to sincerely thank you personally, 'cause—and I mean this from the bottom of my heart—you set in a chain reaction of events that allowed a conclusion to the death of my daughters." Ron's lip quivered and he pulled his chin in tight to hold back the tears. "That truly gave me a lease on life. So, at some level, I owe you my life."

Then, Phyllis spoke to Kara. "One special girl. God put you on this earth for a reason and a purpose. I don't think this has been all of it. I think He has a lot more for you to do. And I think He's going to walk with you every step of the way and take care of you just as He did in this situation. And there is nothing we can ever say or do that can begin to show our appreciation, our love and our caring for you."

Sheriff Lott of Richland County wrapped up the show by explaining the end of Evonitz's life. "They hemmed him up and had him surrounded. He took the coward's way out and he killed himself [. . .] I think justice was served at that time, and he's going to pay for it."

> "Kara deserves all the credit. The strength she showed going throughout this ordeal and afterward has made everyone around her stronger. She provided all the information we needed to get this monster and bring him to an end."
>
> Sheriff Leon Lott, Richland County, South Carolina

Epilogue

The death of his daughters gave birth to Ron Lisk's commitment to help children who had been victimized. This cause, though, was so broad and diverse, Ron felt that to be effective, he needed to narrow his focus. The fate of 3-year-old Katelyn Frazier of Alexandria riveted the attention of many in Virginia to the needs of reform in the foster care system.

Katelyn Frazier lived with her foster parents for two years. They wanted to adopt the young girl. Instead of allowing this to happen, the local child welfare agency, backed by the courts, returned Katelyn to the custody of her mother, Pennee Marie Frazier, on September 15, 2000.

For three and a half months, her mother made no attempt to stop the ongoing abuse perpetrated on her daughter by her live-in boyfriend, Asher Levin. On December 29, Levin beat the helpless toddler to death.

Frazier was sentenced to fifteen years in prison after pleading guilty to child abuse. Levin, convicted of felony murder and two felony convictions of child abuse and neglect, received an eighteen-year sentence.

Working with state delegates in the Virginia General Assembly, Ron Lisk demonstrated an avid determination to change the laws and policies that did not appear to make the safety and welfare of the child the top priority of the system.

On October 1, 2002, the foster care law that placed all its emphasis on the philosophy of family reunification was repealed. Two other laws replaced it. One mandated that a permanency plan be developed for each child where the goal of adoption or custody transfer to another relative were as viable an option as family reunification. The second law provided for background checks of everyone—including the biological parents—in any home where a child would be placed. Through these laws, the ruling principle in Virginia is now the best interests of the child instead of the preservation of the family.

RON AND Patti Lisk adopted two young orphans from Rumania. The two girls did not speak any English when they arrived—an additional parenting mountain to climb. But the Lisks had shown that they had the strength and faith to face any challenge. Their two new children did not replace Kati and Kristin. Nor did they mute the grief the couple felt for their two lost daughters. But their presence in the home gave Ron and Patti the opportunity to channel an abundance of love and nurturing on two children who desperately needed a stable environment and a mother and father who would cherish them forever.

"I WAS raised in this community at a time when I could hop on my bike and ride anywhere without a worry—when doors were left unlocked," said Commonwealth's Attorney William Neeley. "Now the community—particularly the women and children—are paranoid. My daughter grew up in the shadow of this tragedy. She has never done anything unsupervised in her life. She's seventeen now, but still she does not get off of a school bus without an adult present or get on the bus in the morning without being watched."

KARA AND her parents invited Kenya Spry and Cory Thompson out to dinner. They wanted to express their appreciation to the two men who'd rendered assistance to Kara on the morning of her escape. "They didn't have to do that," the teenaged Spry said. "But it was real nice."

• • •

CINDY AND Debra talk often about the impact that the abduction of Kara had on their lives and on those of their
daughters. Everyone felt a lot of pressure and stress in the
aftermath. That made all of their emotions raw and ready to
spill over at the slightest provocation. A distinct strain developed in the mother–daughter relationships of both Cindy
and Heather and Debra and Kara.

"Kids think when you are trying to protect them, you are
being overbearing," Cindy said.

After learning more about Evonitz and his mode of operation, Cindy believed that he was after Heather—that he had
probably staked out their home before and had stalked her
daughter. Kara just happened to be in the wrong place at the
wrong time. That thought gave Cindy nightmares. She told
Debra, "I don't think Heather could have handled it like that."

Debra responded, "I would not have thought that Kara
could have, either."

Cindy worried a lot about the approach of the next summer. She was afraid that summer would never be the same
again. "What happened has changed the way I am with the
kids—it changed my whole life," she said. "I look at people differently than I did before. If anyone approaches me,
I am very leery of them."

Heather and Kara are still close friends. But they had to
give each other a little space—a little time to heal. Being together reminded both of them of what occurred on the day
they wanted to forget. They remain in close contact with each
other—they just are not as inseparable as they once were.

IN THE spring of 2003, Angie Frantz was 23, married and
attending Germanna Community College part-time. She
hoped to transfer to Mary Washington College in the fall and
major in psychology. She bears the emotional scars of her
friend Sofia's death. "I'm still very careful about going anywhere by myself. I carry a can of Mace or pepper spray to
walk around the neighborhood."

She does not know if she ever wants any children. "You never know what could happen—your child could be abducted." Angie is trying to live each day to its fullest. "I try not to take anything for granted. Someone could be here one moment and gone the next," she said. "I know that sounds kind of cheesy." But Angie has learned through her traumatic experience that behind "cheesy" is often a mother lode of truth.

ON THE day before Evonitz's death, Perry Deveaux made his ninth appearance before the parole board in Columbia. For the ninth time, Kathleen Sanderlin's parents, Ella Rue and Dutch Buckheister, made the pilgrimage to the hearing. Fifty others—including Mount Pleasant Mayor Harry Hall, Jr., and Mount Pleasant Police Chief Roddy Perry, the former partner of Detective Eugene Frazier—crammed into the small room with the parents of the victim.

Perry Deveaux was not present at the hearing. His interview with the parole board was conducted via teleconference from the prison. Before every hearing, the Buckheisters distributed petitions to businesses all over Mount Pleasant. They never showed up with fewer than 20,000 signatures to present to the board. This year, the couple had come armed with 268 letters and 46,000 signatures on a petition objecting to Deveaux's release on parole. As always, a good number of the signatories were former students, or the parents of the children who sat in Kathleen's classroom.

The Buckheisters' single-minded determination won the day again. Deveaux's request for freedom was denied. In the beginning of the hearing phase, Dutch and Ella had to travel to the prison in Ridgeville every two years. For recent hearings, they've traveled to an office building in Columbia.

In 1990, a group of inmates sued the state of South Carolina for more frequent parole hearings. As a result, the Buckheisters have to appear before the parole board every year. Gathering signatures is now a year-round occupation, since they only receive a thirty-day notice before the scheduled date.

"We shouldn't have to do this every year," Dutch said. "When you take another life, if you don't get the electric chair, you should have to spend the rest of your life behind bars."

"If he got out of jail, I think he would offend again," said Chief Perry. "I saw no repentance on his part."

Retired Detective Eugene Frazier agreed. "I look in his eyes and I have no doubt in my mind that he could do it again."

In the spring of 2003, the Buckheisters again were collecting signatures in preparation for yet another hearing that they anticipated in June.

MARC EVONITZ's death and the revelation of his crimes left his family reeling. "Initially, I had absolute disbelief about Lisk–Silva. I was horrified that anyone would think that," said brother-in-law Jeffrey Weyand. "By the time that the forensics evidence was presented, I came to the conclusion that it was possible."

Kristen and Jeff's marriage was troubled long before the death of Marc. Soon after her brother committed suicide, Kristen left her husband and her son, Mattie, to live with another man in Chappells, South Carolina.

Kristen is no longer speaking to her mother, Tess Ragin, because Tess had Kristen's new boyfriend investigated. According to Tess, Kristen has taken up "with con artists, liars and thieves who are taking advantage of her. She believes all that man says." He has purportedly claimed to be connected with the Mafia and the heir to a huge estate, and that body-guards are essential to protect his life.

To compensate Mattie, in some small measure, for the loss of his mother from his daily life, Faith Evonitz and Tess Ragin spend as much time with the little boy as work and other obligations will allow.

When Tess learned about Marc's death and the abduction and sexual assault of Kara, she was "devastated" and filled with a "pain you cannot bear." About a week later, she learned of the murders in Spotsylvania County, but at first would not believe the accusations. "Logically, I guess, I have to accept it. Emotionally, it is extremely difficult. I know it is true but I cannot imagine him doing it. It's just mind-boggling." As she spoke, the pain of her ordeal slashed through her voice.

"He was such a great guy, I can't imagine him being this other person. Jen and I still wake up in the morning and can't believe it. It's like a horrible nightmare. We wake up and ask ourselves, 'Did this really happen?'"

Tess has undergone therapy and leaned on her friends— one particular woman who has been in her life for forty years has been an invaluable comfort. But that friend lives in North Carolina and all their hugs are delivered through a phone line.

"The minister's wife here has been very supportive. But most of the people I worked with for thirty years have been absent. I have not heard one word."

The Marc she knew was not the man who killed. "He was very good to me—always. He was very good to his sisters. He was very good to his wife. He worked hard. I was proud of all he accomplished."

Joe Evonitz was baffled, too. For two months he refused to believe it. He mistrusted the police. He was certain that they just needed to solve the crime and were using Marc as a scapegoat. Ezghaharia was "broken-hearted—she loved Marc. She made a fuss over him whenever he came." About his feelings, he said, "I searched my soul trying to find out what in my family life caused him to go this way." He added, "I wasn't an ideal father. I was a weekend drunk. But the past is set. Either people forgive me or not." He concluded, "Marc had a choice. He wasn't a young kid."

Jennifer Evonitz agreed with her father that Marc shouldered most of the blame for what he did. But she added, "My father is partially responsible for what Marc did. People are born with a problem like that and their environment can turn them either way. Putting my father into the equation added a lot of anger and created a greater chance of violence.

"I believe Marc had a chemical imbalance in his brain.

He was sane, but he had abnormal desires that he could not seem to control. If he had grown up in a healthy, loving environment, maybe he could have controlled them."

About her father, she added, "I don't think that it is healthy or wise for me to speak with him anymore. He makes me feel badly. I choose not to have that in my life."

Turning to her mother, Jennifer said, "I feel bad for her because she has lived under somebody's thumb all of her life—whether Dad or Perry or her fears of life. Now this. I love her," Jennifer said. "I just can't imagine living sixty years and being miserable sixty years."

About herself, Jennifer said, "It's very depressing—I didn't want to be in the media. It's been embarrassing, upsetting and humiliating." Worst of all, she said, was how horrible she felt for the victims and their families. "I have nightmares about what my brother did to those girls. I am in therapy and probably will be for some time. I feel awful for the families—what an awful way to lose your children."

When asked about Marc Evonitz, she said, "I love my brother—the one I thought was my brother, not the one who did these horrible things."

Jennifer said that she beat herself up for a long time for not seeing the clues in her brother's past that would have indicated that something was seriously wrong. She also wished she had handled the situation better when he was on the run. "I could have gotten more information out of my brother if I had done things differently."

MAJOR HOWARD Smith found he was in great demand in law enforcement circles since the resolution of the Lisk–Silva case. He made many trips to the FBI Academy to speak to groups of students from all over the world. The topics of his discussions included the case itself, the effective use of the media and how to communicate with the families of victims.

In April 2003, he traveled to a conference in Florida to make a presentation about responding to child abductions at a conference sponsored by the Palm Beach County Sheriff's Department.

· · ·

THE CLOUD that had hovered over Spotsylvania County since the abduction and murder of Sofia, Kristin and Kati lifted, allowing full sun to warm the hearts of its residents—but only for a short time. The cloud descended and engulfed the community again when the sniper struck on October 4.

A 43-year-old woman who resided in the county made her purchases at the Spotsylvania Mall. She loaded her bags into the rear of her minivan in front of Michael's arts and crafts stone. An anonymous shot rang out, disrupting her mundane chore. She survived her injury.

Then, the sniper crept into Spotsylvania County again on October 11—gunning down 53-year-old Kenneth Bridges of Philadelphia. Just a short distance from Interstate 95 to the north and a couple of miles from Courthouse Road to the south, on a strip of U.S. Route 1 cluttered with commercial trappings, Bridges stopped to pump gas at the Four Mile Fork Exxon. He died on the scene from a gunshot wound.

"The sniper revived the fears of Silva and Lisk. It made you realize how vulnerable you were. Some parents had gotten too relaxed and into their routines. Then the sniper brought it all back," said bus driver Pat Stanley. "But the kids were mostly mad because they were locked down and their trips were cancelled."

Once again, the reluctant Major Howard Smith was thrust into the spotlight. National news networks carried his solemn face into living rooms from coast to coast as he delivered announcements from the scene. Smith was now a member of yet another multi-agency task force.

This investigative group got quicker results. John Allen Muhammed and John Lee Malvo were arrested while sleeping in their car at a rest stop in Frederick County, Maryland, on October 24, in connection with the sniper attacks.

Spotsylvania County is third in line to prosecute these men after Fairfax and Prince William Counties. Commonwealth's Attorney William Neeley said that they will decide whether it is practical or useful to proceed after seeing the results of the previous court actions in the other two Virginia counties. Be-

fore making a decision, he would consult with the one sur-
vivor and with the family of the deceased victim.

THE SPOTSYLVANIA County Board of Supervisors passed
resolution number 2002-143 commending the Lisk–Silva
Taskforce on December 10, 2002.

Whereas, the loss of any child affects us all, and

 *Whereas, the killings of three children, Sofia Silva and
Katie [sic] and Kristin Lisk have shaken our community to
its very core, and*

 *Whereas, a group of people known as the Lisk–Silva
Taskforce, rose to this challenge with unending commitment,
and*

 *Whereas, the members of this Taskforce represented a
much broader community than our own County, including
the: Spotsylvania County Sheriff's Department, City of Fred-
ericksburg Police Department, Stafford County Sheriff's Of-
fice, King George County Sheriff's Office, Hanover County
Sheriff's Office, Caroline County Sheriff's Office, Virginia
State Police, Federal Bureau of Investigation, Department of
Alcohol, Tobacco and Firearms, Drug Enforcement Agency,
Secret Service, Naval Criminal Investigative Services, U.S.
Postal Service and U.S. Customs Office, and*

 *Whereas, the various groups and individuals which com-
prised the Taskforce cooperated fully with each other on investigative techniques, equipment and laboratory analyses,
and*

 *Whereas, several representatives of the Taskforce kept the
Lisk and Silva families informed, and*

 *Whereas, after five years and eleven months the case was
solved and the identification of the killer was due in large
part to the efforts of the Lisk–Silva Taskforce,*

 *Now, therefore, be it resolved that the Spotsylvania
County Board of Supervisors commends the Lisk–Silva
Taskforce for its cooperation and collaboration and for pub-
lic service at its finest, and*

 Be it further resolved that the Spotsylvania County Board

*of Supervisors extends to all members of the Lisk–Silva
Taskforce its deepest gratitude for their dedication and tire-
less endeavors for the Lisk and Silva families and for all who
have been touched by these tragedies.*

Anthony W. Barrett, County Administrator, signed the document and made the resolution official.

IN SPOTSYLVANIA County, investigators re-examined the evidence in the unsolved rape of June 1995. A man had broken
into the home, locked an 11-year-old in the bathroom and
raped her 13-year-old sister. All the evidence they had was
taken to the FBI forensics lab for analysis to see if this crime,
too, could be laid at Evonitz's feet. In December 2002, the results were positive. Richard Marc Evonitz's DNA was linked
to DNA obtained from the 13-year-old girl.

ON JANUARY 11, 2003, the Colonel Fielding Lewis chapter
of the Sons of the American Revolution honored Sheriff
Ron Knight of Spotsylvania County. They awarded him with
a law enforcement commendation medal and certificate for
the leadership he demonstrated in the resolution of the
Lisk–Silva murders and during the recent sniper attacks.

AT ARMSTRONG Compressed Air in Spartanburg, South Carolina, staff would hang up the phone the moment they heard
the name of Richard Marc Evonitz. They even refused to
answer general questions about the nature of their business
operations. These callers were informed that the corporate
office would respond to their inquiries. Those calls were
never returned.

THE SENATE of the Commonwealth of Virginia affirmed
Resolution No. 300 put forward by Senators Ed Houck, John
Chichester and William Bolling on January 6, 2003. The
House of Delegates agreed to join their voices to the resolu-
tion on January 24.

On February 17, the Lisk–Silva Taskforce was scheduled

to appear before the General Assembly to be presented with
the resolution. But that day, the blizzard of 2003 brought the
state to a grinding halt. When the roads were clear on February 19, the entire Taskforce traveled to Richmond to appear
before the legislative body. Major Smith stepped forward to
accept the commendation from Governor Mark Warner on
behalf of the Lisk–Silva Taskforce.

As the admiring lawmakers and honored investigators listened, the resolution was read aloud in the chamber.

> *"Whereas, the Lisk–Silva Task Force was formed in 1997,*
> *following the 1996 murder and abduction of sixteen-year-*
> *old Sofia Silva and the 1997 abduction and murder of*
> *fifteen-year-old Kristin Lisk and her twelve-year-old sister*
> *Kati; and*
>
> *"Whereas, these horrible crimes devastated the Silva and*
> *Lisk familes and brought grief, fear and uncertainty to their*
> *Spotsylvania County community; and*
>
> *"Whereas, over the past five years, the members of the*
> *Lisk–Silva Taskforce have worked with great diligence to*
> *solve these crimes and to apprehend the person or persons*
> *responsible; and*
>
> *"Whereas, the Lisk–Silva Taskforce, made up of local law*
> *enforcement agencies, the Virginia State Police, the Federal*
> *Bureau of Investigation, and other local, state, and federal*
> *agencies, has investigated the crimes exhaustively, following*
> *leads, gathering evidence, conducting interviews, conducting*
> *searches, and investigating suspects; and*
>
> *"Whereas, the tireless efforts of the Lisk–Silva Taskforce*
> *finally bore fruit during the summer of 2002, when a report*
> *of an unsuccessful abduction in South Carolina sent mem-*
> *bers of the Taskforce to the scene to investigate the residence*
> *of Richard Marc Evonitz; and*
>
> *"Whereas, the resulting meticulous investigation of*
> *Evonitz, who committed suicide in Florida, involved the care-*
> *ful examination and testing of a large amount of forensic evi-*
> *dence, which led to the conclusion that Evonitz was the*

perpetrator of the Spotsylvania crimes in 1996 and 1997; and

"Whereas, the conclusion, based on hair, fiber and DNA evidence; interviews with relatives, neighbors and associates of Evonitz; and the analysis of evidence recovered from his car and residence, was announced by the Lisk–Silva Taskforce on August twenty-first, 2002; and

"Whereas, the announcement by Major Howard Smith of the Spotsylvania County Sheriff's Office brought comfort to the bereaved families of Sofia Silva and Kristin and Kati Lisk and a sense of relief to the Spotsylvania County community; and

"Whereas, throughout the entire agonizing and prolonged investigation, the members of the Lisk–Silva Taskforce, assisted by Spotsylvania County Sheriff Ron Knight, proceeded with professionalism, sensitivity and dedication; and

"Whereas, the Lisk–Silva Taskforce, consisting of the Spotsylvania County and King George County Sheriff's Offices, the Virginia State Police, and the FBI, was assisted by law enforcement agencies in South Carolina and Florida, by the Drug Enforcement Administration, the United States Secret Service, other federal agencies, and by local law enforcement personnel from Caroline, Stafford, Prince William and Hanover Counties and the City of Fredericksburg; and

"Whereas, all of the professionals involved in the Lisk–Silva Taskforce investigation exhibited behavior consistent with the highest ideals of professional law enforcement and set a new standard for cooperation among diverse law enforcement agencies in pursuit of a common goal; now, therefore, be it

"Resolved by the Senate, the House of Delegates concurring, That the General Assembly hereby commend the members of the Lisk–Silva Taskforce for bringing to a successful conclusion the investigation of the unspeakable crimes visited on the Silva and Lisk families; and, be it

"Resolved further, that the Clerk of the Senate prepare a copy of this resolution for presentation to Major Howard Smith of the Spotsylvania County Sheriff's Office as an ex-

pression of the General Assembly's appreciation and admiration for the exceptional performance of the Lisk–Silva Taskforce."

After the reading, the name of each member of the Taskforce was read. They rose and accepted the applause of the full house.

As of the date of completion of this book, no similar commendations or honors have been bestowed on the officers in Lexington and Richland County Sheriff's Departments in South Carolina or those in the Manatee County Sheriff's Department and Sarasota police.

On March 13, 2003, news from the outside world floated to the surface in Spotsylvania and dredged up the community grief that had settled to the bottom of their collective consciousness. Elizabeth Smart, abducted from her home at knifepoint nine months earlier, was reunited with her family in Salt Lake City.

The community expressed a heartfelt joy at the safe return of this teenager—they knew the anguish of the loss first-hand. The happiness they felt for the folks in Salt Lake City, however, was counterbalanced by the pain of knowing that Sofia, Kristin and Kati were never able to return home to the embrace of their families and friends.

The news hit Detective Twyla Demoranville with a bittersweet intensity. "When the news was announced about Elizabeth Smart, I was very much in shock, because statistics show that missing children cases so often end in tragedy.

"I immediately went back to September 9, 1996, and May 1, 1997. When Sofia Silva and Kati and Kristin Lisk were missing, everyone involved in the investigation saw that story with a different ending. As law enforcement officers, we always see ourselves as recovering children and reuniting them with their families. I so wish our girls could have been brought home safely.

"Statistics show that if a child is not found in the first

twenty-four hours, the likelihood of them being found safely diminishes with every hour. We all felt elation for everyone involved in the Smart case. The whole world celebrated that day.

"It was a miracle. It gives hope to everyone who is out there searching, searching, searching for a missing child. It gives us hope that we can bring them home safely no matter what the statistics say."

Reflecting on her choice to become a member of law enforcement, Demoranville said that she did so because she wanted to help children. "But never did I think in my career that I would be involved in such a heartfelt and emotionally charged case. It changes you. It changed me for the better because of the amazing strength I saw in the families of the victims."

In the fall of 2003, Fred Heblich, attorney for Darrell David Rice, announced that the microscopic investigation of hair found under the duct tape used to bind Julianne Williams and Lollie Winans did not match his client. However, it did match seven to eight percent of the population—including Richard Marc Evonitz. The attorney also claimed that the way the young women were bound was not dissimilar to the bindings in the Silva and Lisk cases. Julianne and Lollie were sexually assaulted but not raped—just like Sophia, Kati and Kristin in Spotsylvania County. It was possible, Heblich said, that Julianne and Lollie were murdered in the Shenandoah National Park in northern Virginia between May 28–30, a few days later than the official estimate. On those days, Evonitz was not at work—he had taken emergency family leave. He did not, however, attend his grandmother's funeral in northern Virginia. Federal Prosecutor Tony Giorno called the theories of the defense a "fairy tale" but nonetheless, requested a delay of trial to allow for further testing of the evidence. In February 2004, he announced that tests did not point to Rice as the killer and the government would drop the charges against Darrell David Rice to pursue new leads in the case.

> *"Death ends a life but not a relationship."*
> Jack Lemmon

Afterword

It was not easy to find the spot in King George County where Sofia Silva's bundled body lay for more than a month after her disappearance. I searched the side of the highway in vain for a sign marking the entrance to Dominion Growers. The ownership had changed since the fall of 1996. It was now Village Farms and instead of filling the world with flowers, they produced tomatoes by the ton.

I turned by the old red barn near the highway and rolled down the small road until I was out of sight of the unending line of cars and trucks stroking down State Route 3. I could not pull completely off the road—the drop on both sides was too precipitous.

I stood on the sloping hill of grass, mere feet from the spot where Sofia rested for thirty-six days. Beyond the gates to the commercial farm, I saw the bustling of people and trucks going about the business of growing food for tables up and down the mid-Atlantic coast. Distance made the sound of their efforts inaudible. The huge glass front of the main building stared down upon me like the eye of God. I did not understand how anyone could stand in that spot and not get the prickly premonition of being watched—and being judged.

The sun streamed down brightly. The muffled sound of traffic roaring by on Route 3 and the babble of birds filled the air. A pungent whiff of stagnant water assaulted my nose—pulling my eyes back to the edge of the woods.

A small white cross marked the spot where Sofia's body

was found—a lonely, weatherworn sentinel guarding her memory, lest we forget. The sun shone brightly on its surface. The trees hanging above dappled it with shadows. Carved into the cross bar were these words: "In God's Arms Forever."

I moved closer and peered beyond the cross. Through a break in the poison ivy, I spotted a body of water, its surface stained an iridescent green. I could visualize the ripples of Sofia's death spreading across it.

In the first circle were her mother and father, Phyllis and Humberto Silva. It is unnatural for parents to outlive a child. Anyone who has suffered this loss through illness, suicide or accident can understand some measure of the pain of these parents. But no one except those who have lost a child to homicide can fathom the depths of their agony. The daily reminders of the empty place at the table. The empty bed in the room down the hall. The haunting horror of imagining her suffering in the last moments of her life. The guilt of not being there. The wistful thoughts of: What would she be doing now? Who would she be? What impact would the passage of time have on the features of her face? On her happiness? On her heart? The wondering never ceases. The pain never ends.

In the next ripple emanating from the center were the other family members and close friends of Sofia. Their lives were altered forever by her death. In good times, they felt blessed to have known her. In bad times, they struggled to banish her from their thoughts and regain a moment of innocence.

Close after them was another ring containing the people who found the body—their dreams haunted always by visions of that discovery. They agonized about being so close to her for so many days, deaf and blind to the cries for justice emanating from her shallow, watery grave.

Then came the circle of the investigators, forensic specialists and others involved in the resolution of this case. For more than five and a half years, they struggled to find the right answers. When a young innocent is the victim, the emotional toll on them is staggering. Years later, the pain still scratched across their voices with the dissonance of a needle traveling across the grooves of a 78 on an old Victrola.

In the next liquid echo was the community at large. In a place like Spotsylvania, there are few degrees of separation between each of its citizens. If someone did not know the victim or the victim's family, they knew someone who did—a friend who went to school with one of them or knew them through business transactions or attended the same church. Sofia's death robbed them of their sense of security and crippled their ability to trust.

In the next circle were the suspects of the crime and their family members. The suspects themselves often were not sympathetic individuals—many brought their fates down upon themselves either by criminal activity or stubborn, foolish decisions. But the families of these suspects were often innocent bystanders caught in the crossfire—like Elizabeth Roush, whose burden was incomprehensible: her daughter abducted and murdered, then, sixteen years later, her son charged with committing the same crime on another young victim.

That ring was followed by the ripple of the family of Richard Marc Evonitz. They did not commit the crime, yet they felt the finger of guilt poking in their chests. Richard and Barbara Evonitz, Marc's aunt and uncle, living in the community where the murders occured were hounded by the media and isolated by the name they shared with a killer.

Then came the final circle. It contained all of us who were aware of what had happened—who cared in principle about the loss of life. The impact of Sofia's death on our lives was subtle. But it was real.

FINDING THE spot where the bodies of Kristin and Kati Lisk had floated unseen for days was an even greater challenge. State Route 738 turned and forked without advance warning. Some twists in the road were not marked at all. At others, signs knocked askew by impact or weather pointed in the wrong direction.

On my map, the road ended at U.S. 1. But when I reached that intersection, I saw that it continued on. And so did I.

I did not know how to find the exact bridge on that long and narrow route except by traveling to where it ended and doubling back for one mile.

I crossed several bridges without pause, but as my tires forded one bridge, my heart raced, and dread became my passenger. I did not know if this sensation was born of imagination or if my subconscious had snatched up a vestige of the sorrow from the past. One mile later, the road ended at a graveled intersection. That was the bridge I had sought. I turned the car around and made the short pilgrimage back.

I stood on the bridge in Hanover County. I heard no sound but the sluggish trickle of the impotent river as it coursed beneath my feet. The sun that hit my body contained no warmth. The flattened carcass of a snake, its shiny colors muted by death, stretched across the roadway like an omen of doom.

Standing there, my breath came in fits and starts. Ice crystals formed in the pit of my stomach. The hair on my arms semaphored warnings to my heart. I stood in the wild, rural version of an unlit city alley on the bad side of town. It was a dark and dreadful place that I did not want to enter alone.

On one side of the bridge, a wooden cross, its grain poking through red, faded paint, marked the spot where Kristin and Kati floated side by side. A white rag doll angel embraced the old rugged cross. Two sets of rosary beads wrapped around the wood. A pair of white angels and a pink puppy sat on the cross bar.

Beyond the cross, I gazed into the water below. Logs, twigs and debris ganged up by the bridge forming putrid green pools. Brown water oozed by the constricted space. There, too, I saw the ripples in the water caused by the deaths of Kristin and Kati.

The inner circle contained different people, Ron and Patti Lisk, whose agony was doubled by the loss of both of their children. Their hearts battered. Their spirits broken. Their grief infinite.

As the ripples caused by the death of these two sisters emanated out from the center, they overlapped with those formed by the death of Sofia—the amount of duplication increasing in a geometric progression as they traveled farther from the center.

The violent deaths of three innocent girls created circles upon circles of pain, transformation and loss. In and of themselves, their deaths were a cataclysmic tragedy.

But most tragic of all is the sure knowledge that; day after day, in one community after another, the ripples are forming again.